D1289720

REDEEMING THE DREAM
Feminism, Redemption
and Christian Tradition

Mary Grey

REDEEMING THE DREAM

Feminism, Redemption and Christian Tradition

INTERNATIONAL EDITION

2000
GUJARAT SAHITYA PRAKASH
POST BOX 70
ANAND, GUJARAT 388 001
INDIA.

This book had 3 editions in Great Britain between 1989 and 1993, published by SPCK, London.

It had also one edition in U.S.A. Translated into Dutch.

© 1999 Mary Grey
    West Mill, Fullerton Rd.
    Wherwell, Hants SP11 7JS
    U.K.

British Library Cataloguing in Publication Data

Grey, Mary C.
Redeeming the dream: feminism, redemption
and Christian tradition.
1. Christian doctrine. Redemption
I. Title
224'.3

Published by X. Diaz del Rio, S.J., Gujarat Sahitya Prakash,
                               P. Box 70, Anand, 388 001, India
Laser-set and printed by S. Abril, S.J., Anand Press,
                               P. Box 95, Gamdi-Anand, 388 001, India.

Introduction

The International Edition of Redeeming the dream by Gujarat Sahitya Prakash, Anand. India gives a welcome opportunity for re-introducing a work now ten years old. Of course there is the strong temptation for self-criticism, for making improvements, for responding to events or criticisms or developments of the last ten years, both in Feminist Liberation theology or Christian theology in general. Whereas this might add to the value of the work, and give a contemporary gloss, (and of course my own thought has developed in this period), my conviction in re-reading Redeeming the dream is that its initial concerns and focus continue to be relevant even to be a matter of life and death for some women.

When, in 1994, the Women's Commission of EATWOT (Ecumenical Association of Third world Theologians) met in San José, Costa Rica, they had invited women theologians from Europe and N. America to join them in an Intercontinental Dialogue on "Women resisting violence — a spirituality for Life." Here, before my eyes was embodied what Redeeming the Dream tried to articulate. Women gathered from all corners of the earth, united in a commitment to eradicate all the death-dealing structures and non-redemptive forces inflicting suffering on the lives of women and all innocent creatures. At the same time women were seeking for all that was life-giving and creative from lost dimensions of Christianity and indigenous traditions. Our discussions — painful at times - witnessed to the complicity — albeit unwitting — of many of us from the northern hemisphere in these very forces of non-redemption, through race, economic position or sexual identity. Yet our liturgies evoked a common hope and commitment to "redeeming the dream" of a life of flourishing for all.

From this experience - and many others, including my times with the village women of Rajasthan, (north-west India), and with Christian women theologians in Bombay — arises the hope that this book still offers a focus on urgent theological issues. Women are poorer than ever and suffer from many kinds of violence: young girls are sucked into the flesh trade in increasing numbers, as I see for myself in Rajasthan, and the toll of deaths from AIDS continues to rise, among women as well as men. Whereas Redeeming the Dream began eleven years ago with a PH.D. thesis and the conviction that God suffered with the whole of creation in travail, I now see that the cross of Jesus, planted anew where places of existence are most vulnerable is, for Christianity, the key to where redeemed life may emerge. But not before the layers of patriarchal and oppressive discourses of many kinds are peeled off and rejected.

Hence the book begins by asking whether the concept of redemption is itself meaningful today, and if so, with what interpretation it could be redeemed. Chapter Two examines the building blocks needed for a new way of looking at redemption: it looks at the psychological strengths of women and a philosophical view of the universe as relational. Chapter Three widens the context of redemption to include the way that human beings draw strength from nature and the environment. Chapters Four and Five explore paths to healing and wholeness using insights from women's experience: can the ancient Via Mystica be reclaimed as a redemptive path for women? Can Redemption as Right Relation offer both a way to transform unjust structures and a new interpretive key to the mission of Jesus? Chapter Six faces the challenge of traditional Atonement doctrines with a feminist critique, while the following Chapter (Seven) begins to re-weave the skeins in a new and positive way. In the final Chapter I begin to envision — albeit in the form of opening up of possibilitis - what difference it would make if we saw redemption as "building right relation".

Since writing this book the networks of relating and connecting have mushroomed into new structures of solidarity and justice-making. I am grateful to the many dear people - family, friends and colleagues — who form for me the powerful knots in this web of relating. I want to mention specifically my son Stephen, a journalist, who reads and critiques my work continually, always hoping that it might communicate better with those I want to reach; my long-standing friends Fr Clyde Harvey, June and Everard Johnston in Trinidad, the West Indies, who keep alive a vibrant image of Christian community. But redemption is about transfiguring and transforming the world, especially its most vulnerable places: so it is to the courage and endurance of the village women of the Rajasthan desert of India that I dedicate the new publication of this book.

Mary Grey, November 1999.

1 Feminist Redemption: Reclaiming the Symbol

A passion to make and make again
where such un-making reigns . . .[1]

So wrote the poet Adrienne Rich, evoking both the intensity and creativity needed for the redeeming of the world. That the forces of 'un-making' threaten the very possibility of people peacefully co-existing is beyond dispute. That there is a hunger for alternatives to military destruction, famine on a vast scale, and the pollution of air and water is also manifest. But the word 'redemption' has a specific origin in Christian theology: it has overtones which ring of suffering, sacrifice, guilt and self-negation, the negativity of the cross of Jesus Christ and the severity of the atonement doctrines which try to explain it. Many would argue that this is a word evoking a concept which no longer 'speaks' to us today. What is more, the question arises as to whether it can still 'speak' to women. The whole feminist agenda focuses on creating an alternative to the patriarchal language of domination and submission, a language which meaningfully addresses the diverse situations in which women find themselves. Does traditional 'redemption' language reach these situations and offer liberating alternatives?

. These are vital questions: they raise the issue as to whether religious concepts must forever be linked with the cultural framework from which they spring, particularly when it is known that certain beliefs of this culture were false.[2] They raise a deeper issue as to the relationship of a statement to the experience it attempts to express. How many women and men have been rendered silent because the words just did not exist to 'hear them into speech'[3]? What is needed is a 'hearing engaged in by the whole body that evokes speech – a new speech – a new creation'.[4]

If we carry on investing our spiritual energies in words which have become over-loaded with the baggage of centuries from which we are attempting to break free, it has to be asked if God's word can still speak to us today with power.

And yet, as a feminist theologian, I believe the entire task of theology is redemptive in a very specific sense. It is redemptive,

1

firstly, because it is an activity of reclaiming. As *Webster's International Dictionary* says, to 'redeem' can mean to 'recover from a state of submersion', 'extricate from futility or meaninglessness', 'reclaim', 'liberate', 'fulfil', or 'realize'. So when we engage in an activity of reclaiming the lost history and experience of women this is truly a redeeming activity. It is recovering 'the underside of history'.[5] It was an activity called for long ago by the tragic heroine of Euripides, Medea, when she cried:

> Flow backwards to your sources, sacred rivers,
> And let the world's great order be reversed. . .
> Stories shall now turn my condition to a fair one,
> Women shall now be paid their due.[6]

More specifically, we are reclaiming today the lost creativity and insights which have been submerged or discarded by a dominant patriarchal tradition. As Professor Catharine Halkes of The Netherlands has said, we are seeking what has been marginalized and trivialized.[7] This is in no sense an attempt to glorify the past but an endeavour to bring into the light what has been deemed negative by the dominant tradition. What difference would it make if these experiences became a source for theology, and if the 'passion to make and make again', the urge to reclaim, save and not to destroy became the accepted ethic of contemporary society? We need to listen again to the words of the poet:

> My heart is touched by all I cannot save.
> So much has been destroyed.
> I have to cast my lot in with those, who, age after age,
> perversely, with no extraordinary power,
> reconstitute the world.[8]

Secondly, in this book I am investigating what this could mean for *Christian* theology. But I am not suggesting that women's experiences should become normative for humanity; nor that matriarchy should replace patriarchy. My belief and hope is that, despite the distorted power models of the institutional Church, despite the suffering of many women within it (through exclusion from ordained ministry and decision-making processes), the creative-liberating vision of Jesus of Nazareth speaks as deeply to us today as it did to his first followers. But the challenge to us today is to uncover the strands of this revelation which have remained submerged throughout Christian tradition.

It is women today who, in the name of the whole of humanity – and in particular, in the name of all marginalized groups within it – are posing the existential question of Hamlet, 'To be or not to be?' And if

I opt for existence, to live – what kind of existence? A way of life which will bring autonomy, independence, some degree of being fulfilled, is our hope. So humiliating subordination and self-negating roles, and the very institutions of society which force women into these, are being challenged. Our agenda must be to uncover what kind of theology, of God-concept, and interpretation of redemption have allowed the degradation of women.

FREEDOM, REDEMPTION, OR LIBERATION?

The question must be honestly faced: if meaningful, fulfilling existence for myself, for others, and, ultimately, for the whole of the universe is the purpose of living – to express the issue at a very basic level – then is 'redemption' still the most meaningful word? Perhaps 'liberation' or 'freedom' or even 'integrity' would be more meaningful concepts within our own secular society. . . ?

If we look around the world, what is immediately striking is the proliferation of life-and-death freedom struggles. Whether we consider the efforts of the Sandainista government of Nicaragua, the sufferings of the people of El Salvador at the hands of the death squads, the struggles of the Palestinians for a homeland or the black people in South Africa for sheer survival, for the oppressed poor of the world, liberation involves political struggles, and, very often, armed resistance and revolution.[9] Liberation means self-liberation and the ethic of protest.

But there are many reasons for seeing this as only a partial solution for human problems. For one thing, revolutions often fail, and, even if they succeed, do not always bring the longed-for freedom or any alleviation in the suffering of oppressed people. As the Filipino liberation theologian, Ed de la Torre, has pointed out, yesterday's disenchanted revolutionaries may become tomorrow's vigilantes.[10] Secondly, however successful the armed struggle, there are areas of human experience untouched by liberation movements. There will always remain the suffering arising from the fact that we are such limited beings, caught in the web of finitude, that we must die, that we will suffer through illness, bereavement and breakdown of relationships.[11] We feel acutely our own failures and mistakes, endure depression because of them, because of the human condition itself. Thirdly, our very ability to sustain the struggle for freedom and liberation is limited. We suffer 'compassion-fatigue'. As Sharon Welch, a contemporary feminist liberation theologian put it, as she reached exhaustion point after a demonstration for the people of El Salvador, 'My sanity was my insensitivity; my humanity was my ability not to care.'[12] Why? What has happened to commitment to liberation? At a certain moment we give up. We reach burn-out point – that is, unless we are sustained by a commitment and spirituality deeper than the ethics of revolution alone.

This is in no way to decry the necessity of opposing tyrannical regimes, or resisting oppression of every kind. What I suggest is that freedom struggles are only part of what we mean by redemption. What I hope to show is that within the very activity of resistance and struggle are other dynamics which contribute more to human becoming and wholeness.

Redemption is deeply concerned with human liberation – and feminist redemption theology asserts itself very firmly as liberation theology. Yes, it is about resistance to oppression and the struggle for freedom, but it is also about human integrity and wholeness. And no word speaks better to that universal human hungering for healing, wholeness, integrity and transformation. Redemption suggests the goal, the process and the method of reaching that desired wholeness. It not only comprehends the personal journeys of men and women to maturity and integrity, the structures of society, damaged and corrupted by vested interests and impoverished vision, but also speaks to the wounds of our damaged planet. It grasps every aspect of the cosmos, every dimension of experience, every aspect of living, past, present and future. It is a word which does not pretend that living is pain-free. In a world which knows genocide and turns a blind eye to the prostitution of small children, a language is needed which honestly addresses the brokenness and despair which threatens life on many different levels. This is one of the problems facing religious language at present: not simply must it 'correlate' with lived experience[13] but must spring directly from it – the experience must inspire the language. Our failure to nurture religious language has meant that it becomes a tool for politicians and that many Christians have discovered their authentic religious experience outside the Christian Church.

THE REDEMPTIVE PATH – FROM CREATION TO NEW CREATION

I speak of redemption from a perspective – to be opened up and discussed further in the following chapter – which understands creation and redemption as a unified process. Creation and redemption are like two sides of a coin. Creating activity *is* redeeming activity. When farmers from around the Zuyder Zee in The Netherlands reclaimed or redeemed clods of earth from the sea,

4

attached them to the land and so built up small farms, they were both creating *and* redeeming. When we make patchwork quilts from hundreds of pieces of cloth from all kinds of garments, we create and redeem. It is the same in the healing of broken relationships. And, on a vast scale, this is the very activity of God in history, always creating and offering new possibilities which are at the same time redeeming ones. We have to 'redeem the time, redeem the dream', as T.S. Eliot would say, and in so doing become the new creation.

To begin from this perspective acknowledges the harm done by separating creation from redemption. If we view humanity, as St Augustine did, as a *massa damnata* – an 'unregenerate lump' – not only have we undervalued the fact that men and women are created in God's image, but we shall be forced to view redemption as coming totally from the outside – yes, from God's action in Christ, but interpreted in such a way that human beings become merely the passive recipients of this action. To hold the processes of creation and redemption together is to see ourselves as involved and responsible in the divine task of transforming the world.

Matthew Fox, the American Dominican theologian, has painted a gloomy picture of what a redemption-based spirituality has done: 'it has put the body down and called this repression holy; it has encouraged private conversions and sentimental pieties. . . It has substituted private righteousness for Biblical justice; it has taught sin-consciousness rather than people's consciousness of the Divine. . .'[14] Fox in his many writings calls for us to recognize and reject the harm that has been done and recover the opposite perspective: a creation-centred theology and spirituality.

From women it is particularly vital to begin from a creation-centred perspective. No redemptive process can begin without a sense of experiencing oneself as God's good creation.[15] One of the tragic consequences of the many crimes against women such as rape, wife-beating, prostitution, being treated as a play-object, as ornament, with sexuality commercialized, is that many women internalize the negative perceptions which society has of women. We begin to doubt whether it is possible to be redeemed from the very fact of being woman. Those who work with women who have suffered rape know how difficult – even impossible – it is for them to recover a sense of self-worth. Being 'redeemed in Christ' does not appear to offer any liberating hope.

But, unlike Matthew Fox, I believe that we cannot separate creation from redemption. One of the themes I will develop is the extent to which women have held on to a connectedness with nature (Chapter 3), and have experienced this very connectedness as

5

redemptive. To hold the two processes together means realistically facing the multiple strands of poverty and oppression in which people live and asking, 'What is creative and redemptive here and now, in this situation?' It is only when engaged in the very processes of redemption and liberation that we can construct an authentic theology of creation. We have to get the structures right – or our creation theology is for the birds and the butterflies alone. The very act of recovering a sense of being created in the image of God, is, for women, a redemptive act, in reclaiming the lost wholeness, and sense of self-worth.

This forces us back to ask of Christian theology, Where are the models for wholeness and self-worth?, and to investigate the meaning of the symbols of womanhood held up as inspiration. Here, another activity of 'reclaiming' is called for: the re-claiming of the symbols themselves. Whether there are other symbols than the Virgin-Mother (Mary) or the harlot (Mary Magdalen) symbol for real flesh-and-blood women to imitate[16] is our question.

By holding together the creative/redemptive processes we open up the possibility of cutting through the many dualisms which have dogged Western philosophy as a legacy of Platonism, and still continue to pose problems. These oppositions have set mind/spirit/rationality over body/matter/affectivity, identifying men with the former, women – needless to say – with the latter. Not that we can hope to eradicate distinctions between 'being' and 'doing'. It is both the way that these are set in opposition, over against each other, which is harmful, as well as the identification of each polarity with a particular sex. Feminist theologians have to be wary of falling into the same trap. In our over-anxiety to oppose the strand of anti-physicality and anti-sexuality found in Christian theology and assert the positive qualities of bodiliness, and in particular, female bodiliness, we can too easily imagine a spirituality formed exclusively from female experiences – such as childbirth – praying to God the Mother, stressing only qualities of nurturing and nourishing – and this at a time when women struggle to succeed in professional spheres, when we seek for ways of identification other than our physical roles. There has to be a way of reclaiming bodiliness and wounded sexuality expressive of the totality of human personality.

If there are ways of knowing, ways of being and ways of relating which are distinctive to each sex these must be brought to light. This investigation will lead me in Chapter 2 into psychology, philosophy and anthropology. Only when it is clear if these are exclusively male and female ways of being and knowing can I discover an accurate language for redemption and begin to understand why

6

the current theological vocabulary does not fit the experiences of women.

'UNTIL EVERY WOMAN IS FREE, NO WOMAN IS FREE'[17]

Under this heading is a specific agenda for feminist redemption. For, within the context of a theology of liberation, feminist redemption is firmly committed to the freedom and liberation of *all* women. In what can be considered a foundational article, 'Feminist Theology as a Critical Study of Liberation',[18] Elizabeth Schüssler Fiorenza claimed that feminist theology is both critical theology and liberation theology, yet is more radical then either, because women span all races and all cultures. She has shown how, although all women suffer from sexism in institutional Church and society, it is Third-World women who constitute the bottom of the oppressive patriarchal pyramid. There will be no toppling of patriarchy, she says, until these triply-oppresed women are liberated. A feminist theology of liberation arises directly from the struggles of Asian, African, Indian and other Third-World women, as well as from the more economically fortunate white European and North American women and those poor white women on the margins of these prosperous countries. Feminist liberation theologians such as Rosemary Radford Ruether[19] and Letty Russell[20] insist on the interlinked nature of the oppressions of sexism, racism and classism. To lose sight of this will cause division within the Women's Movement. Isabel Carter Heyward in fact speaks of an 'unfinished symphony of liberation'.[21]

In fact divisions have already arisen exactly because the interlinked nature of racism and sexism has not been kept in mind. Black women feel that feminism does not embrace the concerns of black women, but focuses on the well-being and success of white women alone. They feel that black theology, too, ignores them, concentrating only on the liberation of black men. Hence a movement is growing in the United States of 'womanist' theology, which is concentrating specifically on the liberation of black women.[22] Womanist theology embraces the liberation of *all* black people, including men and children.

The rise of womanist theology points to a real weakness in feminist theology. Despite the warnings of feminist liberation theologians insufficient attention has been paid to racism within the feminist movement. White women have been insensitive to the fact that their freedom was often at the expense of black women. In the United States women were able to go to classes on feminist theory, while their houses were cleaned and their children looked after by poor black women. In Britain it is more a question of being insensitive to the economic position of black women in British society and of not facing the many situations in which racism has made decent human living impossible. The situation must be honestly faced. If *all* women are included in the agenda of liberation theology, the living conditions of women from ethnic minorities must be at the centre, not at the periphery: this means that an *authentic* feminist liberation theology grasps the nettle of the *two fold* ethic of liberation language and becomes sensitive to whether it is speaking to oppressor or oppressed. It must be sensitive, too, to the fact that women are *both*. Tnat is, with regard to the oppression of sexism women are victims, but as regards racist and economic exploitation, many women must share responsibility for causing misery to fellow human beings. Even within the sphere of sexism itself, women have frequently joined with men in oppressing other women.

Failure to see this leads to inability to answer the question, 'From what are women redeemed?', as well as failure to understand that the dominant strain of liberation theology language is summoning the oppressed groups to resistance: a different language is called for to address those who are maintaining the oppressive structures.

So with liberation theology I seek the redemption of *all* women, and seek an inclusive method which refuses to divide women against each other. But, as I have said, I seek a profounder dynamic than protest and resistance alone. But I am grateful to womanist theology, both for showing the pitfalls into which we fall through a too-narrow vision. I am also grateful for the way in which it embraces man, woman and child within its agenda for liberation. A full theology of redemption cannot stop with one sex alone.

While Rosemary Ruether is right to insist that women must name themselves as the *subjects*, not the *objects* of theology; while, with her, I reject as not redemptive anything which inhibits the full becoming of women,[23] yet I am attempting to develop models of redemption which uncover in divine revelation something important for *all* humanity – not merely for women. There must be ways of being, reclaimed and redeemed, which will offer juster and more fruitful alternatives to a society whose very symbols are sick and atrophied.

That is why it is important to recover the lost experience and creativity, to uncover the hidden ways of knowing. Michel Foucault, the French historian and sociologist, in a way helpful to my theme – and to feminist liberation theology in general – spoke of the recovery of the subjugated knowledges.[24] He saw society as in the control of a dominant form of power and knowledge. Truth, he said, is grounded in the structures of a particular regime – in the mechanism and controls which enable people to distinguish true from false. There

8

cannot be a single way of knowing, but a shifting mass of contradictions. How, then, do we find our way out of this maze?

In a two-pronged method Foucault investigates the whole arena of discourse, its correlation with the institutions of society and the means by which people are excluded or included within it. This he calls 'archaeology'. Secondly, by means of what he calls 'geneology' Foucault examines resistance to dominant forms of power and knowledge. He identifies a strain in history which struggles to present a reality which *opposes* an established form of discourse. This Foucault calls an 'insurrection of subjugated knowledges'.[25] 'Subjugated knowledges' refers to a whole group of knowledges pointing to the specific history of subjugation, conflict and domination which have been lost or deliberately erased by the triumphalist framework. They could include – although Foucault does not tell us – the wisdom of the elderly, of North American Indians, of those skilled in alternative medicine, of the spiritual gurus of different faith traditions, as well as the lost wisdom of women through the ages. So Foucault directs his geneological work towards remembering and bringing into active struggle these lost subjugated knowledges.

Clearly this is a method related to 'reclaiming lost experiences' which I have asserted as a basis for feminist redemption. It has already been used by Sharon Welch,[26] along with the concept of 'dangerous memory' (which she derived from the German theologian Jean-Baptist Metz).[27] Memory is dangerous when it is a memory of conflict and exclusion (as well as of hope, freedom and resistance), of suffering and oppression and of the degradation of women. Memory can also be empowering to redemption (as I hope to show), when based on something other than humiliation.

I part company from Foucault over the significance of the recovered subjugated knowledges. For Foucault – and this is one of the most provocative aspects of his work – does not give a privileged position to either the dominant or the subjugated forms of knowledge. It would appear that for Foucault all is 'fiction'. As he himself says, 'I am aware that I have never written anything but fictions. . . One "fictions" history on the basis of a political reality that makes it true; one "fictions" a politics not yet in existence on the basis of historical truth.'[28]

But this would mean, in applying Foucault's view to liberation theology, a relativizing of its credibility as justified critique of prevailing, dominant discourse. This is unacceptable. Whereas I would argue that protest theology or political theology is the very essence of Christianity, its importance as critique, as recovery of a lost focus on the many groups of people marginalized by society, whom Jesus proclaimed as the very stuff of the Kingdom of Heaven,

9

cannot be lightly put aside. Whereas the policies and distorted notions of the dominant group may well hold scant claim to permanency and truth, the claims of liberating faith spring from fidelity to the vision of 'shalom', or Divine righteousness, which stand their ground despite the quicksands of political systems which may surround them.

And when there is an insurrection of the subjugated knowledges submerged through the subordination of women, what do they reveal, in Foucault's categories? Certainly the memory of conflict and exclusion. But more than that: there are also excluded contents of history which must be brought to light, not as the interesting backcloth of history (its 'underside'), but as central and significant.[29] We have to ask ourselves why it is that men have always needed to keep women in subjection. If, from a very early point in history – and patriarchy is usually thought to be well established by 600 BC[30] – the earlier, more egalitarian relationships which had existed between the sexes had been destroyed, the ethic which allowed this should be highlighted – and rejected.

It is at this level that we touch what I have been reaching for since the beginning of this chapter. It is at the level of broken mutuality that we long for redemption. The level of broken mutuality refuses to be healed by political freedom struggles alone. Indeed, many revolutionary movements which have used the strength of women to achieve their aims, once victory is won, have pushed women right back into their former submissive roles.

Here it becomes clear that my call for the recovery and insurrection of the lost stories, the subjugated knowledges, for the rekindling of forgotten memories of the taste of freedom, is not based on nostalgia for imagined golden ages of female dominance: the central thesis of this book is that it will be through the restoration of broken relationship – the deeply divisive dynamic which has set one sex in domination over the other – that the redemptive processes will be set in motion. But it will not be redemptive in any individualistic sense, but a process enacted in the arena of political and social life. The very activity of reclaiming is itself, as I will show, part of the redemptive process. So I think that Metz is mistaken to speak only of *dangerous* memory. Feminists are discovering that remembering, or 're-membering' as Mary Daly put it,[31] in the sense of putting together, or re-connecting, all the fragmented and dis-membered elements of experience, is part of the recovery of a lost sense of wholeness. In fact memory will play a large part in widening our epistemological base.

So the struggle between the dominant and subjugated knowledges must be thrown into relief, not to relativize and fictionalize oppression, but to display its inadequacy and contradictory nature as

10

preventing full human well-being: when the subjugated knowledges are brought to the light of day, they will – hopefully – reveal the distortions and false consciousness of prevailing values. And the process of reclaiming will itself be part of redemption.

CAN WOMEN ACTUALLY BE REDEEMED?

It must be now clear that a contemporary theology of Christian redemption, such as I am attempting, must open its eyes to an immense range of experiences as its jumping-off point, Incarnational, theology must earth its categories neither in other-worldly pre-suppositions nor in divine-human polarities, but in the richness of created realities, viewed from the perspective of their capacity for growth, becoming and transformation.

In fact, Schillebeeckx has called for seven 'constants' to be borne in mind by *any* theology of redemption.[32] First, he sees the relationship between human bodiliness, nature and the ecological environment as being important; secondly, the dimension of mutuality and communion – which will be my focus – he understands as essential, in a wider sense than interpersonal relationships. Other aspects include relationships with the institutional structures, time-space categories and how theory and praxis interrelate. How religious and para-religious factors affect the human person is also a factor. Schillebeeckx stresses the *irreducibility* of all these factors. Indeed, they must also form a large part of the agenda of feminist theology.

But a question which is often passed over is, Why is there any necessity for redemption, or for salvation, in the first place? It will be objected that the case I have made so far refers more to the purely secular activity of reclaiming lost histories of women, according to a very minor etymological interpretation of the word 'redemption'. But what this has to do with Christian theology is far from clear. And why the process of the redemption of *women* is any different from that of men, deserving of a special category, will seem unjustifiable to many.

My argument is, whether the urgency of the 'reclaiming' task is accepted or not, that there is no dispute over the continual subordination and suffering of women in society. But the particular justification for speaking specifically about the redemption of *women* is that – as I stated at the beginning of this chapter – the very categories of Christian theology have seemed to reinforce the inferiority of women. The Pauline text (1 Tim. 3.11–15) encapsulates the deeply-felt opinion in Christian theology that somehow women are responsible for sin in the world, and can only be redeemed by the role of child-bearer, which, in the time of Paul, meant subordination to the man of the household:

> Let a woman learn in silence in all submissiveness. I permit no woman to teach or to have authority over men; she is to keep silence. *For Adam was formed first, then Eve: and Adam was not deceived, but the woman was deceived and became a transgressor. Yet woman will be saved through bearing children,* if she continues in faith and love and holiness, with modesty [my italics].[33]

I quote this as an example of a strain present in theology which spans the Old and New Testament, the patristic period,[34] emerges very strongly after the Reformation, and again in the nineteenth century. (It has not, mercifully, been the only strain in Christian theology – and can be offset by other dimensions.) But its relevance here is to point to the enormous damage this has heaped on many women, who have felt that their suffering was somehow deserved, their submissive and inferior roles somehow decreed by Scripture. 'Woman', writes Rosemary Ruether, 'through the Fall, and in punishment for the Fall, lost her original equality and became inferior, in mind and body. She is now, within fallen history, subjugated to the male as her superior.'[35] Martin Luther, in a famous passage, wrote that

> Man rules the home and the state, wages war, defends his possessions, tills the soil, builds, plants, etc. . . The woman on the other hand, is like a nail driven into the wall. She sits at home . . . the wife should stay at home and look after the affairs of the household as one who has been deprived of the ability of administering those affairs that are outside and concern the state . . . in this way is Eve punished.[36]

This sentiment of the continuing punishment of Eve has had the effect of blinding society to injustice done to women: 'that she must have "deserved it" defines the basic stance of patriarchy towards assaults on women'.[37] In fact, Susan Brooks Thistlethwaite sees the seeds of wife-beating in the subordination of women to male control, and the way religious institutions support this control. (A report of a Metropolitan Police survey in *The Times*, 2 December 1986, shows that in cases of wife-battering, the police were more likely to side with the batterer than with the victim.)

An example of a frequent church response is cited by another writer:

> When an abused woman was asked why she did not apply for help, she replied: 'I did. Early in our marriage I went to a

12

clergyman who, after a few visits, told me that my husband meant no harm, that he was just confused, and felt insecure. I was encouraged to be more tolerant and understanding. More important, I was told to forgive the beatings, just as Christ had forgiven me with the Cross. I did that too'.[38]

These attitudes are reflected, too, by religious language and by the dual standard with regard to sexuality. Until recently, an unmarried mother was a 'fallen' woman, to be punished even by execution. In certain circles to become pregnant is to have 'fallen', menstruation is frequently referred to as 'the curse', or even as 'Eve's curse', and is certainly a taboo subject in polite society.

Nor is the Judaeo-Christian tradition the only one to attribute evil to the trangression of women. Hesiod tells the Greek myth of Pandora, who opened her box and allowed evil to escape into the world.[39]

The lasting effect on women is that they have been allowed to assume responsibility for suffering and injustice: when confronted by the Christian cross women have so absorbed the ethic of self-sacrifice and the rightfulness of their being punished that they assumed that their rightful place was just there, on the cross with Jesus! This has totally obscured the rightful meaning of when suffering is *authentically* redemptive.[40]

No wonder that when 'Christa', the sculpture of crucified woman by Edwina Sandys, was exhibited in California it immediately struck an authentic chord among many women. 'When I look at Christa I see *me*. That is me on the Cross . . . the sunken, wasted, emaciated centre of the Christa's body, is the emaciated birth centre of my body, rendered incapable of giving birth to the creativity and spirit within me.'[41] Christa was felt to have done what no sermon in words could have done. It had broken down barriers, cut across ethnic lines and powerfully expressed the vulnerability and victim role of women.

And this is why feminist redemption theology has such an ambivalent stance with regard to a theology of the cross and atonement theories. If the central symbol of Christianity contains with it a message which keeps women impaled on that cross, with societal approval, what message of resurrected hope and redemption can it bring?

The way in which women's vocation was one of self-sacrifice and suffering – in the name of all humanity – was brought home to me even more powerfully by a Jewish novelist. I was familiar with the great Crucifixion pictures of the Jewish painter, Marc Chagall, and therefore with the huge symbolic effect of the cross as a trans-cultural symbol for the world's tragedies. But the writer Chaim Potok clearly saw the need to focus on woman as impaled on that cross, eternal victim of world suffering. In the words of Asher Lev, a young Jewish boy, who painted a shocking picture of his mother on the cross – an act which brought him exclusion from his own community:

> For all the pain you suffered, my mama. For all the torment of your past and future years, my mama. For all the anguish this picture of pain will cause you. For the unspeakable mystery that brings good fathers and sons into the world and lets a mother watch them tear at each others' throats. For the Master of the Universe, whose suffering world I do not comprehend. For dreams of horror, for nights of waiting, for memories of death, for the love I have for you, all the things I remember, all the things I should remember, but have forgotten, for all these I created this painting – an observant Jew working on a crucifix, because there was no aesthetic mould in his own religious tradition into which he could pour a painting of ultimate anguish and torment.[42]

Asher Lev's painting, Christa, the tragic heroines of the nineteenth century women novelists focus painfully on my question: How are women to be redeemed? The very central symbol of Christianity itself, the cross of Jesus, must be redeemed from harmful interpretations. The way that it continues to be used in a particularly *non*-redemptive way against women must be highlighted. If there is a particular way in which women have transgressed for which they cannot be redeemed, let it be clarified. If women have sinned in a particularly devastating way, contrasting with the way men sin, let the theological structures reflect this.

14

2 Seeking New Structures: Building New Foundations

This challenge has to be answered. To do so I will tackle the question of whether there is a distinctive way in which women are contributing to the weight of human wrong-doing. I ask what theories of human nature underpin this. I will then embark on a search for new building blocks for redemption theology: What psychological model will provide a new beginning? How can philosophy help?

THE FEMALE SIN – CHOOSING TO BE VICTIM

'This above all – to choose not to be victim',[1] says the protagonist of Margaret Atwood's novel, *Surfacing*, after a solitary and painful struggle to recover a sense of identity. Her conclusion implies that what she is redeemed from is that passive acquiescence in her inferior status, an acceptance of the 'female lot', with its attendant cheapening of her own sexuality, and of complicity in acting out the subservient roles into which women are often trapped. Could this be the 'female sin'?

What is challenging about the way women's experience is being reflected on today is that we have moved beyond the so-called 'kitchen sink' dramas of the early stages of the women's movement,[2] which described the domestic trap in which women are frequently imprisoned to a realization that women have in many ways colluded in their own oppression. (This is not to say that many women are not confined, hopelessly, to the kitchen sink.) But we are led to question what it is about *being woman* which could allow this? Only by understanding if there is a different basis for being female than for being male, can we understand what it is for women to sin, for feminists to sin, and then from what it is necessary to be redeemed.

The journey or quest theme is one of the most popular in spirituality today – but it is not often recognized that the journey for women differs in many ways from that for men. Even in the enthusiasm today for 'holistic' spirituality, for embodied spirituality, it has seldom been recognized that the female body contributes different insights from the male. This is also true in other spheres. Because women have been involved in higher education for a comparatively short time – and in theology for an even shorter – it took a long time for us to realize that what we are being taught in the name of human development did not fit our experience in many instances. Even the psycho-sexual stages of human development – of, for example, Eric Erikson[3] – which are supposed to describe the development of the human being from birth to death, in many cases fit better the experiences of men and boys than they do girls and women!

The insight that sin might mean something different for women has always been implicit in Christian theology, because of the tradition already referred to that woman was responsible for evil being unleashed into the world, and that the punishment of Eve somehow lingers on. Mary Daly, for example, in *Gyn/ecology: the Metaethics of Radical Feminism*, has described the structuring of the suffering inflicted on women by the patriarchal system throughout history, ranging from the footbinding of little Chinese girls to the great European witch-hunt, during which it is estimated that as many as 11 million women died.[4] Daly sees the witch-hunt as a product of the deeply-embedded view of patriarchal society that women ought to suffer:

> In the witch-craze we can see the truth of Helen Diner's insight that 'in Christianity the tree becomes the torture cross of the world. . .' The divine self-centering life of independent women was cut down and consumed. The citizen of the City of God created, staged and acted out the Christian Hell on earth; their theology expressed itself as demonology; their reigning philosophy became an ontology of the damned.[5]

In what I consider to be an exaggerated and melodramatic manner she even relates the apparent indifference to the pain of women in childbirth to a patriarchal wish for women to suffer: 'The lifting of Eve's curse seemed to threaten the foundation of patriarchal religion; the cries of women in childbirth were for the glory of God the Father.'[6]

Daly is right to protest against the systematic structuring of the injustice done to women. But I cannot accept her cruel distortion of the Christian cross into a torture instrument for women – or even, as some have said, a divine sanctioning of child abuse.[7] I look instead, first, to the insights of the liberation theologians, who see the figure of the crucified Christ as their ally, struggling for justice with the oppressed people of Latin America and the Philippines. The crucified Jesus is a most powerful sign that God is involved with the pain of humanity,[8] in the historical struggles for liberation. Nor is the

16

cross of Jesus to be seen as the last word of God, the final sentence – for biblical faith proclaims that 'God raised him up, having loosed the pangs of death' (Acts 2.24).

My task is to uncover the redemptive ethic of cross theology for women, to discover non-destructive meanings for self-sacrifice, to question the possibility of whether suffering can have other meanings than ending up on the cross, as victim, like Asher Lev's mother (referred to in the previous chapter). But to scapegoat all men as the 'evil other', as Mary Daly does, is to remove all possibility of mutuality between the sexes. It is also implicitly admitting that the resurrection history has had no positive impact on human experience.

Christian theology has shown no lack of awareness that women are supposed to be guilty for sin and evil in a different way from men. But there has been no interest or explicit attempt to investigate what these categories could be. The Danish philosopher Søren Kierkegaard was apparently aware that there was a difference.[9] The two forms of sin, he noted, were the sin of defiance and the sin of weakness: 'the one form is, so to speak, the despair of womanliness, the other of manliness'. Quite what he meant by weakness is left maddeningly inexplicit. In any case the sin of defiance and pride has long been regarded as the principal human sin. Adam's pride – at Eve's instigation – was the *felix culpa* which made redemption necessary. Even a recent analysis like that of Reinhold Niebuhr, in *The Nature and Destiny of Man*,[10] sees the fundamental human sin as one of pride. It follows, then, that there can be no redemption without 'the shattering of the self'. Self-seeking, self-assertion and self-realization are all considered by Niebuhr as part of the sin of human pride, only to be uprooted by the sacrificial love revealed by Christ on the cross.[11]

Feminist theologians have not been slow to react. In a now famous article Valerie Saiving Goldstein objected to the prevalent view of sin as pride. She considered this to be much more appropriate to men than women.[12] The danger for women, she says, is that this analysis calls on them to deny what they have never experienced – a sense of self. Women are more guilty of *failing* to take responsibility, of allowing others to act on them and for them. Passivity can be regarded as the female 'original sin'. Women are guilty of 'triviality, distractibility and diffuseness; lack of organizing centre or focus, dependence on others for one's self-definition; tolerance at the expense of standards of excellence . . . in short, under-development or negation of the self.'[13]

I take this analysis of the female sin as passivity very seriously: but it needs to be placed in the context of a proper analysis of human nature. We have to ask whether this is the total picture. What kinds of situation does it *not* cover? For example, was it the sin of passivity which was responsible for racism within the feminist movement? It was certainly not the sin of passivity which drew Myra Hindley into being an accomplice in the infamous Moors murders.

But the sin of passivity seems to suit the neo-Jungian analysis of 'women's nature'. Erich Neumann, for example, links the passivity of women with an inbuilt capacity of biological structuring to give birth. 'The whole of her capacity to realize a conception', he writes, 'may be acted out in a physical, literal conception and birth. . . She may never live out her feminine psyche and thus find her life empty and meaningless, as the outer actuality changes, as her children grow and leave home. This is woman's sin.'[14]

To link passivity with female physiology is highly suspect. It again raises the issue of women's link with bodiliness, with nature and carnality, when this has been viewed so negatively by tradition. The important point made by the analysis of female sin as passivity is that, when it is linked with the Christian ethic of self-sacrifice, of losing a self in order to find it, women are locked hopelessly into a spiral of self-giving, in which no authentic self-development is possible. Christianity encourages them to identify with Jesus' suffering on the cross. Society offers them nurturing, caring and serving roles in which to do this: '. . . women have been invited to participate in and conform themselves to the sufferings of Christ by remaining passive and powerless, because it is these qualities which will humanize the children they raise and the men for whom they provide a home.'[15]

No wonder that the great American feminist Elizabeth Cady Stanton cried over hundred years ago, 'Self-development is better than self-sacrifice!' No wonder that the focus of the activity of women's groups is conciousness raising, in an effort to break this paralysis of passivity as women continue to believe that Christianity's main message to them is to endure whatever God has sent as their particular cross. The process of growth to self-consciousness is the starting point of the spiritual journey – as will be explored in Chapter 4. Even a theologian like Paul Tillich saw that self-sacrifice could be worthless, if there was no self worthy of being sacrificed[16] – but he lacked the sensitivity to apply this to the experience of women. Only if women can see the message of Jesus as invitation to growth and self-affirmation, rooted in a healthy recognition of physical createdness – as call to end crucifixions, not prolong them – is there a chance of recovery of self-denial as part of spirituality.

But this cannot be the last word on sin: a much wider analysis is called for. In this book I seek an understanding of redemption which speaks to *all* human brokenness, violence and oppression. In many parts of the world men and women are locked together in grinding poverty, in a bitter struggle for survival. Sin as passivity hardly seems applicable. Is there not a danger that there is something bourgeois and middle-class about an analysis of sin which sees dominance and pride as masculine, submission and passivity as feminine? There is evidence which we cannot ignore that women in power behave in exactly the same over-assertive, over-ambitious manner as men, even towards other women. Yes, it is undeniable that men have excluded women from power-sharing situations and it is these very situations of dominance which spawn the dynamic which keeps poor people oppressed. But women have colluded in this, as men and women have colluded – perhaps unwittingly – in racist oppression. Upper-class women continue to oppress their servants. A woman may dominate and oppress her own children and even use her inferior status in a manipulative way. There is a sense in which she may keep men oppressed by prolonging her dependent status and financial demands. She may use socially-sanctioned ways to avoid responsibility and become a willing victim to consumerism and materialism. The way society has structured sexual arrangements, says Dorothy Dinnerstein, provides women, like men, 'with a boss for the baby in her, at the same time as it affirms her freedom from the boss she had when she was a baby'.[17] She feels that both sexes collude in mutually destructive arrangements: 'The male rule of the world is not a conspiracy imposed by bad, physically strong and mobile men on good, physically weak and burdened women.'[18]

All this points to the fact that the sin of passivity with regard to the task of self-affirmation is one dynamic in something much more complicated. Yes, feminist thinkers have established that it is time to wake up, to bid farewell to passivity, to 'kiss Sleeping Beauty good-bye',[19] and take responsibility for one's life – the eradication of the roots of evil will require much more than this.

To speak of redemption and the achievement of human integrity we have to understand much more deeply the truth about *human personhood*, and, more specifically, the truth about gender difference.

MYTHS OF FEMININITY

No analysis of sin or redemption could be convincing without a basis for understanding the meaning of human nature. Now, as it is widely accepted that theology and spirituality embrace the whole gamut of human experience, no apology has to be made for delving into psychology, philosophy or sociology to discover, if it is possible, the truth about being male or female. It is certainly a bewildering experience for a woman to try to uncover from the morass of conflicting views any reliable account of female human nature. Where is she to turn? If she turns to the myths and legends of her culture she will usually find them interpreting the experience of men – although I shall look for an alternative layer to some of the legends. It is the male hero who sets out to seek his fortune, win the princess and the kingdom; it is men who seek and find the Holy Grail. If she looks to the female novelists, hoping to find her world described, until comparatively recently she found few who could do this in a creative, independent manner. As we shall see, many fell back on masculine stereotyping of women, and seemed not to be able to give to their heroines the same degree of freedom which they themselves enjoyed.[19] From the developmental psychologists, as I have indicated, she will find that the male will be regarded as normative. Indeed, Freud explicitly says so: 'in its simplified form, the case of a male child may be described' – that is, as norm for childhood experience.[20] That the little girl's 'Oedipal' phase was significantly different from the boy's was not Freud's concern. Small wonder that Simone de Beauvoir has described women as 'the second sex', always looking to men for self-definition: man, she said in a famous phrase, was the norm, and woman was 'the other'.[21]

The kernel of the problem is whether there is one human nature or two, and, if there are enormous differences between men and women, of what, precisely, do they consist? There is an immense range of opinion on the subject. At one end of the spectrum is the view of feminists like Simone de Beauvoir and Kate Millett that all gender difference is socially constructed – one is not born, one 'becomes' a woman – and at the other end we have the myths of 'eternal womanhood' – that somewhere, writ in the heavens is the 'truth' of quintessential womanhood. It is amazing how often this is brought out and used against women when they are contemplating some form of independent action!

In the first place, there is now universal agreement that the Freudian axiom 'anatomy is destiny' is an inadequate basis for understanding human nature[22] and is responsible for many false myths of womanhood. When we speak about the female sin of 'passivity' there is absolutely no connection with the Freudian description of woman's so-called passive sexual role. Secondly, there is a wide consensus today that there is *one* human nature, and that the differences between men and women – apart from the obvious biological ones – are very few.[23] As Rosemary Ruether says, there is no valid psychological basis for labelling certain psychic capacities such as reason 'masculine' and others such as intuition 'feminine': 'to put it bluntly', she says, 'there is no biological connection between male gonads and "the capacity to reason". Likewise, there is no biological connection between female sexual organs and the capacity to be intuitive, caring or nurturing.'[24]

But it is not only feminist writers who want to argue against the two-nature theory. The Canadian Dominican theologian, André Guindon, opposes any attempt at gender differentiation on the basis of psychological differences.[25] His idea that both sexes are oriented towards communion and relationality, and represent two expressions of human living, sets us in the right direction – even though feminist thinkers must reject theories based on complementarity, 'equal but different', as they are usually interpreted in a way detrimental to woman. Each generation, Guindon concludes, must re-make the face of man and woman, manifesting new versions and enrichments of humanity. But to achieve this, the power of choice must be given to women.

Why, then, has the myth of 'the eternal feminine' maintained such a powerful grip on psychological thought, and the way women have been socialized into understanding themselves? I want to uncover the extent to which this is so by showing the different forms in which it presents itself as one of patriarchy's most powerful tools.

The theory's core is that there are qualities which endure that are permanently and quintessentially feminine. These constitute the essence of what it means to be a woman. At the most spiritual end of the spectrum would be the quality of 'maternity', a 'spiritual maternity'. At the more frivolous end of the spectrum would be characteristics such as sweetness, docility, gentleness, femininity – whereas in the middle of the spectrum are qualities like caring, compassion, nurturing, sensitivity, sympathy and empathy.

But where is the theory of 'the eternal masculine'? Not only does there not appear to be one, but the very essential qualities of being woman are dependent on the masculine for their meaning. So 'nurturing', and 'caring' are given expression in caring for men: sympathy and empathy are given natural expression in marriage. The 'eternal feminine' is a useful theory indeed!

'Eternal woman' is given short shrift by Mary Daly.[26] In her critique of the idealizing portrait of woman given by Gertrud Von le Fort – so influential in Roman Catholic thought[27] – she has shown how the focus on the so-called 'symbolic' significance of woman has obscured the actual, historical situation of real women in history. Thus,

the characteristics of the eternal woman are opposed to a developing, authentic person, who will be unique, self-critical, self-creative, active and searching. By contrast with these authentic personal qualities, the eternal woman is said to have a vocation to surrender and hiddenness; hence the symbolism of the veil. Selfless, she achieves not individualization but merely generic fulfilment in motherhood, physical or spiritual.'[28]

So eternal women is shrouded in mystery, her true being given to 'interiority':[29] in order to be a 'luminous and inspiring influence' nature has placed her outside the tumult and the prose of action.[30]

There are three principal ways in which the ghost of eternal woman still continues to haunt. The first is its usefulness to the capitalist system, by which women are made pawns of the labour market and economic forces through essentialist notions of true womanhood. This theory, says Sheila Rowbotham,

> produced a crop of egg-faced, ringleted, bonneted girls, which successfully internalised the role of woman as the helpless, emotional, hysterical angel in the house and was well-suited to the division of labour in a capitalist society . . . [Man] made her an ideal of himself. In her he sought his lost nature.[31]

In fact it is not an exaggeration to say that the more important to a society it is to keep women at home, out of public life, the more idealized become the notions of womanhood.

But the second interpretation is more integral to theology. The spiritual interpretation of eternal woman of certain Orthodox thinkers is its most powerful expression. It is a deeply spiritual notion and has not been specifically addressed by feminist theologians.

For Paul Evdokimov and Nicolas Berdyaev – both upper class Russians who fled the revolution, worked as academics in Europe and reflect in their work a much older Russian religious tradition – 'paternity' and 'maternity' are by no means equivalent notions. Rather, human 'maternity' corresponds to God's paternity in a way which human fatherhood does not. What is behind this is Evdokimov's distress with a masculine-dominated, patriarchal society.[32] Like the feminist analysis he thinks this has occurred through the corruption of power structures. The remedy will be society's recovery of the feminine principle of maternity, which he calls the very 'tenderness of God'.[33] Society has become so masculine, he says, that God cannot be born. So he describes the maternal charism as 'the giving birth to the man-hidden-in-the heart'.[34] It follows from this that Mary, Mother of Jesus, with the title of 'theotokos' – God-bearer – has an iconic role for all women. Indeed, say Orthodox theologians such as Kallistos Ware, this is women's priesthood. Woman should not seek to emulate male ordained priesthood.

This Orthodox tradition belongs to the complementary type of theory of human nature, complementing the masculine Apollonian principle – symbolized as the sun and personalist – with the female Dionysian principle, which is earth-based and communitarian. Similar complementary views of male and female opposed masculine activity with feminine passivity,[35] work (masculine) to source (feminine),[36] egotism (masculine) to altruism (feminine),[37] spontaneity (masculine) to receptivity (feminine).[38]

One could go on. There is a seemingly endless stream of versions of complementary theories of personhood. As I have said, feminist scholarship rejects most of them, as they *both* deny full personhood to women, concentrating on some idealized aspect of her nature, *and* mostly consist of essentialist theory, rather than the historical struggle of real women for independence and autonomy in society. But feminist theology is caught in a double bind by the ambiguity of the Orthodox notion of 'spiritual maternity', and by the characterization of the feminine as nurturing and caring. Mothering, nurturing and caring are such important functions.

It is a similar dilemma to that presented by the Jungian theory of personality types, and by neo-Jungians who want to retain the notion that the so-called 'eternal feminine' will save the world![39] It is similar also to the notion of androgynous being which threatens again to picture 'man' as a split character, forever seeking his lost self! Woman again becomes the necessary completion for 'man' to achieve complete integration of his being.[40]

Again, a neo-Jungian writer like Ann Ulanov will still speak of femininity as 'a cluster of images and behavioural reactions which have a life of their own'.[41] This is in fact the third way in which the ghost of 'eternal woman' still haunts. . . It is undeniable that it is qualities like aggression, competitiveness and domination which are destroying harmonious co-existence: it is surely indisputable that qualities of spiritual maternity and nurturing could be a powerful redeeming force. (In fact I want to build a theology of redemption on these qualities.) But why should these be expressive almost exclusively of women? And why should women accept these qualities as their essential being? Should it be more masculine than feminine to be intelligent?

It is no answer to say that the 'feminine' is a personality type, in theory to be manifested equally by both sexes: in practice myths of femininity are used to control the behaviour of women. If woman steps out of line she is firmly told that she is going against her nature. What we need is to establish a range of human qualities, exhibited by both men and women, to be manifested and striven for in personal and communal relationships, as well as having the potential to transform the fabric of society. Only then could we speak about

23

qualities which truly 'redeem the world'. So when a neo-Jungian writer such as Edward Whitmont, lamenting the mess which patriarchal culture, ideology and myth has made of society, suggests bringing back the myth of the Holy Grail as restoration and celebration of the feminine in our culture, he is telling once again the myth of the eternal feminine in a spiritualizing way.[42] (It is not that Jung's theory of personality types does not offer us valuable insights on human nature, but these need to be worked out equally on the basis of women's experience, instead of on the basis of the male as norm.)[43]

What we seek to discover is whether the actual experience of real women, the way they see the world, feel, think, act and arrive at their own self-definition, *as described by women themselves*, can provide a firmer base on which to build a redemption theology.

IN A DIFFERENT VOICE?

What I now explore – having ruled out essentialist, male-defined theories of female human nature – is whether we can discover from the upbringing, environment and experience of women themselves if a different notion of self might emerge. I then want to explore this against the wider backcloth of a philosophy of human becoming and growth. Only then can I begin to discern the journey of redemption.

My central point is that men and women see both the world and themselves differently not primarily because of inbuilt physiological and psychological differences but because they actually have vastly different experiences and these lead to disparate understandings of their own identities. To come to grips with this will shed light on the degree of guilt and pain suffered by women on the break-up of relationships and also on the nature of the 'female sin' with which I began this chapter.

I have already hinted that the human developmental cycles fit better the development of men than of women. It is felt by many feminist thinkers that Eric Erikson was wrong to put the virtue and achievement of 'care' as the supreme achievement of the developmental scale: this makes little sense for women, who are so deeply socialized into caring from an early age that only gradually do they build up a need for self-discovery and development.

To place the qualities of 'identity' and 'intimacy' sequentially – as Erikson does – as belonging to adolescence and adulthood respectively, again does not fit girls' experience. Girls often do not begin the search for identity until much later.[44] For example, Nora in Ibsen's *The Doll's House* begins a search for self when she is well into marriage. For many women 'the search for self' never takes place at all, as they 'successfully' make the transition from caring for young brothers and sisters to caring for a husband and their own children. Maturity for many women brings the beginning of this search – so the invitation for more 'self-sacrifice' is somewhat redundant, and even positively destructive.

As Carol Gilligan, the American educational psychologist, has so convincingly asserted, there is 'another voice', another layer of human experience which is witnessing to an alternative basis for behaviour, another norm for assessing decisions and evaluating moral judgements.[45] How can this be brought to light? What effect could it have on the developmental schemas?

Suppose that patterns of child-care and rearing mean that the young boy and girl develop differently. Suppose that the famous Freudian Oedipal phase is experienced differently, that it is not just a smooth contrast between boy/father, girl/mother, but that a different dynamic is taking place? Every child is born from the womb of its mother. But the developmental pattern *must* be different for boy and girl. Separation from the mother – which for Freud was the essential step for the boy's growth after the infantile sexuality period – is not necessary *in the same way* for the girl. This means that separation does not define becoming a woman in the same way that it defines becoming a man. Nancy Chodorow – on whose work Gilligan relies – claims that the strength of the mother-daughter relationship in the pre-oedipal infancy years endures during this period, so that her mother is not lost as either internal or external love-object.

But what does the girl learn as a development lesson? A capacity for empathy, claims Chodorow, a capacity for experiencing another's needs or feelings, built into a primary sense of self, in a way that boys do not. Here is where the crucial point lies. Whereas boys develop a 'more emphatic individuation and a more defensive firming of ego-boundaries',[46] girls learn to define themselves much more in terms of relation and connection to other people. Girls become more threatened by separation, boys by intimacy.

The effect this has on the socialization of girls is enormous. 'Empathy' is translated into 'mothering', the role which girls assume also in the world of work – by being a nurse, social-worker or the boss's secretary. But the capacity for mothering can never be totally explained by physiology, hormones or behavioural factors. Mothering is a central and defining feature of the social organization of gender and therefore heavily involved in the construction and reproduction of male dominance.[47]

This means that the capacity for mothering is built developmentally into a girl's psychic structure. She learns that becoming a person is the same thing as becoming a-person-in-relationship. If, for a girl, a basic sense of self consists fundamentally of self-in-relationship, by contrast for a boy it will mean, in a competitive, capitalist society, a curtailing of that primary love and empathy with the mother, in order to achieve more emphatic individuation, and a sense of firmly-defined ego-boundaries. For boys a denial of dependence and attachment to women is deemed to guarantee masculinity and performance in the world of work. In Britain, with the growth of the public school system, this process began with the six-year-old boy being sent to preparatory school. From then on he entered a male-defined world, complemented by experiences in the armed forces and the world of work. In the Catholic Church becoming a priest often used to mean separation from any female influence from the age of eleven by entering junior seminary.

Now it becomes clear why separation, distance and transcendence are viewed as male qualities. Inevitable consequences can be drawn for the image of God. The transcendence of God becomes equated with distance, separation and progress. The immanent God is neglected. Immanence becomes equated with all that is female, weak, vulnerable, dependent and stagnant – a kind of cosmic soup from which the ambitious male must emerge. And what a difficult task those sensitive men of today face when they try to break these societal patterns, to create and maintain more sensitive structures of relating.

The consequences for girls are now also plain. On the damaging side it means that a failure or breakdown in relationship can be experienced by girls as a loss or wound to their sense of self. Even more seriously, a sense of identity may never be developed in the first place. The capacity to empathize and identify with others has never been developed as a strength in society. 'Serving others' has been extolled as a virtue – particularly by the Church – so that women have been encouraged to form themselves into the kind of person who will be of service to others. But there are very few patterns of service which at the same time allow any self-development. Francis of Assisi's prayer, 'It is in giving that we receive', is spoken from the maturity of a man who from a point of his own self-development had discovered a deep spiritual truth. But one has to go through the steps of this journey.

It could mean, says Jean Baker Miller, that the kind of psychic structuring women develop is one of 'mediation' – a kind of psychic reflecting of the needs of others – so that the word 'ego' may not even apply. Women, she says, 'are encouraged to transform their drives into the service of another's drives; and the mediation is not directly with reality, but with and through the other person's purpose in that reality'.[48]

Even if the word 'ego' does apply, there may be such a blurring of ego-boundaries that a woman may be unsure about where she ends and another begins. Couple this with the biblical exhortation that married people should be 'two-in-one-flesh' and we see why women suffer so much guilt about the break-up of a marriage. Is this also why the message of the cross with its invitation to self-sacrifice has such devastating effects on women?

Thirdly, if women act on their relational insights, it may lead them even further into patterns of subservience. *More* mutuality and empathy may deepen the dominance/submission pattern. Is it any wonder that the sin of woman has been named as passivity?

But the positive side of the coin is that capacity for empathy is actually a strength: women have been carrying the torch for all humanity's need and longing for deeper and more satisfying relationships, more effective patterns of affiliation. Yet viewed according to a male-defined developmental scale - as Lawrence Kohlberg's research has shown - girls may appear indecisive and immature. They may seem to be at a lower stage of development. But if Carol Gilligan is right, the reason is that girls are operating from a different ethical base - from an ethics of care and responsibility. Once a situation is seen in terms of relational needs, and not merely in terms of rules and levels of fairness, it can be almost impossible to reach clear-cut decisions. This is not very helpful when a decision is needed quickly - but at least it shows the necessity of making a paradigm shift from clear-cut, linear developmental models to a more horizontal, or even a spiral system based on the relational needs of the situation.

But how do we know that Carol Gilligan is right? Has she taken sufficient account of a class analysis? Poverty and all kinds of deprivation seriously undermine patterns of affiliation. It is possible that gender difference is explained better by variation in education and class than by sex. Perhaps too much emphasis has been placed on early mother-child relationships? Sibling and peer-group relationships are also important in the development of young people. Perhaps there are other ways to learn empathy. . . ?

Despite these objections, what Carol Gilligan argues demands attention and provides inspiration for the way I envisage redemption in this book. She pleads with some force that:

> As we have listened for centuries to the voices of men and the theories of development that their experience informs, so we have come more recently to notice not only the silence of women, but the difficulty of hearing what they say when they speak. Yet in the different voice of women lies the truth of an ethics of care, the tie

between relationship and responsibility, and the origins of aggression in the failure of connection.[49]

If we listen to this voice, how then will it speak of redemption? How will we understand the pattern of redemption which it is necessary to build?

MIRROR, MIRROR ON THE WALL: THE TASK OF RECLAIMING THE MYTH

And when we look with different eyes at certain myths and legends of human development, the mist begins to clear, a different truth emerges. Once we peel away the layers it is possible to see in some instances that the relational strengths of women have been hidden by the way patriarchal society has distorted primary relationships.[50] Hence it has seldom been possible, until very recently, for women to use myth and story as a source of strength for personal development.

As I have admitted, there are few examples of myth centring on the experiences of women.[51] What is worse, the distortion of primary relationships means the mother–daughter bonding is not depicted in a positive manner. The relationship is often one of possessiveness and jealousy. Women are either idealized as the princess at the end of the quest (the eternal feminine) or as the wife/stepmother competing for the attention of the man. For example, the Queen in the story of Snow White who consulted the mirror as to who was the fairest in the land, and was told:

> Thou wert the fairest, lady Queen,
> But Snow White is the fairest now, I ween,

immediately starts plotting the death of her daughter. Bruno Bettelheim says of this tale: 'We do not know why a parent is unable to enjoy his [!] child growing up. . .We do not know why the queen in Snow White cannot age gracefully and gain satisfaction from vicariously enjoying her daughter's blooming into a lovely girl. . .'[52] Yet Bettelheim gives the problem a patriarchal solution, interpreting it in Oedipal terms, as symbolic of the severe problems which may arise between mother and daughter. The solution is given, he writes, by Snow White being kissed to life by the handsome prince. But, as I have been trying to say, it is time for women to find other solutions than being awoken from passivity into other forms of dependence. Kiss Sleeping Beauty goodbye!

But myth and legend, looked at more closely, have more positive messages than this. Greek legend tells of the grief of the wife of

28

Agamemnon, Clytemnestra, at the sacrifice of their daughter Iphigenia, before the Greek fleet sailed for Troy. The whole tragic set of events which culminates in her own murder at the hands of her son Orestes – and his subsequent haunting by the Furies – is set in motion by the sorrow of a mother losing her daughter. As one of the most poignant images of the Bible puts it:

> A voice is heard in Ramah,
> lamentation and bitter weeping.
> Rachel is weeping for her children;
> she refuses to be comforted for her children,
> because they are not. (Jer. 31.15)

The one important exception we have to distorted mother/daughter relationship myths, which is relevant to our theme, because of its significance as a creation/fertility myth and its place in the history of religions, is the story of Demeter and Persephone (Proserpine). The story is well known and stands in contrast with all the great male-centred myths. Demeter, Earth-Mother Goddess, on whom the fertility of the earth depends, is grief-stricken at the rape of her young daughter Persephone by Pluto, Lord of the Underworld. We know that the compromise solution reached – that during the six months in which Persephone must remain underground the earth will be mourning – is an explanation of the rhythm of the cyclical seasons of the year. The rites of Demeter flourished for almost two thousand years at Eleusis, and the Eleusinian Mysteries were the most famous of all Ancient Greek religions. They focus on the three interrelated mysteries of life – fertility and birth, sexuality and marriage, death and rebirth. Because of its bearing on the question of redemption and atonement a question which will need to be tackled later is, Why did the Eleusinian Mysteries eventually give way to Christianity?[53]

Here I want to focus on the possibility that there might be an earlier layer to the story. How could we uncover this from the versions we are given? Charlene Spretnak, a feminist author, drawing on classical scholarship, and the similarities between the Demeter myth and that of Isis, Queen of the Upperworld and Underworld, as well as the Sumerian myth of Queen Inanna and her voluntary descent to the underworld, has created a pre-patriarchal version of the story. In her version Persephone voluntarily descends to the Underworld, to care for the restless spirits of the dead.[54] Also, there would be no rape in this version, and Pluto would not enter the story at all.

Of course this version is in the realm of speculation. Yet it would sharpen the focus on the grief of the mother at losing her daughter, and the consequent rejoicing of the earth at her return. It would also evoke the possibility that there was in this pre-patriarchal period, before the age of military conquests on a vast scale, a time when sexual relationships were not distorted by rape and violence, and when girls were not devalued and humiliated as war-booty, as both the Bible and the Homeric poems depict.

This highlights one of the most important aims of a redemption theology will will be to reclaim sexuality from both the strait-jacket of patriarchal restrictions and the extremes of contemporary permissive society. Feminist redemption tries to envisage other possibilities for experiencing sexuality.

Rachel mourns... Demeter grieves... Clytemnestra cannot forgive her husband... Have we not material here for the recovery of the strength of mother-daughter bonding? That this is essential is not under dispute. (In the contemporary tragic situation of the sexual abuse of children, one of the keynotes for family therapy has been discovered as the building-up of the mother-daughter bond.)

While this is certainly not the only relationship to be reclaimed, it is perhaps a small indicator that redemptive sources are to be discovered in relationships which are distorted by unjust structures. We also see here the immense difficulty in getting behind the text to the truth of the relationship. We see too – and suffer from – the immense power wielded by those who control the transmission of texts.

Myth and legend provide one source, although much is irretrievably lost. The work of women novelists provides another. In societies which prevented women from access to formal theological education, even when women managed to educate themselves informally, what chances did they have of publishing their work? Sadly, not much has remained of women's theological writing – and what we have has been usually edited by the writer's confessor or spiritual director. But if we look at the letters and novels of those with spiritual vision we can sometimes catch a glimpse of that 'different voice' of which Carol Gilligan spoke. This will enable me to explore what I have so far described from a psychological perspective against a philosophical backcloth.

A RELATIONAL WORLD IS A PROCESS WORLD

I believe that George Eliot – Mary Ann Evans – is such a writer. In the novels of this self-educated woman (on which I will frequently draw), philosopher, translator of Feuerbach and Strauss, something struggles to emerge of the different ethic for which I search. In her well-loved novel, *The Mill on the Floss*,[55] Eliot describes the struggles of Maggie Tulliver - a girl with whom she herself clearly identifies - for education, independence and a degree of personal fulfilment. Maggie snatches what crumbs of education she can from her brother Tom. She becomes involved with a hunchback boy, Philip, whose family have a long-standing feud with the Tullivers. Patriarchal norms take over and Tom breaks up what he considers a most unsuitable relationship. But Maggie in her grief gropes for a different ethic: 'I must not, I cannot seek my own happiness, by sacrificing others. . . Love is natural, surely pity, faithfulness and memory are natural too. . . ?'[56] Maggie is trying to break out of a stifling conventional morality by responding to a wider relational scene. She cannot be bound by narrow moral rules, but must, instead, be inspired by 'a life vivid and intense enough to have created a wide fellow feeling for all that is human'.[57]

It is this idea of 'a wide fellow feeling for all that is human' which suggests a different ethical base, and a reason for the pain of Maggie - because a deeper intuition conflicts with an accepted code of behaviour. This, I suggest, is the basis for a feminist concept of redemption. It is not simply that women are contributing skills of empathizing in personal relationships. (I would never deny that sensitive men do the same thing.) It is the intuition that, by witnessing to a profounder ethic for relating, women are actually revealing a world that is relational at its very core. And it is women who have done this, not because of any myth of the feminine, or because of physiological make-up, but being largely left out of the competitive/aggressive/dominance ethic which controls the public arena, these relational strangths - vital for all humanity - have been preserved, developed, but omitted from the transmission of official history.

Now I am drawing close to the heart of what this book is trying to say. Interdependence and relating are the very threads of the complicated tapestry of the world - its warp and woof, to use an old weaving metaphor. So the recovery of that 'different voice', those deeper patterns of affiliation and mutuality, is vital, not just that we may all learn to relate better, and be happier people, but because this is the very raw material of the world. And this is why relating is at the heart of what is redemptive, and what may bring about the transformation of the world, its structures and its patterns of interrelation at every level.

Consulting myths, legends and novels is one thing. But how can I show this at a philosophical level? I need, first, to establish that the 'raw stuff' of the world is relational; secondly, to show how right relationship is at the heart of the redemptive process; and, thirdly, to show that this is in fact the creative divine process at work in history

31

from all time. Finally I will ask what bearing this has on the analysis of 'female sin' with which I began this chapter.

How then could 'relationality' – or the complex interweaving of all created realities – be the raw stuff of the world, when the physicists tell us that it is a question of atoms and electrons? Am I not guilty of a category mistake to mingle two different levels of explanation? True, the Jewish philosopher Martin Buber, in his classic book on relating, *I and Thou*, asserted that 'In the beginning is the relation';[58] but Buber was proclaiming the priority of relating over acting or speaking, and was speaking in philosophical or spiritual categories (it is not quite clear which). Dorothee Soelle, the liberation theologian, in her turn, asserts the primacy of liberation over creation as a primary category, but she is speaking in purely theological terms.[59] Matthew Fox, speaking in the context of spirituality, comes the nearest to approaching what we might call the basic stuff of the universe with his idea of creative energy:

> In the beginning was the creative energy:
> And the creative energy was with God
> And the creative energy was God. . .
> And it was with God in the beginning. . .[60]

Suppose this divine creative energy was the basic stuff of the universe and at the same time it was relational in nature. What could that mean for the world? And could it have scientific coherence and respectability?

I will explore this is in two ways – via the systems theory and with process thought. Here my exploration concentrates on establishing the importance of relating as a primary category, and on showing how the category of process is a vital part of feminist redemption theology. (In a later chapter I will link this with cross theology.)

The systems theory views the world in terms of the interrelatedness and interdependence of all phenomena.[61] It sees all living organisms, societies and eco-systems as wholes – in the sense of being integrated – and yet at the same time as parts with respect to wider wholes. It was Arthur Koestler who emphasized that each 'holon' or subsystem has two opposite tendencies: it has an *integrative* tendency, which enables it to function as part of a wider whole, and a *self-assertive* tendency, which enables it to preserve its individual autonomy.[62] Both tendencies have to be respected for the health of the organism. Systems theory sees all subatomic particles as interrelated energy patterns, in an ongoing dynamic process.

Is it too much in the realm of fantasy to apply these insights to spirituality? Since the shift from Newtonian to Einsteinian physics, we no longer view nature as a fixed, mechanical system to be manipulated by men and women. This, we have realized – too late, in many instances – has allowed a ruthless exploitation of unrenewable, natural resources. But if we reject this, and we no longer accept Aristotle's distinction between substances and accidents, which underlay it, is there is no universally accepted theory of primary matter?

There is now a tendency among some physicists to accept that basic parts of the universe may be interconnected in an immediate way, previously claimed only by mystics and other non-scientific people. It is clearly a theme which fascinates. One physicist has described a theory of super-symmetry, according to which the basic objects of the universe are not particles but 'wiggling motions of strings, like notes on a piano wire'.[63]

What I want to argue is that it is not unreasonable to posit a universe composed of interrelating, interdependent eco-systems: each unit within these will be composed of two polarities or tendencies – integrative and self-assertive. I then want to transfer this to other planes and show how these two tendencies manifest themselves.[64]

For example, a country – like Britain or the United States – also exhibits the same polarities: it interrelates in countless ways with other countries via the market exchange, the World Bank, United Nations, and so on. But it must also maintain its own autonomy. What we usually find is that a country is consumed with self-interest, and does not respect the interrelating function, but shamelessly exploits poorer countries – in the question of Third-World debt, for example. Thus the interrelating tendency becomes exercised in an over-assertive way as power over and domination. When this is applied to individual behaviour it is given a sexist interpretation – self-assertive behaviour is presented as the ideal for men, submissive behaviour for women. Women, says Fritjof Capra, have been forced into roles expressing the integrative function:

> They are the secretaries, receptionists, hostesses, nurses, and homemakers, who perform the services that make life more comfortable and create the atmosphere in which the competitors can suceed. . . All these services involve 'ying' or integrative activities, and since they rank lower in our value system than 'yang', or self-assertive activities, those who perform them get paid less. Indeed many of them . . . are not paid at all.[65]

The second important point for my argument is the process of growth which the systems theory describes. The concepts of growth and change are key parts of the theory – as they are of feminist spirituality. The theory stresses two dynamic phenomena in

33

connection with the self-organizing pole of a living system. The task of *self-renewal* means the ability of living systems to recycle or renew their components. The task of *self-transcendence* means the ability to reach out creatively beyond physical and mental boundaries in the process of evolution.

Where I find the systems theory lacking is in its description of how this growth is supposed to take place. Capra has accurately described the dilemma of women – stuck with an over-development of the integrative pole. But he has not suggested a mechanism for escaping from this dilemma, nor why it should have occurred in the first place. For this I turn to process thought.

This was developed first in Britain by Alfred North Whitehead.[66] After Whitehead's departure to the United States, the centre of interest shifted to Chicago and consequently to the work of one of his disciples, Charles Hartshorne. To some extent process thought is now most popular in California, where John Cobb is Director of the Center for Process Studies at the Claremont School of Theology. My interest is in the way process categories give me a framework for feminist redemption.[67]

The first insight to be gained is the very category of process. As John Cobb said, 'To be actual is to be in process'.[68] The reason this is vital for women, as I will show in Chapter 4, is that as long as they are locked in the despair of the norms of patriarchy, with no opportunity for genuine self-development, there can be no movement forward. We cannot explain away every depression as 'the dark night of the soul'. To be engaged in the process is itself part of the redemption. In the seeking is the finding. As Doris Lessing's protagonist Martha Quest cried, 'The process itself held the keys.'[69]

The second insight from process thought is its emphasis on relating as a primary category. But it is relating as part of the process of moving forward which is crucial. Relating pushes the new existence into being and pushes the new becoming forward to the future. Whitehead, says Marjorie Suchocki, describes existence as a creative response towards the past and the future.[70] So relationships are the beginning and the ending of each unit of existence. Yet within this dynamic of relationality, the tension to which I referred above between interdependence and autonomy must be preserved.

Thirdly, the tension between interdependence and autonomy is described in process terms as *justice*. Self-affirmation and self-giving are held together by seeing the category of relating, or of mutuality, as a basic dynamism. This helps us to see why, at a basic level, there is no clash between justice and love – if the two polarities are respected.

This is an important point for spirituality. Process spirituality can be seen as a maximizing of relatedness. There are no limits to the possibilities for mutuality, which, of its nature, pushes to deeper and deeper forms of communion. But this should mean at the same time actualizing deeper and deeper forms of justice in the world. In this lie the redemptive possibilities of the model. Now we can see why it was so important to hold together the movements of creation and redemption. The strength of the process model is exactly this. The becoming of God and the becoming or transformation of the world are part of the same dynamism. This is because God is seen as *with* the world, not over-against the world, 'feeling' the world in order to offer redemptive possibilities to it. Whitehead saw that the overriding concern of God was for the redemption of the world: 'He [God] does not create the world, he saves it; or, more accurately, he is the poet of the world, with tender patience leading it by his own vision of truth, beauty and goodness.'[71]

The process model depicts the whole world as touched by God, who feels, is present to, and 'prehends' every finite actuality. In Whiteheadian terminology we would say that God's wisdom consists in the integration of God's *consequent* nature – that is, God's nature as turned to and involved in the world – into God's *primordial* nature, which is the completion of all possible harmonies and beauty.

Justice, in the process model, is the responsibility of both God and world. There is a rhythmic interdependence between them. God is always offering redemptive possibilities to the world – in Whitehead's words, 'He is the great fellow-sufferer who understands'[72] – but the world's active response is necessary, otherwise the possibilities which God is offering to the world will never be actualized.

This suggests not the remote God, unaffected by human distress, but the image of the vulnerable God, whose redemptive possibilities are rejected by the human race. . . 'Oh my people, what have I done to you. . . ?' – thus the famous Good Friday reproaches express with pathos the pain of the deity.

So closely did Whitehead see God and world together involved in the redemptive process that he saw the transformed world as literally becoming the body of God. Redeemed human consciousness will become part of divine consciousness. In fact human religious consciousness '*is* God's self-awareness diffused through the eyes and ears and mind of humanity and reunited in the redemptive act'.[73]

Many criticisms have been and continue to be made of process thought even by feminist theologians themselves.[74] Feminist work on process is itself fairly recent. What I take here as crucial to my argument is the way in which the dimensions of past, present and future are held in creative tension by the notion of 'novelty'. Is not 'Behold I make all things new' (Rev. 21.5) the very core of biblical hope?

If we are to have any hope for changing oppressive structures there has to be a way of breaking out of the past, by some means other than a mere repetition of former mistakes in different forms. 'The myth of the Eternal Return' does not offer us much hope: it merely presents us with endless repetitions of the same events in different forms - so women must remain for ever oppressed. By contrast, process thought offers a very positive framework - and it is only the bare bones - for feminist redemption: in the idea of God as both ground or matrix of novelty, as creative source of transformation, as well as vision of ultimate togetherness, there is hope that every situation may contribute to a new harmony, a new depth of relating.

A distinctive feminist process thought can offer much more than the liberation theologians have suspected. I have described the limitations of political liberation alone in Chapter 1: despite the focus of such Latin American theologians as Jon Sobrino - following Jürgen Moltmann - on a God who is crucified and struggling with us against oppression, I have to ask, What hope does this ultimately bring? (Women have frequently experienced a unity with the sufferings of Christ without any experience of resurrection.) Process thought images a God who suffers with us - yes, but more than that. In the very process of divine involvement with suffering and evil (not intervention', we do not intervene in something which touches us our deepest self intimately), God is able to present new, transforming possibilities to the situation. (I use the word 'situation' rather than 'person' deliberately because in Chapter 3 I want to explore freely the context of redemption, and suggest a wider interpretation.) The very fact of the presence of God means that an immense spectrum of factors - from past as well as present situations - can form part of the redemptive process and the very context of redemption.

This brings us full circle. If the relational process is at the heart of reality, at the heart of the great divine creative-redemptive dynamism, participating in this must be what is meant by 'holiness'. So entering into deeper, more meaningful and at the same time juster structures of relating is the kind of redemptive spirituality needed for the transformation of the world. Sin must therefore be acting *against* the relational grain of living. So, how do women sin?

By preserving the 'different voice', by remaining close to a more profound relational scene, women are forming part of the divine redeeming task for the world. But where this is cast aside for destructive and exploitative power systems, the relational truth is rejected and an evil dynamic is set in motion. The assertive aspect has been misused. The other side of the coin is that where a woman or any oppressed person ignores - or is forced by structures to reject - the assertive or autonomous pole of personality, the relational truth is also cast aside..So it is not so simple as merely the 'sin of passivity'. Maggie Tulliver – to use George Eliot's example again – was certainly not passive. She witnessed to the fact that the relational truth was being violated – first when forced to give up Philip, and, secondly, when she was taken off by Stephen against her better judgement. And Eliot had no solution for Maggie. Tragically, she is drowned in the arms of the uncomprehending Tom.

Does feminist redemption theology operate in a wider context? To discover precisely what this might be is my next task.

3 Woman and Nature: A Redeeming Connectedness

'The earth is my sister; I love her daily grace, her silent daring, and how loved I am, how we admire this strength in each other, all that we have lost, all we have suffered. all that we know; we are stunned by this beauty and I do not forget what she is to me, what I am to her.'[1]

'NATURE TOO MOURNS FOR A LOST GOOD. . .'

With this quotation I begin to explore the actual process of redemption. 'Redemption', I have said, encapsulates the yearning of the whole universe for integrity and healing. Women's experiences witness – often in an unarticulated, groping manner – to 'another voice', another strand in human experience which may offer a critique of certain dominating values which hurtle the world on a self-destroying path. If only those subjugated knowledges could be resurrected!

Process theology gives us the bare bones, envisioning God and human co-operation in the redemptive task, which may have different emphases for men and women: but the thread which unites is the need to respect the relational grain of existence and the many aspects of living where this is ruptured.

But in what context is this process enacted? Do we speak merely about relationships being broken? Is this the lost mutuality which must be restored? In this book I envisage a Christian theology of redemption on a much wider scale. In the first place I think the contemporary focus on fulfilling personal relationships can be suffocating, unrealistic, and impossibly demanding. I mean something much wider and deeper by 'relationary' than the intense personal encounter striven for in so many well-meaning encounter groups today. That is the mistake we made when, in rejecting the prison which institutional marriage sometimes becomes, Christian thought focused instead on building personal relationships.[2] This has often raised the hopes of a couple beyond all realistic possibilities. The health of a marriage, this view maintains, is to be defined by the quality of the personal relating. This is a better way to define a marriage than simply as a supposed metaphysical or spiritual bond, which may bear no relation to the actual situation of two intensely unhappy people, but it could make it even more likely that a marriage will break up. It often leads to the cry, 'Why should I stay in a relationship which doesn't fulfil me?' and it fails to take into account that for women the issue is 'Do I have any identity *apart from* this relationship? Am I totally defined by marriage and motherhood?'

I am not trying to argue against strong marital – or other – relationships: I am simply saying that *personal* relationships can seldom bear the immense weight invested in them. Unless we develop our own personal strengths and face our 'aloneness' in the world at quite a deep level (as I explore in the next chapter) our *interpersonal* relating will continue to make unrealistic demands. This has three implications. For women it means not avoiding the task off becoming a 'self', of building a sense of strong identity – referred to in the last chapter as 'the female' sin. It means calling a halt to living a 'mediated' existence. Secondly, for men, it means a conversion from a lifelong attitude of relating to women as extensions of themselves, relied upon for physical, emotional and sexual needs. And, thirdly, it means situating the complex web of interrelating on a much wider plane, including nature and the cosmos itself.

I am not advocating anything as simplistic and sentimental as merely talking to the tulips or relating to the rabbits. I am aware that 'back-to-nature' movements frequently become the hobby of the middle class. Even at the moment the enthusiasm for a healthy 'natural' life-style, with its demand for muesli and organically-grown flour and vegetables – served in stripped pine kitchens lined with Laura Ashley wallpaper! – flourishes among those who can afford the higher prices of these commodities: the luxury of the 'alternative life-style' is not for the poor and unemployed. The matter of 'consulting the stars' before choosing a date for all important meetings is more complex. When we have eliminated all crankiness and craving for quick problem-solving the issue remains unsolved: How are we interrelated with other planets? Is there a wisdom we can tap which could expand our limited possibilities?

But there is a more important issue. Nature, the whole created reality, also hungers for redemption. Nature, too, as Paul Tillich said, watching the ocean rolling towards him – an ocean where smaller fish were being devoured by larger – 'mourns for a lost good'.[3] It is not just that we are estranged from nature – 'Little we see in nature that is ours'[4] (a frequent theme of the romantic poets) – but that nature is part of the whole creative/redemptive process, groaning in travail until the fulness of time (Rom. 8.22). Nature is even *more* endangered by the false philosophies which have allowed her exploitation. Too late we are becoming conscious that the divine command (in Genesis 1.28) to have dominion over all living things has been disastrously misused in the exploitation of the earth's unrenewable resources.[5] The myth of Mother Nature bounteously and endlessly overflowing with her gifts and her fertility, that there is permanently 'the dearest freshness, deep-down things' as Gerard Manley Hopkins once said so expressively,[6] should have ceased to lull us into security and inaction. In reality we are faced with the brutal rape of nature. 'Our mother is dying', as Matthew Fox has put it.[7] And despite the efforts of pressure groups the same exploitative policies carry on.

Yes, we have heard the words of Chief Seattle:

> The air is precious to the red man, for all things share the same breath – the beast, the man, the tree, they all share the same breath. . . What is man without the beasts? If all the beasts were gone, man would die from a great loneliness of spirit. For whatever happens to the beasts soon happens to man. All things are connected. . .[8]

But we do not heed them. The link between cancer and leukaemia – which affects small children and pregnant mothers – and levels of radiation from nuclear reactors, is proved. But we carry on building them. The interest in ecology and environmental issues, it seems – despite the groups which proliferate – still only bites at a skin-deep level. True, hope is offered by Green politics and its idea of ecological wisdom. 'Deep ecology encompasses the study of nature's subtle web of interrelated processes and the application of that study with our interactions with nature and to ourselves',[9] say Spretnak and Capra, echoing the theme of a basic interrelatedness. But their voice and their message – along with the voice of Friends of the Earth and the Alternative Technology group inspired by Fritz Schumacher – is seldom heeded, even for self-interested motives. The destruction of rain-forests continues, causing the uprooting of peoples and immense changes of climate and soil formation.

Not only has the ethic of dominance/submission permitted this destruction but the domination of women has been assumed to be part of the domination of nature. As was seen in Chapter 2, because myths of femininity continually identify female human nature with both physical weakness and with natural processes – which is supposed to form the basis of woman's spirituality – she is justifiably controlled and ordered by men.

Now it can be seen how complex is the redemptive task. If the rape of the earth is legitimized not only by greed and power-lust, but by an underlying philosophy which sees both human and non-human

40

relationships as a question of power and submission – the earth as 'virgin' territory, awaiting violation – then it is at the level of our vision of interrelating that the healing must begin. No amount of demonstrating about saving the rain-forests will make an atom of difference as long as we believe that nature is there to be conquered, tamed and exploited.

All we are left with, if we continue to ignore the rhythms and balance of the natural world, is the tragic symbol – and reality, in so many places – of 'the waste land'. Although this has been given recent prominence through T. S. Eliot's poem,[10] it is a much older symbol: the Old Testament prophets paint the picture of desolation, when it appears that the earth is cursed because the people have forsaken the paths of justice:

> The earth mourns and withers,
> the world languishes and withers;
> the heavens languish together with the earth.
> The earth lies polluted
> under its inhabitants;
> for they have transgressed the laws. . .
> Therefore a curse devours the earth,
> and its inhabitants suffer their guilt. . . (Isa. 24.4-6)

This was Palestine in the sixth century BC. But the ravishing of the earth did not end there. The symbol of the polluted waste land, where all growth is blighted, is a prominent theme in the Holy Grail legends which stem from a range of European countries. In one version of the story – the legend of Perceval, one of the Grail heroes (and Wagner's *Parsifal*)[11] – the plight of the waste land is attributed to the mysterious wound of the Fisher King. Unless Perceval can ask the right question there can be no healing, no vision of the Holy Grail. As I have said, many followers of Jung would see the solution to the problem in the return of feminine values to culture and society.[12] But they do not often realize that there can be a token acknowledgement of female values – and an ignoring of the plight of real women.

Only in one of the Grail stories, in which men play the central roles, is there a hint of allowing autonomy to women. This is the story of Gawain and Dame Ragnell. Although it appears to point to the importance of allowing women the power of choice, it is nevertheless a story which glorifies Gawain as the perfect Christian knight. Gawain and King Arthur were wandering in the forest, Arthur with a problem to solve. An incredibly ugly old hag appears and offers him the solution to the problem if he will marry her. The noble Gawain offers to do so, to save Arthur from his predicament. Great is the mourning in the court when the news is told. The ugly dame insists on the wedding being celebrated at high mass, and then with a feast at which the whole court is present. The author of the medieval text is at pains to describe her ugliness and greed at the wedding banquet – clearly to emphasize the tragedy which has befallen Gawain.

Then comes the dénouement. Alone in their chamber, courageously Gawain offers to kiss her. He is determined to keep his part of the bargain. To his surprise she is transformed into a most beautiful maiden. She then offers him a choice. She may be beautiful for him alone during the night, or for the whole court during the day, but not both. Gawain replies that *she* must choose. 'Because you have given power to the woman,' she says in delight, 'I can be beautiful both night and day!' The enchantment is broken. . . Even though this is a story to illustrate the knightly qualities of Gawain, and is seen through the mirror of distorted notions of the female, yet there is a hint of the importance of the power of choice, which, if offered to the women, could contribute to the healing of the land.

And this is exactly our challenge: What kind of decisions, choices and actions are necessary for the healing of the land? For our context for redemption is the universe itself and the myriad interconnections from which it is formed: all must be enabled to play their part. As an old story puts it:

> It was a chilly, overcast day when the horseman spied the little sparrow lying on its back in the middle of the road. Reining in his mount he looked down and inquired of the fragile creature, 'Why are you lying upside down like that?'
>
> 'I heard the heavens are going to fall today,' replied the bird. The horseman laughed. 'And I suppose your spindly legs can hold up the heavens?' 'One does what one can', said the little sparrow.[13]

But how do we recover the dynamic of interrelatedness, of mutuality with all creation? How is the redemptive process to be set in motion?

ALL THINGS ARE CONNECTED – THE WITNESS OF WOMEN

The key lies in recovering a sense of connection with all living things, that 'wide fellow feeling for all that is human'. It is my argument that, whenever they have kept alive and vibrant a sense of living contact with natural processes, women have been engaging in the work of redemption on behalf of all humanity.

Not only that, but where this process has been reflected on and integrated within a developmental process, as a woman slowly comes to a sense of self, the Christian path of mystical unity can be traced from a feminist point of view (I develop this idea in Chapter 4). Here I will show how, using this sense of connectedness with the natural world, a special form of mysticism emerges, which we might call 'feminist mysticism'.

And the extraordinary paradox is that, although woman's identification with nature has been the very fact which doomed her to carry the burden of degraded sexuality throughout history to this day, branded as whore and seductress, as 'fallen woman', yet through and despite it all women have discovered a healing strength and wholeness through a range of experiences with nature which offer an alternative to the body/spirit dualism characteristic of western philosophy since Descartes.

That women preserve a connectedness with nature, a witness to a more ancient wisdom, is also paradoxical given that theology has usually identified the divine with a transcendence which stood over-against the world, nature and matter. This is the point at which we touch 'another voice'. *Not* that women make any exclusive claim to discovering the joys and beauties of nature – this has been the source of poetic inspiration from time immemorial. Nor have women a unique claim on the discovery of nature as a source of religious experience. We only have to look at 'The Canticle of the Sun' of St Francis of Assisi to see that this is false. But a close look at the way poets and theologians use the theme of nature will often reveal a scarcely-concealed dualism of body/spirit. Even St Francis referred to his body as 'Brother Ass'! In the Great Chain of Being, the hierarchy of living things in which theologians categorized creation, nature and material things are firmly at the bottom, to be dominated by categories of spirit and reason.

Nor does the picture change when Friedrich Schleiermacher – sometimes called the father of modern Protestantism – made experience the source of religion, and identified the world of the sacred with all creation.[14] This was in deliberate opposition to what he saw as the arid scholasticism of the Middle Ages. Yet Schleiermacher – sometimes accused of being a pantheist – was suspicious of identifying nature with the divine and focused much more strongly on the actual consciousness of the divine as creatureliness or dependence. This very consciousness of the divine – whether in nature or in family life – itself constitutes the existence of God, according to Schleiermacher.

This strain was carried still further by Rudolph Otto in his idea of 'numinous consciousness'.[15] The idea of the numinous, which Otto explains is the very content of 'The Holy', or 'The Divine', is certainly to be experienced in nature. But it is experienced in a way totally opposed to the theme of connectedness and interrelatedness which I am developing. For, deep within the experiential moment, which is the experience of God as *mysterium tremendum et fascinans* – as 'mystery which both attracts and repels' – is given the feeling of distance and separation. God, says Otto, is 'wholly other'. He is *das ganz andere*. The deeper the experience the greater the awe and terribleness of God as Wholly Other. Spirituality will then consist in recognizing that one is but dust and ashes before the deity. Just as Moses took off his shoes in the theophany of God in the burning bush (Exod. 3.5), and Isaiah's lips had to be cleansed by a seraph with a burning coal before he could gaze upon the vision of God (Isa. 6.6), so the distance between divine and human will be revealed in a terrifying yet attractive way.

This is totally opposed to what women have experienced. But the challenge in developing my theme is to avoid the well-known snare of identifying women totally with the immanent God, the mystical-communion-with-nature strand in spirituality, which is opposed to any sense of transcendence. This has presented two dangers. First, it engages women in separatism – from men and from the structures of society – in a search for the immanent self, the immanent divine, worshipped as the Goddess. Although I see Goddess-spirituality as vitally important and as having much to teach Christianity – as will be seen later in this chapter – in so far as it turns women totally inward they are not relating to the real world but finding an escape from it. Goddess-religion, says Elizabeth Moltmann-Wendel,

> as a religion of self-discovery no longer has a social, economical or ecumenical perspective. In many places contemplation of one's navel or narcissism has replaced the stimulus of communication. . . Thea – sophy has replaced theology and now becomes a watch-word, and women snuggle up in the arms of the goddess in erotic love.[16]

Secondly, by presenting this as an alternative to patriarchal religion we preserve another dualism – that between patriarchy and matriarchy. If we totally identify immanence with matriarchy, how is the criticism to be faced that female spirituality is stagnant, opposed to movement and separation, the great cosmic soup referred to in the last chapter? In fact John Cobb claims that there would have been no progress in history were it not for patriarchy, because matriarchy tends to stagnation, with its concentration on static principles, on organic immanence.[17] Society needed its explorers and discoverers, he said, in order to evolve.

Feminist spirituality contests this view on many grounds. The first is the question of the dubious historicity of cultures supposed to be matriarchal. It is a pity to oppose old myths of femininity with new ones. The tendency here is for women to assume that before the

44

advent of patriarchy matriarchal societies were the norm. Life-affirming qualities were in the ascendant, there was mutuality between the sexes, no wars – in fact, activity was peaceful and agrarian – women were in positions of authority, and Goddess-worship was universally practised.[18] This is the myth of the Golden Age of matriarchy. My argument is that we just do not know enough about ancient cultures to make such assumptions. The word 'matriarchal' has had many interpretations. Today it is even used of societies where women have sole care of children because they have been abandoned by their husbands: yet these women are often nearly ground into the earth by poverty – being a 'matriarchal' society does not help them very much. To hark back to this supposed era when the Goddess reigned supreme does scant justice to the creativity and courage of women *not* smothered by patriarchy.

In thinking like this women prolong a dualist framework. Rigid, absolutist definitions cannot be defended. Yet we can discern a matriarchal *presence* constant in history. As Rosemary Ruether says: 'There are tensions that define ancient religions – especially between chaos and cosmos, death and life – but divine forces, male and female, are ranged on *both* sides of the dichotomy.'[19] To identify patriarchy with a spiritualizing tendency and matriarchy with a materialist tendency, as does another feminist writer, Carol Ochs,[20] again prolongs a matter-spirit dualism. It would mean that, when a mystic such as Teresa of Avila speaks of values other than the material, she is being influenced by patriarchal norms. Ochs would also equate the matriarchal principle with attachment to soil, settlement and cities, while – as the Bible presents it – patriarchy rejects the transformation mysteries of earth and home and chooses instead exile and wandering. Biblical Jahwism, she claims, offers a spirituality of wandering.[21] The desert is essentially an anti-agricultural symbol, opposed to change or growth. But whereas she is right to associate the desert so closely with Jahwism, she has erected an untenable opposition between the desert-wandering (patriarchal) and city-settlement (matriarchal). We cannot support such un-historical absolutes. It is true that women in Judaism were prevented from wandering by the norms of the times – hence the freedom offered to women by the Jesus religion – and are more associated with settled existence. But the city is a precious symbol for Christianity. Why would the 'New Jerusalem' become the symbol for heaven, if cities represent all that is not patriarchal? The eternal city represents that ultimate homecoming, the journey's end. The desert, too, will be transformed, will blossom, according to the prophetic vision of shalom and righteousness (Isa. 39), and God's people are seen as a fruitful vineyard (Isa. 5). So the argument that Jahwism – and

45

consequently the Judaeo-Christian tradition – is totally patriarchal, opposed to soil, agriculture and settlement, with the exclusion of female symbols, does not hold water.

Nor can I accept the dualism asserted by Cobb between patriarchal activity and progress and the matriarchal organic principle, which, he says, because of its connection with nature, implies stasis and lack of movement. He is limiting the notion of progress and movement to a certain stereotypic interpretation.

But whichever way one interprets progress, women's experience will be intimately bound up with it. To see the organic principle in such a static way, as a permanent sinking back into the primal womb, ignores the change, growth and transformation which are an intimate part of the life-processes. On the level even of the physical processes of pregnancy, childbirth and child-rearing women are bound closely to change and moving forward. Pregnancy should not be seen as a passive waiting, a dreamy co-operation with nature's unseen forces. 'Eternal woman' lurks again. Pregnancy and childbirth are extremely active processes: only in the West, comparatively recently, and mainly among middle and upper classes, has such a misinterpretation been allowed to develop. Women in Asian and African agrarian cultures, when pregnant, are active in the fields and at home during the whole time, birthing being part of the basic rhythm of life and an affair for the whole community.

Women participate in three great transformation mysteries, according to Jungian psychologists, namely, menstruation, pregnancy and breastfeeding (the changing of blood to milk).[22] But this is only one type of transformation mystery. Women are not to be once more identified completely with bodily processes. Embodied spirituality is holistic spirituality. Connectedness with the humblest of things, a sense of care and reverence for the most ordinary tasks, brings awareness of the possibilities for growth and transformation. As Adrienne Rich wrote:

> The enormity of the simplest things:
> In this cold barn tables are spread
>
> with china saucers, shoehorns
> of german silver, a gilt-edged book . . .
>
> this fraying blanket with its ancient stains
> we pull across the sick child's shoulder
>
> or wrap across the senseless legs
> of the hero trained to kill
>
> this weaving, ragged because incomplete
> we turn our hands to interrupted

46

over and over, handed down,
unfinished, found in a drawer . . .

her vanished pride and care
still urging us on, urging on . . .

to help the earth deliver.[23]

This great symbol, '*to help the earth deliver*', is at the heart of my attempt to build a new Christian theology of redemption.

For the moment I want to stress that it is through connectedness, relatedness and faithfulness to the most ordinary of activities that women have built up through the centuries wisdom, strength and possibilities for transformation – especially through activities of herbal lore, healing, cottage industries, gardening and cooking. This fact has been overlooked in discussion about the eligibility of women for the priesthood.

But in maintaining that the gender difference explains the attitude of separation from or connectedness with nature I am aware that there is another factor also involved. Paul Santmire has pointed out that it was Protestant Reformation theology – rather than gender difference – which allowed distancing from the earth to evolve from 'otherness' to 'alienation'.[24] But the issue is more complex than Santmire admits: his analysis, in any case, does not include the experience of women. The increasing industrialization of society and the rapid development of scientific knowledge also added their share to the alienation from nature, as they also contributed to the exploitation of women and children in factories.

The argument has to be seen at a philosophical level. The seventeenth century still saw humanity 'over-against' nature, but also saw nature as inert matter, not as organically connected with human beings. It is remarkable that one of the first philosophers to move to a different view of nature – in fact the strongest influence on Leibniz in his move away from the rigid laws of Newtonian physics – was a woman, Countess Anne Conway. In Anne Conway's philosophy matter was not dead and stupid: there was an intimate bond and unity betwen body and soul. These were of the same substance and nature, except that the soul was more excellent in terms of swiftness, impenetrability and life.[25] She did not build her theology of creation on the model of a machine – which was popular at the time – but on the great hierarchical chain of being. Although she felt that the level of mind and spirit ranked higher than the material level, like Leibniz she believed that 'in every portion of matter there was a whole world of creatures, each one containing within it an entire world'.[26] Like Leibniz too, and in a way helpful to

47

my theme, she based her theory on the interdependence of all creatures under God, 'in a certain society and fellowship . . . whereby they mutually subsist one by another, so that one cannot live without another.' We are still far from Whitehead and process thought, still far from a thoroughgoing understanding of inter-dependence and relationality, and still far from grasping the meaning of embodied humanity. But in Anne Conway's writing – one hundred years before Schleiernacher, and at a time when mechanistic models were prominent – there is some witness to a different tradition, which points to a more organic understanding of nature.

So far I have argued philosophically. I now want to explore the redemptive context of the natural world from a spiritual point of view: What actually has it contributed to the redemptive experience of women?

AFFIRMING THE LOST WHOLENESS

If 'our mother is dying' is a tragic reflection on the contemporary ecological crisis, crying for attention to the destruction of the natural world, what women's spirituality reveals is a continuous thread whereby women have been able to derive strength from nature. This has occurred in different ways, ranging from the 'connectedness' experiences arising from a more embodied way of receiving the world, to a genuine nature mysticism, present as a strand within Christian spirituality. It has been experienced both as part of a quest for wholeness and self-development and as a way of experiencing God when official institutional forms of religion excluded women and female experience. Nature has appeared to offer solace to women when human contact failed them, when institutional religion excluded their experiences, probably because of the very vulnerability and openness of women to such a source for religious experience and the willingness of women to admit and welcome the sacredness of the earth as humanity's true home. Rich and poor women alike have been open to the creativity and strengthening connectedness deriving from natural resources.

Nature as inspiration and expression of divine inspiration is not confined to Christianity, but spans the experience of women through time and across the cultures. In ancient Greece the earth mourned the loss of her daughter with the Earth Mother Goddess, Demeter. In the legend of Psyche, when she is at her most despairing, it is both the reeds of the lake which offer comfort, and the ants who come to her rescue.[27] Not only in the legends of ancient Greece but in more recent works is this theme of drawing strength from nature to be found, for instance, in the pioneering work of the nineteenth-century women novelists.

In Charlotte Brontë's novel *Jane Eyre*, Jane's world falls apart when she discovers that the man she is about to marry, Mr Rochester, is already married. In her isolated, friendless situation it is the moon to which she turns for help:

> She broke forth as never moon yet burst from cloud; a hand first penetrated the sable folds and waved them away; then not a moon, but a white human form shone in the azure, inclining a glorious brow earthward. It gazed and gazed on me. It spoke to my spirit. . .
> 'My daughter, flee temptation.'
> 'Mother, I will.'[28]

This dramatic image of Jane Eyre receiving guidance from what appears to be a moon-goddess raises again the question of theophanies in nature, and in particular the contribution of Goddess-spirituality.

Similarly, it is through nature that the poor servant girl described in Elizabeth Barrett Browning's poem, 'Aurora Leigh', receives her only comforting experience of the divine:

> And, creeping through the golden walls of gorse,
> Would find some keyhole towards the secrecy
> of Heaven's high blue, and, nestling down,
> peer out –
> Oh, not to catch the angels at their game, –
> (She had never heard of angels), – but to gaze
> She knew not why, to see she knew not what,
> A-hungering outward from the barren earth,
> For something like a joy. She liked, she said,
> To dazzle black her sight against the sky,
> For then, it seemed, some grand blind love
> came down,
> And groped her out, and clasped her with a kiss.
> She learnt God that way and was beat for it
> Whenever she went home. . .
> This grand, blind love, she said,
> This skyey father and mother, both in one,
> Instructed her and civilized her more
> Then ever Sunday school did afterward. . .[29]

This is 'the different voice', the grand, blind love' which has been experienced when official religion was found oppressive. It has been expressed in its most passionate form by Emily Brontë in her visionary poems. It seems that, unlike her sisters, Emily did not suffer the deprivations of Cowan Bridge school – immortalized by Charlotte in *Jane Eyre* – from which Maria and Elizabeth died. Nor did she suffer as Charlotte did from the repressive form of Christianity which was imposed on the children by their aunt. Roaming the moors and crags near Haworth, with a freedom seldom experienced by women, then or now, Emily discovered an intense affinity not only with the moorland itself, with every bird and flower which grew there, but also with the deep unity between all creation which was unbroken by death. She believed in everlasting life like the rest of her family, but so strong was her mystical bonding with the universe that she did not believe that the soul needed forgiveness to enter it. In *Wuthering Heights* Ellen Dean, watching by the dead Catherine, says:

> I don't know if it is a peculiarity in me, but I am seldom otherwise than happy while watching in the chamber of death, should no frenzied or despairing mourner share the duty with me. I see a repose that neither Hell nor earth can break; and I feel an assurance of the endless and shadowless hereafter – the eternity they have entered – where life is boundless in its duration, and love in its sympathy, and joy in its fullness.[30]

The tragedy of Emily Brontë was not so much her early death but the death of that intense life within and her visionary powers caused by her grief at her brother's suffering and death and by Charlotte's pursuit of fame for the three sisters.[31] That sense of the power of the immanent deity which is continuous with the world's very life-source is no more powerfully expressed than in her famous poem:

> No coward soul is mine,
> No trembler in the world's storm-troubled sphere:
> I see Heaven's glories shine,
> And Faith shines equal arming me from fear.
>
> O God within my breast
> Almighty ever-present Deity
> Life, that in me has rest
> As I, Undying Life, have power in Thee.[32]

This expressed what Emily Brontë continually pours out: themes of spiritual mystical union with nature and between persons. Heathcliff's wild and desperate love for Catherine was attempting to reach beyond the grave – 'I cannot live without my life! I cannot live without my soul!'[33] Catherine Earnshaw herself had cried in a famous passage, 'Nelly I *am* Heathcliff – he's always in my mind –

50

not as a pleasure any more than I am a pleasure to myself – but as my own being . . . so, don't talk of separation again.'[34]

But the point here is that the mystical union and connectedness with nature is experienced as a conflict with traditional Christianity. In the same chapter in *Wuthering Heights* Catherine tells Nelly Dean of her dream, where she has died and gone to heaven:

> I was only going to say that Heaven did not seem to be my home, and I broke my heart with weeping to come back to earth; and the angels were so angry that they flung me out into the middle of the heath on the top of Wuthering Heights, where I woke sobbing for joy.[35]

Not only is there a tradition of deriving strength from nature and a witness to a 'different voice', there has developed a literary genre whereby women struggle for wholeness and identity through nature experiences.[36] I can illustrate this by examples from the work of contemporary novelists. The protagonist in Annie Dillard's *The Pilgrim at Tinker Creek* achieves a sense of self by simply participating in the rhythms of nature by the side of the creek.[37] This is specifically linked to the process of redemption by Margaret Atwood in *Surfacing*.[38] The problem with the protagonist in this novel is her lack of ability to feel – which also includes a distorted form of remembering. Destructive sexual relationships and the consumer exploitation of society have blocked any capacity for affectivity. The book is permeated with creative-redemptive images. The heroine describes the lake as 'blue and cool as redemption'.[39] But she does not feel free to enjoy it until she has suffered. There is a hint of old sacrificial redemptive symbolism here – even though the writer explicitly disassociates herself from Christianity with 'a roadside crucifix with a wooden Christ . . . the alien god, mysterious to me as ever'. Nature symbols are life-evoking (biophilic), redemptive in the sense of recovering a sense of lost unity or self-wholeness which has blocked her ability to feel. The exception to this is the dead heron, which is both an image of death and a victim of the exploitation of American culture. When, finally, after rejecting every aspect of the consumer culture and identifying as closely as possible with nature she comes painfully to a recovery of feeling and a sense of contact with her parents, it is her cry, 'This above all, to refuse to be a victim', which expresses the redemptive achievement.[40]

To many Christians this affinity with nature will strike a chord. The theological meaning of Easter night, the night of redemption, symbolizes the renewal of the cosmos, with every aspect of creation drawn into the mystery of the resurrection. This is the profound belief of Christianity. But the way this connects with both contemporary exploitative lifestyles and human growth-processes is seldom highlighted, for the philosophical reasons discussed earlier. Instead, institutional Christianity has heaped nature imagery on to the figure of Mary, mother of Jesus: she is named Star of the Sea, Queen of the May, and so on, with many flowers named after her, such as lady's finger, lady's smock, and marigolds. This might have been helpful for the affirmation of ordinary women if Mary had not then been raised to a plane beyond their grasp. On the other hand, Christianity has often wiped out nature imagery altogether, fearing it as pagan and pantheistic, and preferring sacrificial, guilt-filled imagery. Neither alternative is truly redemptive.

It is one of the strengths of women's spirituality to recover a strand never totally lost sight of. The visions of Hildegarde of Bingen, for example, are filled with creative nature imagery. What is even more interesting, she describes creation in terms of very homely images – cream cheeses being one of them. 'I saw the earth with people on it', writes Hildegarde:

> the people were carrying some milk in their vessels, and they were making cheeses from this milk. This signifies the men and women of the world who have human seed in their bodies for the procreation of the human race. Some of the milk was thick, from which strong cheeses was being made. This means the seed which . . . brings forth strong people. . . Some of the milk was thin, from which mild cheese was being curdled. This means the seed which . . . brings forth delicate people.[41]

The same vision uses the image of the will as a fire, cooking bread and feeding people so that they may live. And this is merely a small example of a work permeated with colourful images drawn from the natural world.

What is significant for my theme is that, through the work of the nineteenth-century women writers, through contemporary quest writers as well as through female medieval mystical writings, women who have been victims of the despising of nature are discovering its energizing potential for wholeness and healing. And, what is more important, we reclaim nature's giftedness as God-given graciousness. For this reason – despite the caveats expressed earlier – Christianity must listen and learn from Goddess spirituality.

GODDESS SPIRITUALITY AND THE PROCESS OF REDEMPTION
'I found God within myself and I loved her – I loved her fiercely.'[42]
To speak about Goddess spirituality is to enter a controversial area

for Christians who are sympathetic to the claims of feminist theology, as it seems to represent a contradiction to all that is cherished as Christian faith. Why is it necessary in a search for new feminist models of redemption? I have already argued that to hark back to supposed Golden Ages when the Goddess reigned is to indulge in unhelpful nostalgia, since our sources for the palaeolithic age are, to say the least, shaky.[43] I have also voiced the fear that 'to snuggle up in the arms of the Goddess' might encourage a flight from the real world and the situation of women within it. Yet the stated aim of this chapter is to widen the context of redemption to the natural world as both subject and object of redemption. Since there is a widely-held belief that the Goddess was the source of all natural life, 'the great womb within which all things, God and human, sky and earth, human and non-human beings are generated'[44] (as Rosemary Ruether writes), the contribution of Goddess spirituality to the contemporary redemptive quest cannot be ignored.

When we call to mind the numerous myths which have arisen of the Great Mother, of Sumerian Inanna, of Egyptian Isis, of Babylonian Astarte, of Tiamat of Canaan, and so on, is it not a startling fact that the Judaeo-Christian tradition is so totally and overwhelmingly a Father-God religion, or that there is no trace of the Goddess in the Bible? It is an alarming fact for patriarchal religion to cope with that many of the myths which *do* exist point to the young warrior god having slaughtered the old goddess. For example, the myth which developed in Babylon – but originated in Sumer – tells of Marduk, god of the city-state, who defeats the ancient goddess, Tiamat, and proceeds to develop the cosmos out of her dead body. The theme of victory through death and creation through violence is directly opposed to the feminist model of redemption I am trying to build. But it is important that we bring the witness of other cultures to help us uncover other strands in biblical faith: even though feminist theologians continue to uncover female imagery in the Bible, and liturgical material calling on God as mother begins to emerge,[45] the stimulus of the Goddess movement is needed to envision what redemptive possibilities there are for Christianity, what strands are still hidden within the tradition, what strands need still to be developed.

For women it is important to preserve the principle of solidarity and bonding on which feminist theology is based. If 'until all women are free, then no woman is free'[46] is truly both inspiration and agenda for women, this involves not only tackling the social issues which cause suffering to women – such as rape or racial discrimination – but being willing to listen and learn from spiritualities outside the Christian tradition. It also means being willing to listen to and dialogue with women who are not of a feminist orientation – for example, to understand the dynamic at work which causes women to be ranged on both sides of the nuclear disarmament issue.[47]

The Goddess movement not only involves a historical movement but is an example of vibrant spirituality today. The Christian Church needs to ask itself why it is that so many deeply religious women with strong Christian upbringing experience an affirmation and nurturing relationship with the divine in the Goddess movement, while in Christianity they experienced only rejection and alienation. By the 'Goddess movement' I mean a range of movements and processes, from devotion to particular goddesses, for example within Hinduism, to the Goddess as consciousness-raising principle for women (and men) and to the Wicca or White witch movement. Starhawk, a High Priestess within the Wicca movement, sees witchcraft as an important manifestation of Goddess religion. It is based on the concept that the Goddess is immanent in the world and in all forms of life, so that love for life in all its forms is the basic ethic of witchcraft.[48] 'The Goddess', says Starhawk, 'does not rule the world; she *is* the world. Manifest in each of us, she can be known internally by any individual, in all her magnificent diversity.'[49]

The joy and celebrative life-giving energy discovered by adherents of Goddess religion is based on attentiveness and harmony to the rhythms of nature and the seasons. Hence my stress on rediscovering connectedness with nature as a redemptive strength. It is an energy which brings a new concept of *will* – not merely as an intellectual force, imposed externally by patriarchal moral codes ('Thou shalt' or 'Thou shalt not') – but as energy arising from within, in harmony with the wills and energies of other human beings, attuned to the tasks of the time of the year and respecting the 'seasons of the will'. Similarly, a concept of justice arises from a respecting of the harmonies and balance present in nature. Ethics based on harmony within nature will stress not world-renouncing or body-denying attitudes, but life-affirming, life-participatory life-styles, and values such as integrity, honesty, courage, vulnerability, responsibility and discipline, and above all, says Starhawk, the 'ethics of love',

> because it is through love, of self and others, erotic love, transforming love, affectionate love, delighted love for the myriad forms of life, evolving and changing, for the redwood and the mayfly, for the blue whale and the snail darter . . . that we connect with the Goddess within and without.[50]

For women the Goddess movement offers that celebration and affirmation of female bodily creation submerged by traditional Christian religion. Female bodily experiences, undervalued and abused by patriarchal culture, are valued and celebrated especially by the rituals of the movement. Thus 'Female power is strong and creative' is the message which women receive.[51] A powerful description of the transforming and affirming power of the Goddess for women is given by Adrienne Rich, in a description of early Goddess images:

> These images ... express an attitude towards the female charged with awareness of her intrinsic importance, her depth of meaning, her existence at the very centre of what is necessary and sacred. She is beautiful in ways we have almost forgotten, or which have been defined as ugliness. Her body possesses mass, interior depth, rest and balance. . . She is . . . without age. She is for herself, even when suckling an infant, even when, like the image of Ephesian Diana, she appears as a cone of many breasts. Sometimes she is fanged, wearing a club, sometimes she is girded by serpents, but even in her most benign aspects, the ancient Goddess is not beckoning to her worshippers. She exists, not to cajole or to reassure men, but to assert herself. . . Imagine what sense of herself it gave a woman to be in the presence of such images ... if they did nothing else for her they must have validated her spirituality, giving her back aspects of herself, neither insipid nor trivial, investing her with a sense of participating in essential mysteries. No Pietà could do this, not even the elegant queen of the Amarnian divine family of Egypt. . . The images told women that power, awesomeness and centrality were theirs by nature, not by privilege.[52]

If we can see this affirmation of the female life-cycle as 'redeeming' the centuries of anti-body, anti-nature and misogynist tradition, when women were described as more carnal, more earthy than men, and as such, responsible for sexual sin, then the value of Goddess spirituality is indisputable. At a time when official Churches complain of falling numbers – especially among the young – women, bruised and battered by both society and Church, are slowly awakening to the possibility for wholeness offered by the healing rituals of Goddess worship.

The movement stands also as a powerful critique not just of the misogynism in Christianity but inherent in Western culture itself – for example in its lack of respect for the ageing woman. The old woman has often been associated with evil, for example, in the figure of the wicked old witch, burnt at the stake. Even though most legends depict the old witch as evil, there are still traces of the Goddess as old, wise, woman, in some tales. Cassandra, daughter of King Priam of Troy, is a wonderful example of the wise woman and prophetess, ridiculed and deemed mad by the patriarchal norms first of Troy and then of Mycenae, when she becomes a captive of Agamemnon.[53] The Bible, too, gives the example of Saul seeking out the witch of Endor, at a time of crisis in his life – and after he himself had attempted to rid the land of witches and wizards (1 Sam. 28. 7-25).

But lest it be thought that Goddess spirituality is merely replacing a male god 'out there' with a female goddess 'within', symbolizing the mysterious harmonies of nature, and women's connectedness with it, or even that the Goddess is simply and solely a rallying-cry for the consciousness-raising of feminists, I want to return to my theme of redemption within process theology and show how the Goddess symbol functions within it.

First, Mary Daly has described the importance of being human in the world as the task of 'naming the self, the world and God'.[54] But in the very task of naming the self, there is a reaching out beyond the boundaries of finite existence. As Daly says, 'There is a dynamism in the ontological affirmation of the self that reaches out to the nameless God.'[55] Daly has called for a radical new naming, a moving forward from empty symbols and oppressive structures to a search for new transforming images. It is the process of this new naming wherein lies the power and significance of the Goddess movement. Daly thinks it even necessary for Christian feminism to move away from the word 'God', because the ghost of Jahweh will always be lurking within it.[56] Whether one accepts this or not, it has always been true that Christianity admits the limits of its God-symbols. Paul Tillich called for a God-above-God, warning us against the absolutizing of symbols and the danger of idolatry of our images, sacred objects, and our very conceptualizing of the divine.

When we link this with the fact that the spiritual journey will always require the purifying of God-images and that the developmental paths of men and women also demand that we widen and deepen our childish images of God, then, we can accept that 'The Goddess is a way of confronting the trivialization of exorcizing the male "god", and of affirming a different myth/reality.'[57] The method offered by process thought demonstrates how this happens and how the becoming of God and world are bound up together in the process. The element of novelty is the intuition presented of the divine intuited as female. The process of concrescence invites the individual and community to reflect on and order past experience in the light of this intuition. If the individual is female and has suffered from exclusion in the Christian Church she can react in two ways. She can reclaim from the past those occasions of experience which enhanced her well-being (for examples, stories from the life of Christ which affirm the female, or experience of prayer in a spirit-filled community); she can allow these 'occasions of experience' to interact with the present intuition to thrust out towards the future in the creation of a Christian theology richer for its affirmation of the female. This again will make an impact on perceptions of God, self and world, but it will also demand commitment to a long process.

Or she can reject the intuition, the element of novelty presented. Because of a timorous disposition, long trained to accept what she is taught without questioning, or because she is locked into a life-style which leaves her no mental or physical energy, or because the notion of rejecting a male God makes her feel far too insecure – she is happy in well-structured situations – the 'physical pole' which represents the past, described in Chapter 2, will also represent the main thrust into the future, except that it will be strengthened by the element of novelty – the female deity rejected. Hence when that idea reappears – as novelty in a new occasion of becoming – it will encounter stiffer resistance, unless her circumstances have changed. Perhaps she has done some reading – of the Bible or medieval spirituality. So she discovers that Jesus referred to himself as a mother hen (Luke 13.34), that both St Anselm and Blessed Julian of Norwich prayed to Jesus our Mother, and that even the God of the Old Testament uses images of God the Mother (Isa. 49, Jer. 31). She is then more open and receptive to the next intuition. What often happens is that she encounters some personal tragedy which threatens her old image of God and grasp of faith. 'Where is God?' cry the anguished mothers watching at the bedside of the dying child. Female images of the divine never suggest that suffering and tragedy are sent to try us, to make us better people, as is often suggested in traditional Christianity, rather that God is the immanent divine presence, nurturing and affirming – Whitehead's 'fellow-sufferer who understands' – empowering us to take from the situation and bring to it whatever is creative and healing.[58] This will involve a re-imaging of the death process itself.[59]

What the metaphor of the Goddess is here offering is the dawn of a new reality, the ushering in of new revelations of the divine. The framework of process thought encourages this, by holding together the becoming of God and human beings and the dependency of one on the other. By using verbs rather than nouns – 'Be-ing', 'Becoming' – for the divine, we emphasize the dynamic interaction intrinsic to the process. The critique of feminism offers fertile soil for the process because of its chosen role of critique of patriarchal structures. It is the very vulnerability and openness of women, with the ability to draw strength from simple aspects of human life and the natural world and to seek alternative power sources, which keeps the process moving.

But how does this affect the becoming of God – the God of Christianity? All that I have said about affirming the divine female would suggest that Goddess spirituality and recovering lost connections with nature as source of strength works well for the affirmation of women – but how does it affect the becoming of God? The answer to this question goes also to the heart of the dynamics of the redemption process. In all situations it is the creativity, the love and wisdom of God providing the element of newness, the novelty, or 'initial aim' in Whiteheadian terms. God has prehended or 'felt' the situation in its entirety and is offering the best solution possible, to lead a person to wholeness. But the response is open to the ididvidual as I explained above.

The vulnerable God allows and suffers the possibility of rejection. God is absolutely dependent on us to give concrete shape to redemption. But where the initial aim is responded to and integrated within a person's life-situation, new redemptive possibilities can take flesh. Giving expression to the divine in female imagery means that the significance of incarnation takes on new dimensions.

God needed both the vulnerability and active co-operation of Mary of Nazareth for the incarnation of Jesus. Jesus in turn enfleshed new possibilities for humanity. This is the joy of God spilling into the world, as people participate in greater and greater forms of fulness. God is glorified in the life-affirming structures. It did not give God glory when half of humanity was excluded from the splendour of being human, where women's very selves are degraded and commercialized by the culture, as it does not give God glory when white people exploit black, and human beings hunt animals to extinction.

But we need a naming of the divine which envisions alternatives *and calls them into being*: we need a seeing which calls sacred what has been despised – female sexuality – and which from the interdependence of all things makes this the basis of the ethic of a new lifestyle, seeing this as part of the very process of redemption.

And this is precisely what many women writers have been groping after. Not that it is so admirable *in itself* to be open, vulnerable, sensitive to relational connections, or even connected with nature's rhythms; but to participate in the process which this can set in motion is the divine dynamic for the transformation of the world.

George Eliot intuited this in her greatest novel, *Middlemarch*, in the character of Dorothea.[60] When confiding her idea of religion to Will, whom she eventually marries, she hints at the mutual dependence of God/humanity, and the need God has of human responsiveness:

'I have a belief of my own and that comforts me.'
'What is that?' said Will, rather jealous of the belief.

'That by desiring what is perfectly good, even when we don't quite know what it is, and cannot do what we would, *we are part of the Divine power against evil*, – widening the skirts of light and making the struggle with darkness narrower.'

'That is a beautiful mysticism. . . .'

Yes, it is a mysticism of redemptive mutuality, the dynamic of creating and saving. That it seems to express both the strength and vulnerability which comes from entering the relational situation can be seen in the sufferings of Dorothea with regard to Will:

> There were two images – two living forms that tore her heart in two, as if it had been the heart of a mother who seems to see her child divided by the sword; and presses one bleeding half to her breast while her gaze goes forth in agony to the other half which is carried away by the lying woman that has never known the mother's pang. . .[61]

Here is a woman who struggles between the two polarities of interdependence and consequent call to self-sacrifice, and the opposite pull to autonomy and personal happiness:

> She yearned towards the perfect right, that it might make a throne within her and rule her errant will. 'What should I do – how should I act now, this very day, *if I could clutch my own pain*, and compel it to silence, think of those three?'[62]

And when Dorothea comes to resolve the situation, for her the redemptive moment (what Whitehead would call the completion of the occasion), Eliot shows us how that 'different voice', that 'wide fellow-feeling for all that is human' experienced through connectedness with all that is created, is the very raw material of redemptive grace:

> It had taken long for her to come to that question, and there was light piercing into the room. She opened her curtains, and looked out towards the bit of road that lay in view, with fields beyond, outside the entrance-gates. On the road there was a man with a bundle on his back and a woman carrying her baby; in the field she could see figures moving – perhaps the shepherd and his dog. Far off in the bending sky was the pearly light; and she felt the largeness of the world and the manifold wakings of men to labour and endurance. She was part of that involuntary, palpitating life and could neither look out on it from her luxurious shelter as a mere spectator, nor hide her eyes in selfish complaining. . .[63]

Dorothea chooses new clothes to wear, symbolic (and initiatory) of her new resolve to move forward: strengthened by the awareness of being part of a much wider life-process, she was able to sacrifice her private joy. This sense of connectedness with natural process of the dawning light and the rhythm of human labour empowered her to withstand a loss of self.

This now raises the question of what I mean by redemption and how a person comes to it. Is redemption synonymous with self-development and autonomy? How is the mystical sense of connectedness balanced with the need for autonomy and for the self to stand alone? How does this fit with a Christian theology of redemption? Now that we have looked at the context for redemption it is time to address the process.

60

4 Affirming Self-Redeeming Self: Redemption as Self-affirmation

The inadequacy of existing categories to interpret the experience of women is now clear. These categories permeate theology, myth, legend and developmental theories as well as the attitudes of ordinary people. It is my claim that there is a 'different voice', witnessing to another scale of human values which has made it difficult, if not impossible, for women to reach that sense of selfhood which is a prerequisite for any experience of redemption.

What I now explore is the process of coming to that sense of identity. Chapter 3 showed that this process builds on a sense of connectedness with the natural world – indeed I will show that where this is lost it is to the detriment of the redemptive path. Here I will try to discover if the relational sense of self discussed in Chapter 2 can become a redemptive strength instead of being an obstacle to any self-development.

So the focus here will be, 'Who is woman *for herself?*' It will not be her search for identity as 'wife of', 'mother of', 'daughter of . . .' It will rather attempt to move away from woman's 'mediated existence'. By this I mean the frequent assumption that woman's role *is* redemptive – but consists in redeeming *others*. How she herself achieves fulness of being is simply not the issue. For example, Dostoevsky in his novel *Crime and Punishment*[1] presents the idealized picture of the girl, Sonia, who becomes a prostitute to save her starving family; she represents the only saving grace in the life of the murderer, Raskolnikoff, and, still trying to redeem him, she follows him to Siberia. But Dostoevsky never asks, 'Who will save Sonia? Who will relieve her destitution and help her recover her sense of self-worth, lost after being pushed into prostitution?' A more surprising example is that of George Eliot's novel *Adam Bede*.[2] Here the central character is the preacher Adam, who represents good sense, reason and solid dependability. Dinah is also a preacher, a Methodist, whom Eliot depicts as being motivated by sentiment and feeling. Like Maggie in *The Mill on the Floss* and Dorothea in *Middlemarch* she is full of compassion and witnesses to that 'other voice'. One of the homely characters in the book says of Dinah, 'She'll never marry

anybody, if he isn't a Methodist and a cripple.'[3] When Dinah is
finally convinced that it is God's will that she marry Adam, it is clear
that Eliot sees the match as providing Adam with what he lacks –
deep feeling and sense of compassion:

> 'It's like as if it was a new strength to me', he said to himself, 'to
> love her and know as she loves me. I shall look to her t'help me to
> see things right. For she's better than I am – there's less o' self in
> her, and pride. And it's a feeling as gives you a sort o' liberty, as if
> you could walk more fearless, when you've more trust in another
> than you have in yourself. I've always been thinking I knew better
> than them as belonged to me, and that's a poor sort o' life, when
> you can't look to them nearest to you t'help you with a bit better
> thought than what you've got inside you a'ready.'[4]

What the match will do *for Dinah* is clearly not the issue.

Our difficulty in charting woman's path to self-development, or to
becoming a responsible, self-directing personality, capable of
responsible choices specifically within a Christian context, is the lack
of suitable role-models: whereas the quest theme in spiritual
literature is a popular one, and theology as story or narrative is now in
vogue, the problem for woman is that her story is reflected through
the male author – or not reflected at all. When Luke's Gospel tells us,
'But Mary kept all these things, pondering them in her heart' (Luke
2.19), we are not told what she thought or felt. Mary is prominent in
Christian tradition as Mother of the Saviour, Mother of Redemption,
and Mother of the Church, but seldom is the question asked, 'Who is
Mary for herself?'[5]

It is true that feminist theologians like Elizabeth Schüssler
Fiorenza have embarked on 'reclaiming the lost stories' of women in
the New Testament, reclaiming what is background and presenting it
as foreground.[6] Others like Carol Ochs and Phyllis Trible have made
valiant attempts to recover the stories of Old Testament women such
as Hagar, Leah, Miriam and Deborah.[7] But the difficulty is not only
the scarcity of material, and the filtering of the story through male
eyes, but that the women selected as heroines are outstanding
according to masculine and patriarchal standards of excellence: 'The
few Biblical women who have been regarded as heroines either
function in traditional masculine modes, as do Deborah (a judge),
and Judith (who decapitates an enemy general), or fulfil a male idea
of feminity, as does Esther (beauty).'[8]

There is still an enormous amount to be gained by studying
Scripture in this way, especially as the women selected show courage
and independence in the face of abandonment and rejection – Hagar
in being thrown out into the desert (twice!) by Abraham, and Leah

by being rejected by Jacob in favour of her sister Rachel. After all, tragically, abandonment and rejection are still the situation of many women today in many parts of the world.

But rather than trace the path to fulfilment of a few medieval women – even such famous ones as Catherine of Siena or Hildegarde of Bingen – my exploration will be through contemporary stories and protagonists, linking them where appropriate with examples from Christian heritage. What I want to discover is whether the contemporary heroine's struggles for identity, the search for the feminist self, can genuinely be seen as spiritual quest. To test this I will use the five traditional steps of the mystical journey, as presented by Evelyn Underhill in her study of mysticism.[9]

That this is an essential process for women has already been seen in the context of the 'female sin'. Even if I want to broaden the analysis of the female sin as being more complex than merely self-negation and passivity, it has never been denied – even if it has not been encouraged – that redemption requires a degree of self-development and awareness: '. . . this matter of self-knowledge must never be neglected', wrote St Teresa of Avila:

> no soul on this road is such a giant that it does not often need to become a child at the breast again. . . And self-knowledge with regard to sin is the bread which must be eaten with food of every kind, however dainty it may be, on this road of prayer: without this bread we could not eat our food at all.[10]

Catherine of Siena, too, repeatedly emphasized the necessity of self-knowledge for the spiritual journey.

But because I write within a liberation theology context, what I ask of a mystical journey cannot remain on the level of the individual and God, but most hold together the solidarity of all oppressed peoples before God. If self-awareness is linked with a communal consciousness of oppression, self-development must be linked with the corporate redeeming process of the community: this will be one of the challenges of the models I explore.

FIRST MOVEMENT: THE AWAKENING

Here I chart the journey to self-identity of Doris Lessing's protagonist Martha Quest in her five-volume saga *Children of Violence*.[11] Although Doris Lessing is not working within a Christian framework, her novels raise all the prominent Christian redemptive themes. Martha Quest is growing up in South Africa, a typical example of a girl with no self-image and no role-model to inspire her. Her story unfolds against the background of the violence of the times, two World Wars, a racist society in South Africa, and, eventually, the threat of nuclear destruction.

But Lessing gives no indication that this is a political novel – she focuses entirely on the personal struggles of Martha. Only in the final novel, *The Four-Gated City*, does the reader become aware that the struggles of the universe are actually being played out in the struggles of Martha – that the two are interlinked. For the first four novels Martha Quest simply drifts, avoids responsibility and decision-making, is passive and 'acted-upon': she drifts into marriage and out again, into communism, into another marriage – with a German alien in an act of confused goodwill – into love with a German refugee, finally setting out for London. It is only in the final novel that some coherence is formed, and sense begins to be made of earlier experience.

How then does the Martha Quest saga function as a myth of redemption? It is clear that she fits into the classic picture of a woman with no self-image. As Carol Christ has written:

> The spiritual quest of a modern women begins in the experience of nothingness, the experience of being without an adequate image of self. Her drive to pursue her quest beyond the experience of nothingness, without being trapped in a compromise with a prevailing mythology is rooted in a vision, and an experience, however fleeting, of *transcendence* which she identifies with the vision.[12]

Thus Martha Quest's sense of confusion, of nothingness and of yearning for something different, which she cannot articulate, is the unexpressed beginning of a search. This is in contrast with the normal masculine images which use the literal journey image: Perceval searches the Waste Land for three years, as Arthur's knights seek the Holy Grail; Christian and Hopeful journey towards the celestial city; and Frodo the Hobbit – in Tolkien's contemporary saga, *The Lord of the Rings* – sets off on a real journey. But woman's journey is often inwards, with none of the custmary landmarks.

Martha – like the heroes of old – has three gifts or 'graces' present to her on the journey. The first is the occasional experience of nature mysticism, that 'wider feeling for the whole of life' observed in George Eliot's heroine, Maggie Tulliver – which in terms of the Christian mystical way can be called her 'awakening'. In Chapter 3 I explored the significance of discovering nature as strength. Annis Pratt has claimed that 'naturistic epiphanies' usually give heroines a sense of authentic selfhood – more than they do to men. For Martha this came in a joyous experience on the veld, and a second experience later, in the mud, in a rainstorm – which she promptly forgets. Lessing, as Carol Christ observes, repeatedly shows us the link between maturity and developed personhood with the capacity to remember, connect and integrate experiences. It is only after deep searching that, in the last book, Martha is able to reconnect and rediscover this sense of unity with creation: 'The sky, O the sky! And the trees in the square whose branches moving in the square sent her messages of such joy, such peace, till she cried "Oh trees I love you, and sky I love you!"'[13]

It is not simply the discovery of joy and connectedness with nature which is important for the spiritual journey: it is the capacity for remembering which triggers off a deepening of consciousness that accompanies the experience:

> Suddenly the feeling in Martha deepened, and as it did so she knew she had forgotten, as always, that what she had been waiting for like a revelation was a pain, not a happiness, what she remembered always was the exaltation and achievement, what she always forgot was the difficult birth of a state of mind.[14]

The part played by empowering memory in the redemptive process can hardly be over-emphasized. It is not that memory is the special prerogative of feminist writers. One only needs to think of the imaginative use of memory made by Proust in *A la Recherche du Temps Perdu*,[15] and Wordsworth's notion of recollecting and remembering emotion in tranquillity. Poetic imagination has always used remembering as a tool. But in the feminist quest the subject remembers or deliberately recalls 'moments of being' *from the existential situation of non-being*. For the depressed woman, overwhelmed by feelings of inadequacy and non-achievement, it can be the remembering of earlier moments when she felt strong and hopeful, before she contended with the dragons of the patriarchal world – the struggle for education, for job, for a sense of being valued in relationships. Virginia Woolf referred to this as 'deep remembering', as 'moments of being . . . embedded in many more moments of non-being'.[16]

The un-blocking of memory may bring surprising revelations. It is an area worked on today by many forms of spirituality and therapy. The healing of memories must form part of the redemptive path.[17] But what I see as vital here is the very process of coming to know. It is this, says Carol Christ, which fascinates Doris Lessing. Martha is unable to shape her life by these 'naturistic epiphanies' or moments of transcendence, 'because she does not "remember" them as moments of transcendence. . . The long detours in Martha's process of self-knowledge represented in the first four novels of the series reflect this mysterious quality in the process of self-knowledge.'[18]

The task of 're-membering', of painfully putting together the fragmented bits of self, is part of acquiring knowledge, or wisdom. This is not the acquiring of mere facts or cognitive knowledge. It is the 'redemption' of feminist wisdom, a deep knowing, discernible in myth through the figure of the wise woman. It is the wisdom handed on through the ages by our 'raging stoic grandmothers',[19] blocked both by structures of knowing which opposed matter to spirit and trivialized the world of the female to the private sphere.

Even when a discerning poet like Charles Williams, who explored so brilliantly in his novels the interconnections between divine and human spheres, speaks about knowledge, and specifically about the knowing of the body, it is to downgrade flesh-knowing as opposed to spirit-knowing:

> Flesh knows what spirit knows,
> *but spirit knows it knows* – categories of identity:
> women's flesh lives the quest of the Grail. . .
> Blessed is she who gives herself to the journey. . .[20]

The same poem argues that women should not be priests, because they are already on the altar in the capacity of victim.

> Well are women warned from serving the altar
> who, *by the nature of their creature*, from Caucasia to Carbonek,
> share with the Sacrifice the victimization of blood.[21]

I quote this to show how a theory of womanhood – 'by the nature of their creature' – has not only been used to present female biological processes (referred to earlier as transformation mysteries), as weaknesses, but to dictate woman's position in the Church. (What this means for atonement theories I will show in Chapter 6.)

My point here is that, if we try to overcome dualistic thought-patterns, we have to recover and use the kind of 'deep knowing' which resists and transcends cheap polarization. Woman's knowledge is often sneered at as 'feminine intuition', as instinctive and emotional. It is true that snap, instantaneous decisions based on hunches, guess-work and mental laziness do not qualify as 'deep knowing'. But one of the reasons for the legendary female skill in herbal lore and healing is the 'knowing' which addresses the total situation of illness and reaches beyond the symptoms to the suffering person. It is this 'knowing' which inspired Cicely Saunders to found the Hospice of St Christopher and Elizabeth Kübler Ross to work for the bereaved and dying.[23] Both have refused to separate body from spirit, and focus instead on the needs of the whole person in the midst of their family situation. They pay attention to the whole relational situation because the healing required both includes and transcends the disease from which the person is suffering.

This brings me to the most important point about memory as a tool for 'deep knowing' or wisdom in the feminist journey. It is the notion of 'transcendence' or transcending the self – Martha Quest experienced it several times but was unable to use it as a tool to move forward – which is crucial for the moment of 'awakening'. In it lies the possibility of solving the dilemma of 'self-development or self-sacrifice'.[24] In the experience of transcending the self – the feeling of being part of a wider whole – comes authentic self-realization, yet a corresponding vulnerability to victimization. (It is this dilemma which is responsible for many feminist writers' rejection of any notion of self-sacrifice and abandonment of a theology of the cross for women.)

This was Dorothea's experience when, in realizing that she was part of a teeming, palpitating life-process, she was able to grasp her own pain and move forward.[25] It was Mary Craig's painful journey when, angry and rejecting a God who had sent her two mentally-handicapped sons, she was able to participate in the suffering of the Polish refugees and work for their well-being, thus realizing she was part of a much wider process.[26] The experience of transcending the self as part of the process of self-realization often comes linked with an experience of the divine. Dorothea's mystical moment, referred to in Chapter 3, made her feel as if she wanted to be part of the divine power 'widening the skirts of light'. As the process model describes, God and humanity are closely interwoven.

The second 'gift' which Martha Quest receives for her journey is the presence of 'The Watcher', who is 'that part of herself which observes, understands, becomes conscious of the deeper dimensions of her experience'.[27] Yet the Watcher's presence is only occasionally noticed: that deeper level of consciousness which the Watcher could provide is hardly made use of to move further forward. But at last, in *The Four-Gated City*, when Martha is walking by the Thames, she knows herself as 'a soft, dark, empty space, a soft, dark receptive intelligence, a quiet, empty space, behind which stood an observing presence.'[28] This clear-lit space, experienced before, but not retained, is the location of insight, the dwelling-place of the Watcher, the old friend whom she later describes as 'that part of me which watches all the time . . . the only part of me that's real – that's permanent anyway'.[29] The Watcher enables Martha to assess whether what she is doing is in touch with her deepest self. It is the Watcher who enables her to value experiences of awakening, of lucidity and of self-knowledge which she has not as yet learnt to use to beat back the darkness. The key to this process of self-transcendence is the idea of 'waiting'. Much of Martha's waiting is a passive drifting, but the waiting which moves her into a deeper level of consciousness is a kind of focused attention during which Martha learns to grow from experience: 'Waiting is not a passive activity', writes Carol Christ,[30] 'Martha waits with purposefulness. She does not know what she is waiting for, but she recognizes it when it is given to her and she takes active steps to explore it further.'

Here is an area of richness for feminist spirituality. Not that I want to glamorize 'waiting'. Everyone is aware of its tragic dimensions: waiting in dole queues has become part of the weary routine of the unemployed; waiting for meagre groceries in long queues is still the lot of many people in the Communist bloc; waiting for the expiry of prison sentences, for the return of the missing sons and husbands in Chile and Argentina. One could go on. The poor know all about waiting. But on the plane of spirituality 'waiting' can become a tool charged with hope. The spirituality of Simone Weil was inspired by 'focused waiting' or attentiveness:[31] 'Attention', she said, 'is the rarest and purest form of generosity. It is given to very few minds to notice that things and beings exist.'[32] This focused attentiveness of waiting – which in Simone Well reached mystical levels – is not opposed to action. It is one way which women's spirituality offers of bridging the gap between being and doing. It is the one activity in which women have been engaged from time immemorial – waiting at the sick-bed of a child, waiting with the dying, keeping vigil with the dead, standing outside embassies pleading for the missing. . . A fresco by Fra Angelico in one of the cells of the monastery of San Marco in Florence even testifies to the legend that, when the apostles slept in the Garden of Gethsemane, when Christ asked them to stay awake and pray, two women, Mary and Martha, were awake, watching and praying at the gates of the Garden.

The women waiting at Greenham Common witness to 'active waiting' as a very high form of activity. Not only by their practical actions of Cruise watch and local peace education work, but by their very presence they are witnessing to a different set of values in the world. To use an explicit theological category, they are an eschatological presence: they are a tangible sign of hope of a different world – and the very tangibility is the hope that this world will be a reality.[33]

The third 'gift' on the journey of Martha Quest is the vision of the city. Like the Grail knights whose quest for an external goal is linked with their personal need for growth and purification, Martha's 'vision' is an external image, yet connected with her need for self-image. In the first book, the vision is at the level of a daydream:

There arose, glimmering whitely over the harsh scrub and the stunted trees, a noble city, set four-square and colonnaded, against its falling, flower-bordered terraces. There were splashing fountains and the sound of flutes; and its citizens moved, grave and beautiful, black, white and brown together. . .[34]

I have already alluded, in Chapter 3, to the significance for Christianity of the redeemed city. For Martha Quest's journey, says Carol Christ, the vision may rather be reflecting the fact that women develop in relation to the environment, not over-against it. Here is the theme of connectedness once more. It is this vision of the city which loosely influences Martha's decision to marry and to be active in the Communist Party – in the hope of bringing the city closer: Martha and Jasmine (a co-activist) at the sight of a ragged, hungry urchin, smile, since

> because of them, because of the vision, he was protected and saved; the vision they dreamed of seemed just around the corner; they could almost touch it. Each saw an ideal town, noble and beautiful, soaring up over the actual town they saw, which consisted in this area of third-rate shops and sordid little cafes. The ragged town was already a citizen of this ideal town, a citizen with themselves.[35]

However many times the vision must be reshaped and purified (the moment of purgation), its abiding significance for the feminist quest is the importance of hanging on to hope, however dismal the reality: '. . . after all', says Martha.

> the vision's the thing. And keeping your mind firm on the vision, as if it were an entity, a thing quite separate from the minds and personalities which created it, you overlook the lies, the exaggerations, the sheer damned lunacy, because you know in your heart that you haven't the spark. . .[36]

Thus, awakened by a vision which endures despite disastrous mistakes, by moments of natural ecstasy leading to the possibility of self-transcendence, and the slow building up of wisdom, and thirdly by the capacity to reflect on and integrate experiences – at this point the second step is embarked upon . . .

THE VIA PURGATIVA

Suppose that with the spiritual awakening comes the need to burst the bonds of the structures which constrain. The protagonist of Kate

Chopin's novel *The Awakening*, which caused such a stir at the time it was written, trapped in a meaningless marriage, flung herself into the sea, because no other solution seemed available.[37] Spirituality offers more hope. It suggests embarking upon the *via purgativa*, the way of purification, the second step on the traditional mystical journey. But here I will depart from the masculine notion of a linear journey upwards and forwards. The feminist journey is as much about diving deep, spiralling, moving inward, as it is about moving upward and forward. A movement which seeks to recover and reclaim must seek alternative symbols and images.

So the tools for the journey remain the same as for the first movement. Not for women is the sword of Excalibur the usual weapon, but vision, connectedness and sources of self-transcendence remain constant resources. The task is the 're-membering' of experience which will be redemptive. Here we discover this to be not so new to the Christian tradition. For Meister Eckhart, the thirteenth-century Dominican monk, the whole activity of redemption was the task of remembering. for Eckhart Christ comes as *reminder* more than *redeemer*: 'For this reason, therefore, has the wisdom of God wanted to show our redemption by himself assuming flesh – in order that our instruction in divine, natural and moral matters *would be remembered*' [my italics].[38] Christ, Reminder of God's wisdom and purpose for humanity is the inspiration for this movement. Holding on to a consciousness of being made in the image and likeness of God is to be empowered in the redemptive path, especially when one has lost all sense of being God's good creation. Women know what it means to feel ashamed of the body, and therefore to believe that asceticism is the only path to holiness.

'Remembering' for Martha Quest is more a sense of recollecting, of holding together forgotten images and experiences in her deepest self in order to move forward.

But traditionally, the *via purgativa* demanded a stripping away of the false notions of the self, the distorting absolutizations of the self. But if the female sin is the lack of sense of self, or self-abnegation, how is the *via purgativa* to be experienced by women?

For Martha Quest, the *via purgativa* is experienced only after years of passive drifting. Yet here I think it must be questioned whether the so-called passive drifting is always so spiritually unformative. If we compare the period of Teresa of Avila's life which she describes as one of superficiality, frivolity and variety, in very self-condemning terms, we observe that this period apparently prepared her for the next step, and gave her the insight as to what had been previously wrong:

70

> For the first week I suffered a great deal. . . For I had already become tired of the life I was leading; and even when I offended God I never ceased to be sorely afraid of Him . . . and my soul began to return to the good habits of my earlier childhood and I realized what a great favour God does whom He places in the company of good people.[39]

Living in apparent spiritual stagnation and passivity can create in a woman an enormous hunger for spiritual nourishment. Like the legendary Sleeping Beauty she may at a subconscious level be preparing for the great awakening – although not necessarily for the kiss of the prince.

In contrast to the stripping away of the false self, the feminist *via purgativa* can often require the integrating of positive images and experiences, together with the rejecting of the destructive ones. For Christian women it means seeking the biblical images which encourage these positive images. The task of building a sense of self will be slow and painful. For Martha in *The Four-Gated City*, it meant 'paying her debts', as she put it, which meant trying to recover the vast quantity of experience unreflected upon and integrating this with a developing sense of self. For Margaret Atwood's protagonist in *Surfacing*, it meant a literal stripping away of all aspects of contemporary materialist and exploitative culture, while opting for the starkest 'natural' existence, not so much in a nostalgic bid to rediscover lost innocence in nature, but to unblock the capacity to feel and remember.

Carol Ochs describes this movement of purgation in a way more suited to the development of women, as the stripping away of all that stands in the way of our relationship with reality – such unworthy goals as wealth, fame and status, fears of failure, ridicule or isolation, and such habits as irresponsibility, laziness or forgetfulness.[40] In the journey of spirituality described by Meister Eckhart this is the movement of 'letting-go' (*abgeschiedenheit*) in order to facilitate in us the 'birthing of God'. As Matthew Fox quotes him,

> Who are those who honour God? Those who have entirely renounced themselves, and who do not in the least seek their own in anything . . . who do not look below themselves or above themselves, or at themselves, who love neither goods, nor honour, nor comfort, nor joy . . . but have renounced all this.[41]

But Eckhart's Way neither takes account of those whose sense of self has already been stripped away – or who may never have developed any in the first place – nor does it allow the notion of growth experiences through delight, affirmation and happiness. Yet

71

to strip away false notions of the self in the effort to reach a 'centred self', to preserve the two poles of relating (interdependence and autonomy), described in Chapter 2, this is the challenge of the *via purgativa*.

The part played by anger, conflict and suffering will be crucial. Carol Osiek has described the maturity necessary to take on the *via purgativa*:

> Suffering will be the cost of acting rather than remaining passive. The results will do violence to her sense of well-being. Her needs for relatedness and connectedness must at times be sacrificed in order to allow independent action. . . Her need to be cherished and valued must be sacrificed in order that she come to value and cherish herself.[42]

If we are furious about rape and wife-battering and senseless loss of life in war we are more likely to protest and act effectively against it, we are more likely to seek for ways to end crucifixions, than if we assume we are meant to endure all and end up on the cross with Christ. The redemptive help which women need is in handling the inevitable conflicts which arise when self-assertion rocks the boat. Women are traditionally meant to rock cradles, not boats, after all!

But the reward of perseverance in recovering the wisdom which builds self-development will be to reach the stage of illumination.

THE *VIA ILLUMINATIVA*

The reward of perseverance is the dawn of a new consciousness. True, the need for purgation and the stripping-away process will continue and the pain of increasing conflict will bring us into the Dark Night. For women these states are not necessarily successive – and certainly not linear – even if at a given moment one aspect predominates. The more light and illumination floods the very being of woman the more her sense of vision will throw her into conflict with those around her.

For the mystics of Christian tradition, such as Catherine of Siena, Brigid of Sweden, Teresa of Avila and Hildegarde of Bingen, this is the well-attested visionary period. For George Eliot's heroine Dorothea it was the mystical insight that we are part of the divine power against evil. For Simone Weil, whose life does not seem to have been blest with much illumination, it was an experience in the abbey at Solesmes:

> I was suffering from a splitting headache, each sound hurt me like a blow; by an extreme effort of concentration I was able to rise up

above this wretched flesh, to leave it suffer by itself, wrapped up in a corner, and to find a pure and perfect joy in the unimaginable beauty of the chanting and the words. This experience enabled me by analogy to get a better possibility of loving divine love in the midst of affliction.[43]

This experience of Simone Weil will need further discussion, as it leads us deep into the meaning of suffering, and away from the tension between self-development and self-sacrifice.

It is the breakthrough into deeper levels of consciousness which is here the issue.

What happens to Martha Quest is that, through the influence of the 'Watcher', she learns self-discipline, experiences sexual transcendence and develops prophetic-visionary powers, as a direct result of a concentrated focus on the problems in the house. She, who had abandoned her own little girl, becomes the mother – for twenty years – of a collection of children with serious emotional problems. This for her is not a regression to a more conventional role, but a time for gaining more insights. (In a similar way George Eliot's heroine Romola chose the role of motherhood, without its biological reality and conventional stereotype, when she adopted the orphan boy Benedict.)[44]

The most remarkable advance which Martha makes is with the help of the poor, mad woman Lynda. While watching Lynda trying to escape from the prison of madness, she realizes that she, too, was part of Lynda, in trying to escape beyond the barriers of ordinary consciousness. She is able, through Lynda, to plug into this vast, impersonal, sea of energy, which Martha realizes can be used for good or evil. When the energy accumulates in Martha, she has the experience of 'crossing the sound barrier', which terrifies her:

Her whole body, organism, vibrated, shook, was shattered to bits by the force of the sea of sound which entered her. Her head was a jar, a bedlam; but, as she was about to cry out, scream, let go of control, perhaps bang her rioting head against the walls, she looked at Lynda . . . and remembered . . . [Lynda] had remarked, 'I must get through the sound barrier'.[45]

The effect of what is in fact an entry into a kind of mystical consciousness is to make Martha aware that she has been asleep for most of her life: most ordinary people, she feels, are not tapping into this source of energy, but are rather behaving like 'slugs'. Martha also discovers within herself 'the self-hater', or source of evil exterior to her who could destroy her, as it is destroying Lynda. This breakthrough is significant for the spiritual path because Martha

73

discovers within her inmost being that all the evil which she has projected on to society is actually located within herself:

> ... Martha comes to recognize that this 'hating ... is the underside of all this lovely liberalism'. Finally she recognizes that nothing human is alien to her.
> 'I am what the human race is. I am "The Germans are the mirror and the catalyst of Europe"; also "Dirty Hun", "Filthy Nazi".'[46]

This is in fact the climax of the five books: to recognize the hater's power, not to succumb to it but to see it in connection with the violence of the times and to remain, in it and through it, in touch with the deepest core of one's being. All the searching drives Martha back on herself, in one of Lessing's most searching statements of self-illumination: 'Where? But where? How? Who? No, but where, where? . . . Then, silence and the birth of a repetition; Where? Here. Here, where else, you poor fool, where else has it been ever?'[47]

Lessing's description of the self-realization of Martha Quest is remarkable for many reasons: most poignant here is the realistic way in which Martha is able to come to terms with the evil of the times. My fear in being content with a notion of the female sin as passivity was that feminists would produce a new contemporary version of the myths of femininity: while scapegoating men for all that is wrong with the world, we would claim all the nurturing, compassionate qualities as female, and women as the 'great innocents of history'. To do so is to fail to take responsibility for all the evil in which women have participated and continue to participate.

Spirituality today sees mystical experiences as a possibility for all, and not the privilege of an élite. Whether it be in 'making the most of our natural ecstasies' as Matthew Fox puts it[48] or in the political mysticism experienced by those involved in action potentially transforming the world – like the peace movement – or in the ecstasy of relationship, new ways of self-transcendence are being discovered. And discovered as participation in divine life.

But what happens when the light goes out? When despair, tragedy and affliction take over. . . When nothing is experienced and, once again, God is absent. . . In other words, what happens when one enters 'The Dark Night'?

THE DARK NIGHT OF THE SOUL[49]

> You must go by a way wherein is no ecstasy,
> In order to arrive at what you do not know,
> You must go by a way which is the way of ignorance,

wrote T. S. Eliot,[50] and this is certainly the experience of anyone who tries to advance along the spiritual and redemptive path. The celebrated expression, 'the Dark Night' comes, of course, from St John of the Cross.[51] He describes the schooling given by God to purify and draw the human person deeper into the mystery of divine love: 'In the process of affective redemption, desire is not suppressed or destroyed but gradually transferred, purified, transformed, set on fire. We go *through* the struggles of human desire to integration and personal wholeness.'[52] St John describes the purifying of the 'dark side' of human desire; he shows how it is that in the very experience of joylessness and darkness, in the withdrawal of all comfort, the actual transformation of desire takes place.

At this point I leave the explorations of Martha Quest to focus on the Christian mystical path, although Martha, too, experiences her Dark Night, as she chooses to remain in the underground room, working on insights received with Lynda. I want to explore a different Christian feminist interpretation of the Dark Night, asking whether this can be redemptive for Christian women according to the model of redemption as self-affirmation. At the same time I will try to discover if the process model contributes to this understanding.

There is one obvious practical interpretation of 'the Dark Night'. The feminist cry, 'take back the night', is a demand to be able to walk freely and with safety in darkness, without fear of attack and violation. For the truth is that for young children, both boys and girls, and for women the night is no longer theirs. (Perhaps the legends of witches and moon-goddesses hark back to a time when women could move freely at night-time. . . 'She walks in beauty, like the night. . .')

Spiritually speaking, 'take back the night' is a call to reclaim and redeem our spiritual heritage. As Mary Giles says:

> We only claim a night that is the spiritual birthright of every person, irrespective of sex or profession, a night that is ours but that for want of adequate commentary from the point of view of women today may seem the exclusive property of theologians and cloistered religious.[53]

Secondly, the experience of the Dark Night, the place of impasse and despair, is a very real one for Christian feminists. A fierce loyalty to and love of Christianity, an expectation of continuing commitment and service to the Church are frequently the background of Christian feminists: most people assume women are angry and depressed because they are not allowed to be ordained priests. But the Dark Night comprehends a *much deeper* level of alienation and despair. It is a darkness born of a lack of nourishment by the liturgy, prayer-life and

75

doctrine of the Christian Church. It is the pain of the distorted symbols and lifeless rituals which exclude the humanity of women; it is the making of the Christ-mystery into something un-related to human living and the controlling of this by a class of clerical elite, many of whom live in a style remote from ordinary people; it is having no form of prayer which connects with one's experience, having the life of the Spirit choked back and still-born. . . It is seeing the Church one loves stifled by corruption, afraid to act for justice and freedom. . . The total impasse of the night, the experience of being made mute and inarticulate – not in the silence of loving contemplation, but because the language sought for has not been brought to birth – descends with shocking immediacy.

Imagine that the awakening to the presence of God in new ways and images has brought new hope and excitement to a woman's life. For some women there has been a new affirmation in parish life, as well as through education and job responsibility: the incipient, felt need for self-development has inspired activity in the form of joining a consciousness-raising group, a women's spirituality group, perhaps, or political commitment in terms of working for peace, anti-racism, or in a rape-crisis shelter. The recent spate of writing on biblical themes from a women's perspective may have increased the belief that the new dawning consciousness which she experiences will be universally shared. The Jesus of the Gospels who numbered women among his friends encourages her to participate in ministry. She is hopeful that what women are discovering about female sexuality will be integrated with spirituality and transform relationships.

In the spirit of this awakening and enlightenment period she has willingly pursued the *via purgativa*, not only stripping away those faith images which deny her very being, but seeking to give her new-found consciousness political and social expression, and working for tangible expressions of it. It is in the very purifying of her vision that she is plunged into darkness. Because most of the people she encounters will not understand the radical nature of the vision which she tries to bring to birth. They think it means the assumption of power for women, not a transformation of the very concept of power itself. As yet the vision cannot see the light of day because the human categories – thought-patterns and affectivity alike – do not exist.

The aloneness, loneliness and anxiety which this brings lead her into the Dark Night. Like Hagar (Gen. 21. 8–21) who, despite having experienced the light of God's revelation through the promise of the birth of Ishmael, is cast into the desert for the second time,[54] she is in the wilderness. She is plagued by anxiety and guilt. Not only do women carry the unjustifiable burden of supposedly being responsible for all human sin, they must now carry the guilt of upsetting existing norms of behaviour and role stereotypes. They may be married to – or living and working with – men who are content with the status quo: they cannot understand women's pain in hearing continual please for vocations (male) to the Church, when they have offered their services and been rejected, or why women should call for alternative images from those of God as Father, Judge and King. Developmentally, as I have explained, women are geared to considering the whole relational scene and acting on behalf of wider interests, which means that the temptation to fall back to submissive patterns of relating is very great.

The worst aspect of all is the absence of God. The 'God of power and might' who sent *his* Son to save all *men* no longer brings any comfort – in fact it increases her loneliness when the congregation around her sings *his* praises so lustily – but new images are tentative, the energy which they call forth is dead. In fact all passion is dead. The anguish of all this is heartrendingly expressed by Celie in Alice Walker's novel, *The Colour Purple*:

> What God do for me? I ast. . . He give me a lynched daddy, a crazy mama, a lowdown dog of a step pa and a sister I probably won't ever see again. Anyhow, I say, the God I been praying and writing to is a man. And act just like the mens I know. Trifling, forgitful and lowdown. . . All my life I never care what people thought bout nothing I did, I say. But deep in my heart I care about God. What he going to think. And come to find out, he don't think. Just sit up there, glorifying in being deef, I reckon. But it ain't easy, trying to do without God. Even if you know he ain't there, trying to do without him is a strain.[55]

How can there be a way out of the impasse of this Dark Night today? Mythologically, it is suggested that the Dark Night is the time spent – like Psyche and Persephone – in the Underworld, yet seeing this as a time to consolidate, to work on insights, just as the apparent death of winter conceals a hidden growth. Perhaps it is time to work on dreams, to let the rich material from the unconscious be absorbed into conscious life. Adrienne Rich describes this psychological growth as the the 'work of winter':

> Force nothing, be unforced,
> Accept no giant miracles of growth
> By counterfeit light
> trust roots, allow the days to shrink
> Give credence to those slender means
> Wait without sadness and with grave impatience. . .[56]

This expresses the positive aspect of the Dark Night but does no justice to the degree of pain and confusion present. Nor do the paradoxes of religion, which tells us that light will only be found in darkness, help us. The Dark Night was experienced by Simone Weil in utter desolation, experienced as affliction – although in her case, it was the weight of the oppression and suffering of the world which afflicted her: the insight she gives us that is that it is only in this experience of affliction that truth will dawn: 'I have the inner certainty that this truth, if it is ever granted to me, will only be revealed when I myself am physically in affliction, and in one of the extreme forms of affliction that exist at present'.[57] For most people it is as if the ground has been swept from under one's feet: the certainties of the old faith have vanished, to be replaced by – what?

I think the first seed of hope is to remain within the growth processes, both physical and psychological. We need to ground ourselves as firmly as possible in living contact with the different birth-growth-death cycles which surround us, and to use these as resources for the journey. As I have said, for women this redemptive journey is not linear, the resources for the journey remain constant. Cyclically, too, women are conscious of a rhythmic connection with nature which must be claimed as a strength, not a degrading nuisance in a technological age. The will, too, has its seasons, as does the spirit. There are so many interconnections to be explored. This means hanging on to the hope that the insights which arise from the new consciousness are to be trusted.

Secondly, the insight of process theism that God is with us in this growth process can be seen as strength. But how can God be present in such anguished experiences of aloneness? To believe that God is present in absence may be simply wishful thinking. . . If it is true in nature that the birth of a new state of existence is actually hard work, and means sloughing off old skins (like snakes or caterpillars), it is just possible that, just as the baby must endure the darkness of the tunnel of the birth canal to come screaming and blinking into the light, the aloneness of the Dark Night is when God is 'luring' us forward into a deeper level of consciousness. As Marjorie Suchocki explains: 'In the flashing moment of existence, every momentary concrescence is followed by a transitional relation, and every transitional relation is followed by a concrescent aloneness. Con-crescence is like the breathing space in the sea of relationality. . .'[58] 'The breathing space in a sea of relationality' points us to a possible feminist re-interpretation of the Dark Night: it suggests that what is experienced as utter aloneness and confusion is far from the reality of being abandoned by God but is actually the empty space where God is challenging us further.

So the consciousness of what 'might be' – the dimly felt new images of God breaking in – is the presence of God meeting us in the concrete situation of the 'finite occasion' – the present moment – integrating what we have chosen to become within divine awareness. This is why the 'loneliness', the 'dark night of the soul' has such a mystical dimension. It is the contrast between the *depth dimension of God*, which is intuited in the new images and symbols springing from women's experience, and the feeling of being pushed back to the everydayness of the ordinary world, where the pain of exclusion and unjust structures threaten to crush.

But we have to be able to discern whether this is truly the Dark Night and not just the various psychological depressions of the life-cycle – or possibly a mixture of both. In the first place what is experienced as enduring is a passionate love and hunger for God, which increases even as all supports and props are dragged away: for a woman this can mean the crumbling of the close relationships which have been the mainstay of her life, and the guilty bewilderment which floods her when traditional liturgies block her incipient deeper experience of God.

Secondly, although the actual existential situation is one of anxiety and confusion, which is well recognized by psychologists as a serious condition and a threat to the very value which the self holds necessary for existence,[59] yet in experience of bonding and community-creating with other women, women have sensed divine presence as 'the cosmic matrix of novelty',[60] the lure or challenge inviting them to transcend the experienced reality of sexism. Here it is very evident why the female sin should have been named as passivity: with this impasse which we name spiritually the Dark Night comes a numbness and 'imaginative shock' which can induce a frozen immobility.

How then to move forward into the light? Constance Fitzgerald has suggested that change and growth will come, not through rational analysis, but through a second-order response – implying that breakthrough will be the fruit of unconscious processes:

> The psychologists and the theologians, the poets and the mystics, assure us that impasse can be the condition for creative growth, and transformation *if* the experience of impasse is fully appropriated within one's heart and flesh with consciousness and consent; if the limitations of one's humanity and the human condition are squarely faced and the limits of one's finitude allowed to invade the human spirit with real existential powerlessness; if the ego does not demand understanding in the name of control and predictability but is willing to admit the mystery of its own being and surrender to the mystery. . .[61]

It is to hang on to the insight that we are touched by God, who as the process model suggests, is taking the initiative. We have lost that all-pervasive sense of divine presence: but we are touching and being touched by the dark knowing of God, only made possible in the shattering of existing sexist and power-ridden images, and by our experiencing existential loneliness so that new growth will occur.

So to claim back the night is to claim darkness as a time for growth and transformation. It is to free darkness of its overtones of evil and sin and see it as potential richness, fertility, hidden growth and contemplation, as nature broods and contemplates in winter, seemingly inactive, yet preparing for the birthing of spring. It is in darkness that a new vision is born. (The real evil is the pervasive injustice of the structures which spawn sexism and racism.) But, just as 'the work of winter' is indispensable, so the period of darkness has its own tools and activity.

Although there is no comfort and even no real hope experienced for the future, and memories of the past bring no security, the process demands that we move forward: with anger, rage and grief our tools, the solidarity of support groups our resource, trust in the absent God our guide – to an alternative we have no name for, only yearning. . .

And will there be a breakthrough? Shall we 'know' the unnamed God?

THE *VIA UNITIVA*

This model of redemption now moves to the traditional unitive moment, the end of the journey out of darkness. It asks, How will there be an end to the process in the fulness and joy of the presence of God? The wisdom of both ancient and contemporary spirituality tells us that there can be no end-of-journey, until, in the attainment of the beatific vision, God's transformation of the world is complete. The feminist vision in any case sees the spiritual path not in a linear but a cyclic, rhythmic way: just as Martha Quest had discovered that the whole redemptive process could take place nowhere else but within herself, and T. S. Eliot has written

> We shall not cease from exploration
> And the end of our exploring
> Will be to arrive where we started
> And know the place for the first time[62]

so any achievement will be in terms of an ever-deepening vision of the interconnectedness of divine and human becoming. Rhythmic and cyclic movement onward does *not* mean, however, the Nietzschean myth of the 'endless return', the despairing repitition of the same mistakes. Redemption is redemption after all.

So the painful acquisition of wisdom must mean, at the very least, that through the *via purgativa*, through recovery of memory, through integrating and connecting what we have learnt, a new freedom is possible.

The problem is that it is scarcely possible to articulate with any lucidity something not yet fully formed, something for which we hunger, for a new beginning which demands, the same poet said, that we make 'a raid on the articulate'.[63]

But it is not just a question of waiting in the dark, even if the darkness is of God. We have been given a way of seeing in the dark, if we trust to the insights and resources given to us, if we go with the process of 'diving deep' to the murky depths. In the 'nothingness' we shall find the immanence of the vulnerable God, we shall discover graces unimaginable: if we go, suffering, with this dark knowing of God we are liberating the very being of God for more redeeming possibilities. Eliot's darkness captures poignantly the delusion of pre-empting the outcome of our spiritual search:

I said to my soul, be still, and wait without hope
For hope would be for the wrong thing; wait without love
For love would be of the wrong thing; there is yet faith
But the faith and the love and the hope are all in the waiting.[64]

What we will recover is the sense of self-affirmation for which we have searched, our connected self, blocked by years of superficiality and passivity. While the journey of self-affirmation continues, the sense of being a unified personality should be a basic affirmation all our lives. While we can never hope to overcome the tensions between the two polarities of connectedness and separation – they will remain a lifelong tension, part of 'the unitary, restless, creative motion of life itself[65] – yet redemption in this sense will mean that we are able to hold the two tensions in creative balance. The notion of being held in a wider whole, in other words, that there is a reality greater than oneself, will be the deepening experience which holds the two poles together. This is the redemptive sphere of the vulnerable and creative God. The task ahead will be to maintain this sense of 'connected aloneness', to be self-affirming as a choice-making, judging and acting individual, and yet to maintain that vital interconnectedness with the rest of creation. Eliot, again, puts it very piercingly:

Blessèd sister, holy mother, spirit of the fountain, spirit of
the garden,
. . .

Teach us to care and not to care,
Teach us to sit still
Even among these rocks,
Our peace in His will
And even among these rocks,
Sister, mother,
And spirit of the river, spirit of the sea,
Suffer me not to be separated,

And let my cry come unto Thee.[66]

THE REDEEMED SELF – MODEL OF CHRISTIAN REDEMPTION?

But now we have to ask if the recovery of the connected self is actually what is meant by the fulness of Christian redemption. We need to know if the right balance between self-affirmation and self-sacrifice, the holding together of these two polarities, will bring about in Christ the longed-for liberation and transformation of the world. I suggest that the strength of this model is to demonstrate that the discovery and affirmation of the self – honest self-love – are a pre-requisite for the process of redemption and transformation. But what I want to emphasize is that there are aspects of the Christ-mystery still left untapped. For one thing, there is no evidence that relationships will be transformed by the end of the process. Martha Quest does not seek her abandoned daughter, or seek reconciliation with her dead mother. Atwood's protagonist does not aim to transform the quality of her relating with her associates.

The model is also imbalanced in its attitude to the past. Whereas there is much to be 'reclaimed' in terms of blocked memory and lost sense of self-worth, there is an assumption that the creativity of women has always been thwarted by patriarchy, apart from the exceptional few who managed to beat the structures. This assumes that women since the dawn of time have always been unfulfilled and that the men they lived and worked with have always prevented their development. This forces one to question whether history has been a total vacuum as to the creativity and achievement of ordinary women.

Alice Walker, in a moving essay, searched for the lost creativity of the black women of the American deep south, which she knows must exist. She sees in the Smithsonian Institute in Washington DC a quilt depicting the crucifixion made from bits and pieces of worthless rags, a portrayal of deep, spiritual feeling, made by

an anonymous black woman in Alabama, a hundred years ago. . .
And so our mothers and our grandmothers have, more often than

not anonymously, handed on the creative spark, the seed of the flower they themselves never hoped to see, or like a sealed letter they could not plainly read.[67]

This points to the reclaiming of an actual historical past, not a rejection of it as totally negative, being sensitive to its gifts, as well as its sufferings and injustices in an effort to create a better future.

Thirdly, this lack of a vision of mutuality with the whole human and non-human community is characterized by a focus on transcendence as self-transcendence. Whereas it is important to stress wholeness, connectedness, holistic integration with bodily processes and to build a concept of redemption on female goodness rather than on fallenness, the vision of mutuality and transcendence which results is severely limited. Nor can we realistically confront the structures of injustice which prevent the creation's redemption, because the process focuses almost exclusively on personal development.

I think this model also falls short for another reason. In Chapter 2 I sketched the relational strengths of women, the capacity for empathy and compassion, pointing out how few patterns of caring and service existed which were at the same time opportunities for self-development. Redemption as self-affirmation leaves this aspect unexplored. Suppose a model of redemption focused on this opposite polarity, asking how relational strengths could form its basis and at the same time reveal unexplored dimensions of the ministry of Jesus, specifically the vision of mutuality and transcendence it contains. Perhaps here would be a way to reappropriate the realities of suffering and sacrifice as a real strength for the developing self as well as for the transformation of the world.

83

5 'With you ... the fires can burn again': Redemption as Right Relation

We are now seeking a model of redemption which pushes beyond the boundaries of the conscious self. I have shown that the whole cosmos is the arena for the creating and redeeming task. I have argued that a feminist theology of redemption reclaims as part of this task the strengths and experiences of women, lost or suppressed by the dominant theological tradition. I have also argued that the journey of self-awakening, of the recovery or formation of the 'connected self', can take place within the steps of the traditional Christian mystical path, exploring this by appealing largely to secular literature. But I want to discover whether there can be a model of redemption which *both* includes the journey to self-discovery, *and* builds on the relational strengths of women, yet doing this in such a way that these can be redemptive and transformative of society as a whole: what is more, I want to explore whether these relational strengths can be seen to be a dimension of the Christian redemptive mystery – as part of the life and ministry of Christ.

A RELATIONAL WORLD – REDEMPTION'S RAW MATERIAL

So this chapter will have two aims: to discover whether redemption can be seen as the building of right relation, and, secondly, to see whether this meaning can truthfully be drawn from the ministry, death and resurrection of Jesus. To explore this I work within the context of both the systems theory and process thought, which already, as I discussed in Chapter 2, sees the basic units of energy of the world as interrelated, God and humanity as linked in a process of mutual becoming. I am also drawing on Carol Gilligan's call for a 'different voice', but here specifically seeking that the relational situation, its resources and strengths be recognized as the redemptive scene, and that the focus of this be widened from self-development alone – although it will be included – to the transformation of the very structures of society.

First we have to make clear what kind of relating is being talked about. In Chapter 3 I widened the context from interpersonal relationships alone to embrace the natural world both as resource and as itself in need of redemption. I wanted to take some of the weighty expectations away from intense personal relationships, yet at the same time widen the relational possibilities by including nature in all its manifestations.

To speak about the redeeming of the dynamics of relating is certainly not new. Martin Buber's assertion of the primary category of existence as relationality is famous – 'In the beginning is the relation'[1] – as is his twofold division of patterns of relating into I-Thou and I-It. Nor did Buber confine himself to relationships between people, but spoke of the threefold level of I-Thou possibilities: between people, nature – his example of the tree is famous – and the Eternal Thou, or God. The question has to be posed: What is the point of claiming that the fundamental category of existence is relationality? Even if it could be proved, it has to be asked what difference would it make. Would it make any difference to the understanding and experience of redemption?

Buber's paraphrase of the beginning of John's Gospel, and its reinterpretations by Matthew Fox as 'In the beginning was the creative energy', by Dorothee Soelle as 'In the beginning was liberation', and by Buber himself elsewhere as the primacy of action over speech, are all attempts to uncover the raw material of existing, the dynamics not just of human experience but the key to all change, development and growth. When we speak of creation and redemption there is another dimension from that of the individual's experience alone: this is the context of the wider whole, the divine source and ground of the universe, and God's will and vision for the end of the process of development. We no longer focus on an individual's self-consciousness as a pivot of all reflection. So this is why, in spirituality, we speak not only of a person's self-awakening and development, but this in relation to a profounder process. Thus the climax of Martha Quest's journey was to link her own developed awareness with a cosmic energy, to be harnessed for good or evil and to develop her own visionary powers to prevent this threatened disaster.

The problem is, however much we try to transcend dualistic divisions between matter and spirit, there is no way at the moment that we can relinquish either category. (In any case, what we want to eliminate are the distortions of these tensions.) Again, with the best will in the world to own our links with the plant and animal world – 'Remember man that thou art dust' – to identify myself with a stone, a lump of pastry, a chestnut tree or a bumble bee may not particularly inspire my progress, spiritual or otherwise. Respecting the value of the connectedness of ourselves with all living organisms does not mean this, but something deeper. 'To be is to respond', as another process thinker, Daniel Day Williams, wrote.[2] 'Love is known in ultimate depth as the mystery of personal communion,' he said, '. . . Communion is another word for love.'[3] Charles Hartshorne, another process thinker, saw the future in terms of openness to new forms of relating: 'To be is to be available for all future actualities.'[4] What all these thinkers – and others – are hinting at is that the dynamic energy which connects all living organisms is *relational* in character. Even the use of a word like 'dynamic energy' is an attempt to transcend a matter/spirit dualism. What I mean by relationality as a basic category is a mutuality, a dynamism, a responsiveness expressed in a myriad of different ways. It has been seen as an evolutionary force, for example, by the Cretan writer Nikos Kazantzakis, in his evocation of the great Cry, blowing through history, stirring the lower forms of life to develop and evolve.[5] John Taylor saw the Spirit of God, the *ruah elohim*, as the dynamic, elemental yet relational force ceaselessly active in history, drawing human beings into deepening forms of encounter and mutuality.[6] He sees the annunciation story as a paradigm of these encounters – in fact this theme has similarly inspired many poets:

> See, they have come together, see
> While the destroying minutes flow,
> Each reflects the other's face,
> Till heaven in hers and earth in his,
> Shine steady there. . .
> But through the endless afternoon,
> These neither speak nor movement make,
> But stare into their deepening trance
> As if their gaze would never break.[7]

But it is not merely mutuality as a dynamic force, a flow of energy, between persons which is its claim to be redemptive. If relationality is a basic category of existence, then it is also the basic dynamism of the divine nature, since all creation participates in the being of God. Christianity has tried to express this through the doctrine of the Trinity – a God in relationship, whose being consists in that flow of circular energy which the Greeks called *perichoresis* (or *circumcessio*, to give its Latin name). So God must *be* the divine ground, the limitless creative source of relationality. Could it not be that creating forms of deeper mutuality within society is also redemptive? That God *is* that ground and source and challenge of our search for deeper and more just form of relating?

If that is so, then in one fell swoop we have linked the being and very existence of God with the creation and making-tangible of just structures and forms of relating. Then God *is* the 'passion to make and make again' which I quoted as inspiration for this book. This is precisely the insight of many feminist theologians. It is the key to a theology of redemption, because, as I have written, redemption seeks to transform the world at a deeper level than do the movements for freedom and liberation – yet it must include them. No one can stand aloof from the engagement and struggle for liberation at the most basic of human levels. If broken mutuality and broken relation underlie all injustices, it is there that the redemptive task must begin.

But, as I stressed in Chapter 3, 'Nature, too, mourns for a lost good' – the natural world is both subject and object of redemption, both victim of broken relation and resource for healing. The political and social world, too, cries out for redemption. The very structures of our language, thought and consciousness are distorted so as to limit our possibilities of mutuality. So how does mutuality or building right relation apply here? Again I speak of a process from midway within it, from which no clear solution has yet emerged and whose tools are clumsy and born of the very fragmentation from which I try to escape.

My problem is that the concept I want does not exist. For 'mutuality in relation' implies a reciprocity in relating which may be the ideal but, sadly, is beyond the grasp of most people. Relationships for most people are characterized by a lack of mutuality. Love accepted and returned is sheer grace which cannot be elicited or grasped by will alone. Like Buber's 'Thou' it comes unexpectedly as total gift. Hence encounter groups today speak more of intentionality and willed commitment in marriage relationships. The miracle is that people have the courage to stay in relationships where mutuality is absent. (Where mutuality is totally absent, where the basis of a relationship is *injustice*, it should be more clearly recognized that God's call may be *out* of a relationship.)

As Sharon Welch, quoted in Chapter 1, despairingly recognized, sanity often lies in blocking levels of sensitivity and mutuality, because the pain of its absence cannot be tolerated. We seek anaesthesia in a variety of ways: our compassion is all too limited.

Yet 'building right relation' is also too limiting a phrase for what I mean. It works well as a basis for ethics but its effectiveness will depend on whether the vision of 'rightness' or justice is itself inspired by a mutuality which embraces all dimensions of the situation. What I seek is a concept which includes a dynamic flow of passionate energy, capable of being nourished between persons, through sexual relationships or friendships of which sexuality is a dimension (to be explored in Chapter 8), but also in other ways because it is the *fundamental creative and healing energy of existence*. It is also the very

87

ground or truth of existence because it flows from the being of God. This is why I find Tillich's definition of God as the 'Ground of our Being' is inadequate. It tells us nothing. In what does the 'Ground of our Being' consist? If it is the limitless and creative source of relational energy which pushes to mutuality and justice-making, if the very being of God is a passion both for justice-making and deeper forms of mutuality, then we are given *content* to the phrase 'Ground of our Being'. We are also given content to the phrase 'creation in the image of God' and summons to deeper participation in divine life. As we increase our passionate energy for justice-making and juster forms of relating we increase our participation in the divine creative ground of our existence: we become more like unto God whose existence is made more tangible in the world. What is more vital, there will be a concept of God which unites feeling, energy and action for justice. God will be a God of wholeness of being and doing.

This is exactly the strength of what many feminist theologians are saying. This is the importance of listening to the 'different voice', the intuition that relational strengths should not lead to victim but redemptive roles in society, that aggression should not be responded to with more aggression, but with an alternative ethic. This is the insight that there are other forms and sources of wisdom to be followed, that there are expressions of sexuality other than that which leads to the domination and exploitation of women. Most importantly, that sexual feeling can even be harnessed as energy for justice-making. As Isabel Carter Heyward puts it:

> With you I begin to realise that the sun can rise again, the rivers can flow again, the fires can burn again. With you, I begin to see that the hungry can eat again, the children can play again, the women can rage and stand again. It is not a matter of what ought to be. It is a power that drives to justice and makes it. Makes the sun blaze, the rivers roar, the fires rage. And the revolution is won again. And you and I are pushed by a power both terrifying and comforting. And 'I love you' means 'Let the revolution begin!'[8]

GOD AS POWER-IN-RELATIONSHIP AND PASSION FOR JUSTICE-MAKING

Although many feminist theologians either develop the theme of mutuality, or, like Rosemary Ruether, see it as central, no one has developed it like the American dogmatic theologian and ordained priest in the Episcopalian Church, Isabel Carter Heyward. In her book *The Redemption of God*, which – without agreeing with

88

absolutely everything in it – I regard as inspirational, the theme of mutuality in relation is developed principally as a means of reclaiming the concept of God from distance and otherworldliness. Carter Heyward reclaims the God who stands over-against humanity: by contrast, God is interpreted as source of relational power: further, our lives here and now are seen as constitutive of our experience of God and of our experience of redemption, which is seen as voluntary participation in making right relation here and now among ourselves: 'With us, through us, God lives, God becomes. God changes, God speaks, God acts, God suffers and God dies in the world.'[9] To claim this power-in-relationality, she writes, we need the encouragement of people whose 'passion for' is 'passion with', or compassion, or a sense of relation characterized by empathy. In a beautiful passage in another work compassion is described relationally as

> our way of bearing with one another in our work and relationships, at home, in the office, in the larger society. Compassion for those to whom we are called to speak judgement is only possible when we realize the radicality – fundamental character – of our bonding with our sisters and brothers and the extent to which the world we share is being called into question/judged. The judgement we speak of is of and to ourselves as well as 'them'.[10]

This interpretation of compassion is derived from the root meaning of passion or suffering as 'to bear', withstand', or 'hold up'. Compassion thus means, writes Carter Heyward,

> to 'bear up' God in the world. To withstand or 'stand with' God is 'to be in solidarity with God'. . . to go with God in our comings and goings. This vocation involves pain, as Jeremiah, Jesus and all bearers of God have known – but not only pain. To be passionate lovers of human beings, the earth, and other earth creatures; to love passionately the God who is Godself, the resource of this love is to participate in an inspired and mind-bogglingly delightful way of moving collectively in history.'[11]

Clearly this positive redemptive understanding of passion and suffering is of great significance for feminist redemption theology which, while rejecting all forms of institutionalized victimization of women, and recognizing passivity as a form of female sin, seeks to discover how to come to an understanding of suffering and sacrifice in such a way that the process of self-development and coming to personal fulfilment is not mutilated.

Redemption will be to take responsibility for all the forms of relationality in which we are involved, personal and political. Redemption will be building right relation here and now; it will mean seeing that this power-in-relation which we claim is redemptive here and now – not a passive waiting for better things in another world: it will be especially to take responsibility for the pain of broken relationality – including our own.

For, like the process thinkers, Carter Heyward realizes that this drive to mutuality and justice takes place in a world filled with injustice and fear. The source of the pain and anguish which we see all around us she sees – as Marjorie Suchocki had done – in the breakdown and distortion of relationality on all levels and spheres:

> Terrified we see. It is terrible, what we see. And it is good that we see together that we are not alone. We see broken body-selves crying to be healed, separated people, yearning for relation; suffering humanity raging for justice; nations, strangers, friends, spouses, lovers, children, sisters, brothers with us, we begin to remember ourselves, compelled by a *power in relation* that is relentless in its determination to break through the boundaries and boxes that separate us. We are driven back to speak the Word that spills among us: 'Without our touching there is no God. Without our relation, there is no God. Without our crying, our yearning, our raging, there is no God. For in the beginning is the relation, and in the relation is the power that creates the world, through us, and with us, and by us, you and I, you and we, and none of us alone.'[12]

In a powerful and moving manner Carter Heyward has evoked the connection between the existence of God and a passion for mutuality and just relating. She has linked the absence of God in the world with the distortion of relation and consequent suffering. This, she would even say, points to the non-existence of God. God died in Auschwitz, she claims, using the novels (semi-autobiographical) of the Jewish writer and Nobel Peace Prize winner, Elie Wiesel, to illustrate this.

Although the Holocaust is not the only tragic example of appalling evil inflicted by one group of human beings on another, Wiesel showed Carter Heyward what could happen if the category of relationality was totally obliterated. For Wiesel, as for all Jewish people:

> The Holocaust is experienced as negation-obliteration, total destruction of relation. To the degree that, for Wiesel, relation is radically good, the Holocaust is experienced as radically evil, the extinction of the meaning and value of human experience; the nullification of human existence; that which is utterly without relation.[13]

The Final Solution of Hitler is seen as the ultimate triumph of structures of dominance and hierarchical power in which all categories like 'love', 'relation' and 'human experience' disappear for both dominant and submissive alike. We only have to look at the world today to see that the disappearance of the category of relationality makes possible the treatment of the Vietnamese Boat People, the dispossession of North American Indians and the marginalization of Aids sufferers. . . Sin as denial of relation, failure to claim power-in-relation surrounds us. It is logical to see this equally as denial of God. This tragedy, argues Carter Heyward, is the key to the category of redemption needed: if a dominating deity led to the annihilation of humanity in Auschwitz, it is the affirmation of humanity which is the only way to the affirmation of God.

No contemporary writer has described the link between the sin as denial of relation and God as the source of relational power more evocatively than Isabel Carter Heyward. She has also made very clear the danger of believing in a God 'out there', remote from the world and the existence of evil within the world. Sin means that we are unwilling to claim our power and passion, to bear up God in relation. Because we seek solutions to what should be mystery, because we seek to impose rigidity and order on what should be spontaneity, pluralism, choice and difference, we destroy relationality. Failure to claim this relational power – and thus admit our deepest yearnings to touch and be touched – means that we are tempted to project it on to someone else, be it guru, hero, public figure or God, and thus we have failed to join in the common enterprise, with God, to create the universe.

Having begun with Carter Heyward's insights, I now want to develop them further for the redemptive process. For how can she be right to assert that 'God died in Auschwitz' because, it appeared, relationality died? No words of mine can possible describe the anguish of those who died or participated in any way in that tragedy and none except those who survived can know the heroism of its victims. But was relationality *totally* eclipsed? Many would say, on the contrary, God was present in the extraordinary experiences of bonding and solidarity which were experienced even in the death-camps. Even in Wiesel's heartrending story of the death of the young boy, the 'sad-eyed angel', which provoked the cry, 'Where is God?' we find the presence of a God who suffers with us, in his own answer, choked out, 'There He is, hanging on the gallows. . .'[14]

For even in conditions of being reduced to a mere cipher, where, as Wiesel wrote, categories of relation seemed annihilated, where the last scraps of being human were being removed, examples of courage, mutuality and bonding did occur, and provided a basis for protest and resistance. God as theologians of the cross like Jürgen

Moltmann have told us,[15] shares our suffering. 'God weeps with our pain', as Kwok Lui Pan, an Asian feminist theologian has written.[16] Stories have emerged of women grounding their power to resist in the reality of relationships. One story relates how four sisters enabled one another to survive:

> To have sisters, not to be alone, was a blessing, too, but fraught with tests, daily, hourly; when this day ends, will there still be four of us? If you are sisterless, you do not have the pressure, the absolute responsibility to end this day alive. How many times did that responsibility keep us alive? I cannot tell. I can only say that many times when I was caught in a selection, I knew I had to get back to my sisters, even when I was too tired to fight my way back, when going the way of the smoke would have been easier. . .[17]

Claiming power-in-relating as strength to resist and survive – surely God is in this too? Again and again experiences of women in prison have claimed mutuality-in-relating, not merely as survival tactic but as spiritual witness, born of shared commitment. Elizabeth McAlister has written of the community of women in prison because of a commitment to peace, and of the joy that was created:

> . . . a community was born among us – a blessed event, a gift. It was not a formalized community – it couldn't be. We sought out each other – spent time together. It had a flow to it, an openness to others. At the same time, there was need in it. We all needed to be with people who cared deeply about our world, about the life of the Spirit, about the life of the mind.[18]

Yes, this is America, not Auschwitz – the gas-chambers did not await the women of this story. Nonetheless, it is one example among many where the shared value of commitment to peace created a new mutuality amid dehumanizing conditions.

It is certainly true that for many people in the world the overwhelming weight of grinding poverty and sickness within political systems which offer no hope, makes the God of traditional theism appear totally absent. No miraculous help is forthcoming. No philosopher has yet produced a convincing solution for the problem of evil or satisfactorily explained God's involvement with it. But the God who is power-in-relation, the source of redemptive energy, is through us and with us in every disaster which the human condition has dreamt up. It is often the poorest communities who have the strongest faith. It is false consciousness, bad faith, which makes us look outside ourselves for slick, artificial solutions. Diving deep within ourselves, to the healing resources deep within us and in the mutuality of human experience and solidarity we will discover the healing possibilities which are God's longing for our fulness of being. This is why the process model sees the edges of God as tragedy – that part of God which identifies with the travail of the universe (= consequent nature) – and the inner being (= primordial nature) of God as total joy. This is the clue to the duality at the heart of all our experience. This is why we can know deep sorrow amid intensity of joy and vice versa. Progress in the spiritual life seems to imply feeling these contrasts in ever sharper intensity. And our culture offers us many anaesthetizing, pain-avoiding possibilities. But, like Hans Andersen's Little Mermaid who wanted to be human to gaze on the Prince she loved, we have to endure the piercing of the sword to keep moving downward and inward to draw on our inner strength.

One of the main objections to this call to discover redemptive mutuality here and now in this life is that there seems to be scant justice available for those who die each day of hunger, violence and warfare, from drowning or road accidents – or indeed for those throughout history who appear to have lived totally meaningless existences. To dismiss this problem by saying that they must all be part of the learning process seems heartless indeed. The traditional solution that all be will be put right in the next world by divine justice seems much more satisfying. This is the greatest challenge which redemption theology must face and I return to it in the final chapter.

But rather than speculating *why* there is a basic duality or tension permeating all existence (the life-death processes which underlie all movement forward), God's presence in any situation means that we have to *claim* this energy and relational power with its transforming potential *now*. And this is all the more difficult when the misery which engulfs us removes energy of any description. As one of the sisters in Auschwitz said so despairingly, it was easier to go to the smoke than to struggle to survive. And in ordinary life, how much easier to accept existing norms and compromises, to be the reconciler, rather than the one who challenges the system, to seek the drug which makes depression bearable rather than face its underlying causes. In all things, hold the system together rather than rock the boat. But the divine source of the energy of mutuality is also the source of the power which drives to justice and the power that judges the false consciousnesses which tolerate injustice.

RECLAIMING SUBJUGATED MEMORY AS AN EMPOWERING TOOL

Here the importance of empowering memory as a tool for justice-making is evident. It was Jean-Baptist Metz who introduced the concept of 'dangerous memory' as a tool for doing political theology.[19] Metz interpreted history – as I am doing – as the arena where redemption or non-redemption occurs, but he did not totally identify redemption with the historical struggle. He saw the vital element in the freedom struggle as the memory of suffering as negative consciousness of future liberation, and as a stimulant to operate within the freedom of this horizon, so that suffering is overcome. I discussed in Chapter 1 how Michel Foucault's concept of 'the insurrection of the subjugated knowledges' can similarly be focused on the dangerous or subversive memory of the subordination of women in history. I have also focused on the importance of the process of recovery of the memory of 'moments of being' blocked by patriarchal structures and consciousness. Edward Schillebeeckx found Metz's theology lacking because Metz in fact identifies all human history with the history of suffering.[20] What we are trying to discover is the value for healing and redemption in the re-membering of the subversive struggle against being dominated. Seeking to remember in order that our desire for vengeance will never be weakened can hardly be consistent with Christian forgiveness. (It would mean that the wrongs perpetrated achieve a kind of destructive immortality in human society.)

What we need to do is to fill out the content of subversive memory in such a way that it drives to greater mutuality and justice-making here and now. Whereas it is true that the experience of solidarity in prisons quoted above was only one strand of experience present, and certainly stories of affection and solidarity cannot replace the tragic experiences of others, yet what is undeniable is that, within what appears as a history of suffering, there are *other* memories, of relating, tenderness and courage. The theology of re-membering for which I argue will recover these redemptive memories as a powerful strand in the Christian tradition. The memory of creative and transforming relationships is more redemptive and hope-giving than the memory of suffering and failure. It is a question of the *content* of subjugated memory. Both Foucault and Sharon Welch – who used Foucault's ideas of uncovering the content of subjugated memory – fail to examine this content. We have to discover fragment by fragment, in every category of human experience, if there is a memory preserved which is *discontinuous* with the dominant historical memory and yet continuous with itself.

Many historians would now say that the memory of women throughout history would be the underside of history, history from the angle of the conquered, not the conqueror. But even within this there are discontinuities. For many women – particularly middle-class women – have certainly adopted the prevailing consciousness and have been separated from the experiences of poorer women, even collaborating in their oppression. So, while it would be impossible to discover a memory continuous with the experience of all subjugated women, the memory of smaller groups of women in history can certainly be called into existence. (Within the Christian tradition, communities of religious sisters, the Beguines, Quaker women are all examples of this.) Not only conscious, recorded memory, but *unconscious* memory lies buried in myth, legend and archetype and can be brought to light.

My point is that the content of the memory and the purpose of remembering are as important as the methodology. The memories of violence, struggle and failure are insufficient, not just because they eventually cease to empower, but because they are not the full truth of humanity in relationship. Even within the feminist movement itself it could be said that the earlier resistance movements based on the 'sisterhood is powerful' slogan were a limited success, because 'communities of resistance' was an inadequate ethic. Surely feminism meant much more than struggle with – or against – men. Surely it must be more about offering alternative values. And. . .if this is true, then something of these values of the dynamism of mutuality and solidarity must be evident both in the struggle – as a critique of prevailing values – and in the way women related with each other and with men.

But before pursuing the content of 'dangerous memory' further, the question must be asked whether the redemptiveness of mutuality and making right relation is expressed in the life and death of Jesus, who is, in Christian theology, the redeemer of humankind.

JESUS: LIVING EXAMPLE OF MUTUAL EMPOWERING IN RELATIONSHIP?

If God creates, heals and redeems by enabling us to claim power in relationship, a power which at the same time drives to justice, we would expect to see that manifest above all in the life and ministry of Jesus. 'God', says Carter Heyward, 'is nothing other than the eternally creative source of our relational power, our common strength, a God whose movement is to *empower*, bringing us into our own together, a God whose name in history is love. . .'[21]

Mutuality-in-relating will express something vital about Jesus' relationship with God; it must be the key to Jesus' developing personality, self-awareness and relationships with the men, women and children of his life, as well as the drive to his understanding of his mission to save the world – in fact to the central question of the meaning of salvation.[22]

Can all this be seen in the four Gospels? Can we see the dynamic of mutuality-in-relating as the salvific energy of God's creating/redeeming will? If God is truly the liberating God of Exodus, the God of action-for-justice witnessed to by the Old Testament prophets (see Mic. 6.6), then the creative energy of mutuality-in-relating could be the very alternative way of living which is called into being when the experience of being slaves under the oppressor is brought to an end by God's liberating initiative. This will then be seen as the very heart of the message of freedom to which Jesus witnessed and of which he was the embodiment.

We can never know by what means Jesus himself grew to that fulness of meaning of redemption to which his final actions witnessed. I think we can discern three distinct periods in the development of Jesus' consciousness of the meaning of salvation. We know there is evidence to suggest that for a time Jesus explored and discarded the meaning of freedom and liberation lived out by the political freedom movement of the Zealots.[23] The famous passage of Luke's Gospel (Luke 4.18–30) where Jesus picks up the scroll in the synagogue and clearly identifies himself with the task of Isaiah (61.1–2) to

proclaim release to the captives,
and recovery of sight to the blind,
to proclaim liberty to the oppressed,

suggests all the fire of a young freedom fighter. This is the phase characterized above all by urgency and immediacy. The Gospel of Mark tells that after his baptism Jesus came up out of the waters 'and *immediately* he saw the heavens opened. . .' (Mark 1.10). Then the Spirit '*immediately* drove him into the wilderness. . .' (Mark 1.12). When passing the Sea of Galilee, he calls the sons of Zebedee to be his disciples: 'and *immediately* they left their nets' (Mark 1.18). That first chapter in Mark carries on with a breathtaking urgency, until Jesus takes his first break – to go out to a lonely place before daybreak to pray.

But in a second phase the Jesus of later passages in Luke, who – in stark contrast, apparently abhorring violence – heals the ear of the High Priest's servant (Luke 22.50), is the Jesus who cries, 'The Kingdom of Heaven is in the midst of you' (Luke 17.21). Here we encounter a man who knew that redemption meant being spoken to in the depths, with immediacy:

'Today, salvation has come to your house', he tells Zacchaeus, a personal salvation which still included the restitution of money wrongfully extorted from the poor. The rich man who built bigger and bigger barns is condemned not merely for extravagance, but because his heart is on the wrong things. By redemption is meant the total transformation of the inner and outer person – and neglect of the inner processes of growth in wisdom is totally condemned: 'Now you Pharisees clean the outside of the cup and of the dish, but inside you are full of exhortation and wickedness. You fools. . .' (Luke 11.39).

Jesus well recognized the inner processes of coming to self-knowledge as the beginning of the redemptive path, which we described in Chapter 4, when he cried: 'Woe to you lawyers! for you have taken away the key of knowledge; you did not enter yourselves, and you hindered those who were entering' (Luke 11.52).

But self-knowledge and conversion/awakenings would burst spontaneously into a seeking of forgiveness (Luke 15: the Prodigal Son), and a living out of the justice and compassion of the Kingdom of God (The Good Samaritan, Luke 10.30–37). This is a man who is fearless in using the insights of nature as resources in the journey to wholeness – the lilies of the fields, the birds of the air, the foxes in their holes, the fig tree in flower and the seed growing to maturity are all contributory images.

But in the third and final phase I think Jesus envisions the redemptive task in global terms. Images of the Kingdom begin to suggest more and more that its values are in total conflict with the world's values – we must receive it like a child (Luke 18.17), the rich will find it hard to enter (Luke 17.24), and the contribution of the poor widow is the shining image of total giving. Frequent reference to his own coming suffering and the disaster about to befall Jerusalem (Luke 19.41; 21.20), depicted in cosmic apocalyptic terms of ultimate disaster, suggest that what is needed can never be achieved by merely individual conversions and efforts, but by a turning back at its very root of the tide of evil and violence, which would transform the universe on a cosmic scale.

But because creation and redemption are ultimately God's work, this could be set in motion only by someone who had discovered and manifested the divine source of creative, relational energy in a way powerful enough to draw the whole world with him. And this is the origin of the redeeming power of Jesus: first, that it was divine in origin, and secondly, that it was relational and mutual in its nature and operation.

In Jesus we see a person rooted in God as source and resource of relational energy, wanting to draw his friends into this relational matrix, (John 17.20–26). The intensity with which Jesus loved his Abba–Father (the most important God-symbol for him) was part of the same divine source with which his friends were also loved – 'for the Father himself loves you, because you have loved me and have believed that I came from the Father' (John 16.27) – which was also

97

to be their source for loving one another. Teaching them to pray and to keep on praying (with the image of the harassed judge, for example), was part of drawing them into this resource of relational flow, for prayer is one significant way of entering the dynamism of mutuality in relating. But if God is the liberating and creative source of mutuality-in-relating, then we would expect Jesus too to break the ethic of domination/submission and to reach out to those rejected by the values of those in power. From the beginning of his public life this is indeed the startling thing about Jesus. He is a man who eats with tax-collectors and prostitutes. He ministers to women and children. He makes the healing of outcasts such as lepers his special task; racial groups detested by the Jews – like the Samaritans – are not only ministered to (as is the women at the well in John ch. 4), but made central images of the Kingdom 'the Good Samaritan'). The poor, he says, are the very stuff of the Kingdom of Heaven – though not because it is wonderful to be poor or marginalized. Jesus showed himself to be very concerned that people should be fed. But only with those cut off from the ambition of becoming powerful, rich and exploitative of those less fortunate, could the divine redeeming energy of mutuality do its transforming work.

And this is the significance of Jesus' encounters with the women of the Gospels: if it is true that women remain close to relational processes, and in the time of Jesus were cut off from positions of authority, then the vulnerability and openness for the flow of relational energy was present to them in a significant way. That same soil of vulnerability from which compassion – the ability to 'bear up God in the world' – is born and which can so often turn women into society's victims is found in the poor and oppressed of the world today, as well as in the sensitivity of anyone towards a loved person in a relationship. 'Only when persons begin to act on the ideals of openness,' says Marjorie Suchocki, 'turning what is possible into actuality, can God integrate that new actuality into a vision which will elicit still further relevant models of openness for the world.'[24]

But the problem for us is to discern through the information which the evangelists give us whether the mutuality-in-relating for which women have potential played any part in the life and learning processes of Jesus.

It has been argued by both Isabel Carter Heyward and Elizabeth Moltmann-Wendel that the Gospel of Mark preserves an earlier layer in the memories of the way Jesus reacted to and related with people. The latter has shown that what was depicted relationally by Mark, in terms of the reactions between Jesus and his disciples (for example, in Mark 10.35, where the sons of Zebedee ask him for the privilege of sitting at his right and left hand when he enters his glory), in Matthew and Luke has already lost the dynamics of encounter and mutuality: '. . . even Matthew and Luke no longer wanted to note such signs of independence and personal activity. . . The dynamics of encounter and movement, the fact that Jesus clashes with them, the fact that they are a group and represent something in themselves, is no longer of interest.'[25]

We can see this especially in the Marcan story of the woman who suffered from the flow of blood for twelve years (5.21–43). It is an amazing story, sandwiched in the middle of the story of the raising to life of the daughter of Jairus. It contains so much of the shame and embarrassment of the haemorrhaging woman, who was getting worse, not better, and did not dare to approach Jesus openly. It is a story of the flow of healing energy awakening Jesus himself to touching and being touched. For Mark is attentive to the self-consciousness of Jesus in a way which the other evangelists are not. Jesus, 'perceiving in himself that the power had gone forth from him,' (5.30) is able to respond to her reaching out, and the relational energy and healing response is called forth from him. But the important point is that there is a dialogue, an encounter, and Jesus *learns* from the experience. This is absent from Matthew who depicts Jesus making a formal response: 'Take heart daughter; your faith has made you well' (9.22).

What we also notice is that because women in the Gospels are so often presented silent and in the background, it would seem that often their communication with Jesus is non-verbal, through symbol and gesture. The woman who anoints Jesus (Mark 14.3–9, Luke 7.36–50) is silent and unnamed.[26] She communicates her recognition of who Jesus is by the lavish, extravagant gesture of pouring perfumed ointment over his head (Mark) or his feet (Luke). In the Marcan story the symbolic intent of this gesture again awakens a dynamic response from Jesus, as he hails her action as prophetic – indeed forever linked with the proclamation of the gospel.[27] Again Mark hints that Jesus actually *learns* from the encounter. The Lucan story shows Jesus responding to the almost embarrassing gesture – the women won't stop weeping and kissing Jesus' feet – in answering her great love for him by forgiveness. But we get the impression that this is Luke using the story to bring out his theme of conversion/ forgiveness – the mutuality of the Marcan story has disappeared.

The theme of the silent – often unnamed – women in Luke's Gospel is startling, right through from Mary, 'pondering these things in her heart' (2.19), to the other Mary who sits silent at the Lord's feet (10.38–42), where Martha is presented in a negative light as 'being busy about many things'. This is in stark contrast with the

99

picture of Martha in John's Gospel, where the most significant confession of Jesus as 'the Christ, the Son of God, who is coming into the world' (11.27), is on the lips, not of Peter, as in the synoptic Gospels, but of Martha. And yet she has gone through Christian history as the sanctified domestic, a kind of holy floor-scrubber.[28]

Widows are a group of people who clearly aroused the compassion of Jesus: it is possible to trace a connection between the roots of his compassion for the widow of Nain (Luke 7.11–17) and Jesus' response to the situation of his own mother Mary. She, too, was apparently now a widow; he, too, was presumably the only son – yet he was totally engrossed in the ministry of the Kingdom, a mission which would lead him to suffering and death. Small wonder that he had compassion on the widow of Nain.

Luke also presents women as disciples, following Jesus from a distance (8.2–3), and they are given no voice. The daughters of Jerusalem weep for him as he treads the Via Crucis and his response to their weeping is in terms of the global tragedy: even the worth of motherhood is called into question in the context of the world's rejection of all that is innocent and good. But the silent recognition and response to Jesus of the women of the Gospels reaches its climax with the cross vigil: 'And all his acquaintances and the women who had followed him from Galilee stood at a distance and saw these things' says Luke (23.49). And Mark tells us, in closer and more relational terms:

> There were also women looking on from afar, among whom were Mary Magdalen, and Mary the mother of James the Younger, and of Joses, and of Salome, who, when he was in Galilee, followed him, and ministered to him; and also many other women who came up with him to Jerusalem (15.40).

Here relational strengths and empathy with Jesus' situation are visible as ministry, in fact as a very high form of action. Here we see a way to cut through the dichotomy between feeling and action. It was the only form of action possible in the situation. And yet it was relational, mutual energy which was its characteristic. Standing at the foot of the cross, in grief-stricken empathy, women found the strength, the focused attention, to 'stand with', 'withstand' the situation, with the necessary openness and vulnerability to 'receive' Easter morning.

And the reason that it is redemptive is because – as can be seen if we use the process model – that is the way in which the 'with-ness of God' is present to the situation. A mother watches over the bedside of a sick child, empathizing with the child's feverish tossing, or a baby's fretfulness, can yet imagine a tomorrow when that same child will be running in the garden, eating ice-cream. Even if she knows her child is dying she may be overwhelmed with grief, yet, owing to the relational understanding of the self, may not see tragedy as the situation's *only* dimension. One grief-stricken mother, whose two daughters had died in Auschwitz, had only one thought – to find some way to turn this tragedy into possibility for forgiveness and harmony. Being a talented violinist, she played her violin around the world, to forge bonds of reconciliation and fellowship, until stiffening joints meant that she could play no more.[29]

In the same way, God is with the grief of the moment, in empathizing sorrow. But that is not all that the divine presence means. God is also offering alternative possibilities, strength and hope in the midst of the struggle, protest against the appalling existential realities. Watching at a sick person's bedside may be a *hidden* way of 'bearing up God in the world': standing at the foot of the cross of a 'criminal', watching at the gates of Greenham or Molesworth, standing in vigil outside the South African embassy in London or Washington are highly politicized forms of redemptive mutuality. It is thus that 'all things begin in mysticism and end in politics . . . only to begin again'[30]

But if silent empathy or symbolic presence is a prominent female form of gospel witness, it is also when women actually speak and encounter Jesus that we see how the energy of mutuality is an integral part of his developing consciousness. Here I explore only two examples of this, the first a Marcan story, the second from the Gospel of John. It is Mark again who is sensitive to relational dynamism. In the story of the Syro-Phoenician woman whose little daughter was possessed by an unclean spirit (Mark 7.24–30) Jesus seems irritated and embarrassed: she is clearly nothing to do with him and he gives her an answer in terms of what the Jews think of Syro-Phoenicians. But her response is needle-sharp – and she takes his own insulting image: 'Yes, Lord; yet even the dogs under the table eat the children's crumbs'. And again the relational energy is called forth from Jesus – his consciousness has leapt forward in mutuality as he realizes that the passionate flow of healing divine power is no respecter of narrow political boundaries!

Secondly, we can detect this mutuality set free by honest confrontation, this time in John's Gospel. In the story of the Marriage Feast of Cana (John 2), commentators now see this as the first of the seven signs which the writer of John's Gospel has selected to illustrate the essence of Jesus' ministry.[31] Here the Messiah is presented bringing the new wine of the Kingdom. The new reign of God is inaugurated. In this story the Mother of Jesus is instrumental in awakening his attention to the situation of no wine. The theme of

Mary who misunderstands the nature of Jesus' person and mission has been a favourite one for commentators, especially among those who claim that her position is grossly over-exaggerated in the Church. But if we re-envision Mary as an independent woman, fiercely committed – as was her Son – to the work of witnessing to the Kingdom, and to her own role in this: if we envision her as responsive to the energy of relating, steeped in the Wisdom and prophetic traditions (as the Magnificat shows), reflective as to what all this meant for her own life and that of her Son's, quite a different picture emerges. This is no lonely, clinging mother, unable to cope when her child left home, following the crowd pitiably, in hope of the occasional glimpse of him. This is a woman as passionately committed to God's creative and redeeming plan as he was, a woman who had set him free for his work, as she was free for hers. When she is with him she is as set on God's work as he is. The breaking-in of the Kingdom of Heaven is where Jesus is, so Mary is there too. But this is no example of 'He for God and she for God in him': Mary – like all women – must be liberated from mediated existence.

We do not know whether she was present in the crowd when the woman cried out, 'Blessed is the womb that bore you, and the breasts that you sucked' (Luke 11.27). But Jesus' response – 'Blessed rather are those who hear the word of God and keep it' – far from being a rejection of Mary, could very well have been learnt *from her*, as in her prophetic discernment of events she realized the necessity of setting him free for wider bonding than the family situation alone.

The wedding at Cana shows Mary's perception of the relational scene – the potential embarrassment for the host and consequent unhappiness of bride and groom – and her lack of fear of presenting this to Jesus. However we translate his irritable response, it is clear that he did not wish to assume any responsibility for the scenario. Mary thought he should and risked confrontation. His words do not represent a putting-down of an interfering woman, as has been suggested, but a wrestling with his developing consciousness of what God wanted of him – and when. A sense of the ripeness of the moment – the *kairos*, the 'sunset touch', or what Charles Williams calls the 'Beatrician moment'[32] – is crucial for John's Gospel. He responds to Mary's sensitivity of the rightness of the moment by an action which will continue to inspire history with its many-levelled symbolism. But it was called into existence by response based on mutuality-in-relatedness.

This means that the power which characterizes the life and healing miracles of Jesus is not the power conferred by virtue of institution or external authority but the free-flowing relational and passionate energy of God's Spirit, which transcends boundaries and human

102

categories and forever seeks moments and means of breakthrough into history.[33]

RELATIONAL POWER AS BREAKTHROUGH TO REDEMPTION

Re-imaging Jesus as influenced and learning through the dynamic energy of mutuality-in-relatedness has not yet fully shown why this is the energy of divine redemption. Relational power seen as passion for justice-making has to be shown as the driving force of the death and resurrection of Jesus, as well as the elemental yet redeeming force by which God operates in and through us; possibly even the special giftedness of God's presence among us at the present time: 'A passion for justice, shared and embodied, is the form God takes among us in our time.'[34]

The special contribution of feminist theology has been to see that the alternative vision offered does not mean the surrender of power to the dominators in order to join ranks with the oppressed but the re-imaging of power itself, in order to change this destructive dynamic . . . If power is seen as originating in relational dynamism, which can be developed for good or evil, sin, as blocking and distorting this flow, stimulates new images of power and thus a new Christology, when Jesus is envisioned in relational terms.[35]

Thus the re-imaging of power as mutuality in relation – which is crucial for the theology of atonement I will develop in Chapter 7 – is first of all a power which brings to birth. This means a bringing-to-birth of what is already there, empowering people in their own powers, in the way Jesus was constantly empowering and sending people to heal, exorcize and preach, but emphasizing the dependence of this power on deep faith.[36] Secondly, it was the power of awareness, sensitivity and affiliation or bonding, which drove Jesus to be with people in their grief – for example, in the story of the raising of the son of the widow of Nain (Luke 7.11–17), and to call for new forms of relating. (In fact the whole gospel story is one of a call to a new dynamic of community-relating: 'A new commandment I give to you, that you love one another; even as I have loved you, that you also love one another' (John 13.34).) Thirdly, it was the power of compassion, linked with the creative passion of God which seeks to bring-to-birth new dynamics of relating. Next, it was the power of anger, which drives to justice-making, as seen in the casting out of the money-makers from the Temple (Matt. 21.12–14). It was also the power which drives towards healing and wholeness. It was a power, finally, which has been described – in a somewhat unusual interpretation – as erotic power. Erotic power, says Audre Lord, means 'the creating, enlarging and sustaining of relationships'.[37] it is the power which, at its deepest roots, understands joy and refuses injustice, 'because the deepest celebration is the union with others, and the clearest protest against oppression comes not from an abstract commitment to principles, but from the experience of suffering, caused by oppression'.[38]

To live in the relational process is to claim this redemptive power, which is also erotic power, which transforms, saves and empowers. Claiming this power is part of the very reclaiming exercise for which this book is written. It is re-sourcing, reclaiming, redeeming lost creative energies. As Sally Gearhart has written,

> There is a source, or kind of power, qualitatively different from the one we have been taught to operate with; further, the understanding of the development, the protection of that source and allowing of it to reach its full dimensions could mean the *redemption of the entire globe from the devastation of the last thousand years* (my italics).[39]

Put in these terms, it becomes clear that mutuality-in-relating is about far more than improving one's personal relationships: it is about touching a deep source of relational energy in such a way as to liberate God's own passion for justice.

And it is this breakthrough in the life of Jesus which set the redemptive events in motion for the Christian tradition – in a uniqueness not previously experienced. The breakthrough was itself made possible because, as I have explained, the world is relational in its most basic units, because the very nature of the divine is to be the inexhaustible ground of relational energy, and because there is a remarkable co-inherence between all spheres of existence which allow interpenetration and breakthrough on all levels.[40]

Rosemary Haughton, in her book *The Passionate God*, uses the image of romantic love to describe this exchange of energy and life between all spheres of existence.[41] Romantic love pinpoints this exchange, she says, because love is concentrated at one point, where it is enabled to break through all the defence mechanisms and barriers which human beings erect to block mutuality with each other. Breakthrough can occur, she says, through the beauty of shared commitment, so that, for example, Christianity was able to use the Romance language of twelfth-century Provence to evoke the giving and receiving of divine/human loving.

The insight of Haughton that I find the most valuable – for I think it is a mistake to build too much on romantic love, particularly as it appears in such debased forms today – is the idea of divine energy as passionate force seeking the 'soil of vulnerability', the cracks in consciousness, the response of mutuality, to break through with a changed vision of relating. This is once more the vision of God's creative vision or *ruah*:

> It is about an energy that smashes through the surface of everyday awareness and makes possible the exchange of spiritual power and knowledge which not only penetrates the lovers through every aspect of body, mind and spirit, but reaches far beyond them to transform every other relationship of the material world.[42]

This passionate force, which drives to deepening levels of experience, is the very essence of incarnation or 'flesh-taking'. Inspired by the model of the divine Sophia-Wisdom encountering and co-inhering with the whole of creation, not only the falling-in-love situation, but every human encounter carries the possibility of breakthrough of God's passionate energy. Hence the word 'passion' moves, as it did with Carter Heyward, from the guiding image of the sexual experience to being the passion which fuels our caring and justice-making, 'the power which drives to justice and makes it'.[43]

With a re-envisioning of the gospel story, we can see how this power drove Jesus to justice-making. The same force can drive us today. With a new understanding we can discern the raw material of redemption. The dynamics of mutuality evoked a re-imaging of power in a man totally open and vulnerable to divine passionate energy for justice-making. This was a man whose relationships were characterized by intimacy, immediacy and intensity, whose vision was of its essence one to be lived, shared, and made accessible to the poorest on the face of the earth. Here we can see that tradition's one-sided focus on the cross is missing out on the very heart of the trail which Jesus blazed and which we have to reclaim. It is in the reclaiming of the resources of Jesus' *life* that we understand that what sacrifice really means is a total response in mutuality to justice-making in a particular situation. It is passionate energy for justice-making which calls for that self-transcendence, that total self-offering we call sacrifice – not a passive putting one's head on the block in a masochistic self-martyrdom.

So it was the mounting intensity of the struggle, the increased sense of urgency of his life – 'I came to cast fire upon the earth, and would that it were already kindled! I have a baptism to be baptized with and how I am constrained until it is accomplished!' (Luke 12.49) – which increased Jesus' vulnerability towards those in whom the forces of evil were vested, and made the end inevitable. So was it with the early martyred followers of Jesus, with Gandhi, with Martin Luther King and all who oppose the vulnerability of sheer mutuality-in-relating with the refusal of exchange.

Haughton's greatest contribution is her analysis of the resurrection as the breakthrough of passionate love, making possible in history endless possibilities of exchanged love: although at no point during his life do the gospel writers indicate that his followers understood Jesus – or perhaps they did, at levels too deep for conscious awareness: it seemed that just before his death was a time for them of increased intimacy and depth of relationship. Haughton sees the Last Supper as at the centre of many kinds of exchange, a point at which it was possible for the group to reach a new level of intensity of presence to each other. I think there was another level of exchange or dynamic of relating for Jesus: there was a consciousness, as never before, that the ripeness of time was *now*, to halt the great refusal of exchange which we call the power of evil. The very breakthrough in love which his lifestyle was calling into being was also evoking that judgement which calls for justice. That new level of intensity of relating brought him, as it would bring his followers, to new levels of suffering, as it clashed with the meanness and superficiality of what passes for ordinary relating.

What the great prayer of John 17 conveys is the intensity with which Jesus was consumed with divine mutuality. What I see happening at the Last Supper is his attempt to discover an enduring way – through a shared meal, the simplicity of historical gestures of blessing, the spontaneity of friendship fused with time-honoured ritual – of bringing together these many levels of divine relatedness. He sought to provide means of an enduring breakthrough into human experience, so that the human passion of friendships, of romantic love, all the tenderness towards children and patient nurture of the sick, all enjoyment of earth's goodness, could be caught up into his experience of being held by the passionate intensity of divine energy. But afterwards, these moments of intensity and illumination, which appeared to be the climax of his earthly life, were followed – as we saw in the previous chapter, in the way the *via illuminativa* was followed by the Dark Night – by the desolation of the Garden and the apparent abandonment of the cross:

> The cry of Jesus was the cry of awareness that all indeed was accomplished, brought to consummation. He knew that he could, at last, give back to the One He loved, the unshackled fullness of love, and in so doing, *carry with him* on the surge of that passion the love which is the essential being of all creation.[44]

Yes, it appeared that Jesus was abandoned, as everyone in a situation of desolation feels totally abandoned. But we know that God's love is present to *every* situation: Blake's wonderful drawing of the Trinity shows the dying Christ as held in the passionate love of God:

ultimately God *is* resurrection and through resurrection was able to halt the great refusal of exchange.

But if the analysis I have presented is correct there are three consequences. If sin as denial of relation – 'refusal of exchange' in Haughton's terms – is present in the structures of bureaucratic society, in our prison system, health care, our pollution of air, sea and earth, the fact that we allow so many poor people to live homeless or in inadequate housing and so on, this means that the dynamics of redemption – a passionate energy for justice-making – are equally vital today. We too must become 'points of exchange' (Haughton again), not in the sense in which city monetary life depends on commercial exchange, but in the sense of openness to deeper levels of mutuality. Charles Williams himself has played on this parody of the image of exchange:

This is the way of this world in the day of that other's;
make yourselves friends by means of the riches of iniquity;
for the wealth of the self is the health of the self exchanged.
What saith Heracleitus? – and what is the city's breath? –
dying each other's life, living each other's death.
Money is a medium of exchange.[45]

Yet in another poem Williams describes the exact opposite, the way of exchange as the joyous ethic of a small company of knights, who did live each others' life and die each others' death, taking on what he called the 'one adored substitution'.[46]

Not only is openness demanded, but a readiness to claim power in relation, to be willing to become vulnerable, and voluntarily accept suffering for the sake of juster forms of relating. Secondly, the philosophy of empowering memory I have been building up will take on a new dimension. Jesus' call to 'Do this in memory of me' involves not merely a command to die the death that he would die, as Haughton thinks, but to live the life that he did by responding in all the fulness of mutuality of which we are capable. This is indeed the content of 'dangerous memory' which was discussed earlier, because the dynamics of relating, if entered upon with intensity, will clash with that great refusal of relation so evident around us.

Thirdly, to assert that claiming the uniqueness of incarnation and resurrection would *weaken* relational power in history, as Carter Heyward does, is to undervalue the actual *history* of the breakthrough of resurrection in history. 'I suggest', writes Carter Heyward,

that female Christians, black Christians, poor Christians and gay/Lesbian Christians participate in the perpetuation of our own oppression insofar as we allow our visions and energies to be drawn towards a heavenly man and away from our human situation as sisters and brothers, by fixing our attention on the spiritual accomplishments of a divine saviour rather than on the spiritual possibilities of a concerned human commitment that can be inspired by the Jesus story as a human story.[47]

Focusing on redemption as claiming power-in-relation here and now, which is also interpreted as divine passionate energy for justice, *is* claiming resurrection energy for the world. To deny uniqueness to resurrection, as Carter Heyward does, to say that Jesus was merely a remarkable man for his time, as Rita Brock does, Jesus as 'a distant partner who participates in our search for life, whole and healed',[48] does not do justice to the fact that it is not merely memory of an event in which we engage, but a remembering and reclaiming of a living force which has empowered the lives and relational possibilities of so many Christians for two thousand years: it is not a question of slavishly imitating Jesus' life, but being empowered by the same redemptive dynamic set in motion by the Calvary event. It is part of resurrection history that this power continues as living force: our task is to claim it as liberating for women and all oppressed groups.

But if the recovery of all that leads to self-development and then to deeper possibilities of mutuality-in-relation, to energy for justice, is at the heart of redemption, it has to be asked why Christian theology has concentrated all its efforts on the meaning of the cross event. Jesus saved us by dying on the cross and opening the gates of heaven, we are told as children: so it is to the doctrines of atonement that I turn, to explore ways of reclaiming atonement for feminist theology.

6

The Placating of the Deity?
The Unravelling and Re-weaving of Atonement

All reflections on Christian redemption centre on the passion and death of Jesus on the cross. It is such an in-built focus of theology that, when the question is asked, 'But *how* did Jesus save us? *How* exactly is he our Redeemer?' – without hesitation comes the response: 'By dying on the cross'. Although there are many examples of Christian art and iconography which represent incarnation in the form of Jesus' nativity, by far the greatest number focus on Calvary and cross, even in contemporary art. Because for so many people suffering *is* the only reality they know, the cross is the symbol par excellence with which they can identify. Even resurrection – although theologically of primary importance – has taken second place in popular spirituality. It has sometimes even been seen on the level of Jesus' God-given reward for 'going through with it'!

CAN ATONEMENT BE RECLAIMED FOR FEMINIST THEOLOGY?

The many interpretations of the 'how' of redemption are known as 'atonement' doctrines. Here we will meet interwoven strands of theologies of grace and sin, guilt and freedom, and will be challenged by the question as to what we mean today by being 'saved' by anyone. If being 'saved' is an authentic experience, we need to understand the mechanics of soteriology. (Indeed, as Carter Heyward suggested, we should even ask ourselves if the hero/saviour concept is itself a false construct, since it enables us to project our guilt and powerlessness on to someone else.) I have already explained some of the pitfalls of cross theology for women. Yet I have also asserted that a Christian feminist notion of redemption, and, specifically, redemption as right relation, is reclaiming lost and potentially enriching elements of the Christian tradition which might, conceivably, unite the notions of redemption as divine gift, and redemption as liberation or emancipation. As Marjorie Suchocki has said, reflecting on the contribution of women to Christianity: 'If the energy of women has gone into the weaving of this religion, then that energy might be honoured or reclaimed by unravelling the fabric and weaving it into new patterns.'[1]

We have already seen how the dynamic of mutuality can be a key to the interpretation of the life and ministry of Jesus, as well as an inspiration to ourselves to 'claim our own power-in-relating'. We now explore whether the notion of 'redemption as right relation' or as 'mutuality-in-relating' can function as the *how* of Christian redemption, or in other words if it can function as a doctrine of the atonement. This means investigating the dynamic in terms of the saving function or *soteriology* of the cross event.

To explore this I have to look critically from a feminist point of view at the most important atonement doctrines. I have to ask if feminists can accept an atonement doctrine at all, in view of the disastrous consequences this has had for women. Then I will ask if atonement can be re-envisioned and woven into new patterns, according to the dynamic of mutuality-in-relation, which is the strength of the feminist theology I develop. To do this I will first briefly sketch three main classifications, the Greek Patristic model (the earliest form of the doctrine, when Fathers of the Church first began to reflect on the salvific meaning of the cross event), secondly, the Latin or Western model (often associated with St Anselm), and thirdly, the atonement within the framework of individual subjectivity[2] (often associated with Friedrich Schleiermacher). This is no attempt to give a full history of atonement doctrines or interpretations. However, without an exploration of and an evaluation of the strengths and weaknesses of these beliefs, which are so deeply-rooted in our faith tradition, we cannot see whether the model I am trying to develop can actually bear the weight of what an atonement doctrine must do, which is to offer a realistic language of sin and grace and face responsibly the entire reality of evil with which we struggle in our personal and communal lives. Above all, we need to see how such a doctrine relates to our experiences as women and men today. Only when this is clear can I begin to sketch an alternative model.

THE GREEK MODEL OF ATONEMENT

Four basic motifs are important in the Greek, or Patristic, model of atonement. First, atonement is seen as the example, teaching and new direction given by Christ. By his formative and educative activity he brings new knowledge, and so opens the way to imitation and participation with him, and leads humanity away from darkness, error and death. Atonement through education has actually become a popular contemporary theme.[3] But in the thought of St Irenaeus, Bishop of Lyons about 125 AD, we can see the whole salvific work of God as a pedagogic process through which the image of God, now corrupted in human beings, can be restored as they are led to greater freedom.[4] At this stage, it does make a difference for our argument that for Irenaeus, though he stands in contrast with Augustine's view of fallen man as having completely lost the divine image, nevertheless, the final achievement of freedom and perfection will come in the next world: already there is a degree of undervaluing of the claiming of right relation here-and-now.

Secondly, the atonement means the repetition for us of the life and death of Jesus. In Christ was 'recapitulated' or summed up all human actions and achievements, so, as he acted on our behalf, now we can share and be drawn into his actions.

Thirdly, the struggle of Jesus against the devil and the demonic forces shows that atonement is not achieved by pressure of divine power but by victory through a genuine struggle. (This is the *Christus Victor* motif of atonement which Gustaf Aulen preferred and made popular – possibly because of the influence of two World Wars.) It is this idea of the struggle which generates the need for 'ransom money' and Jesus himself as ransom price, as well as the notion of humanity enslaved, in bondage through sin and evil and in desperate need of liberation. (The theme of bondage is the reason why some psychiatrists see the motif of *Christus Victor* as valuable, because they see a link between the bondage of sin and the bondage of a mental illness, both of which need the healing processes offered by the atonement doctrine.)[5]

Fourthly, atonement is about the divinization of humanity, about community with God, the forgiveness of sins and true life – all motifs which can be drawn together under the idea of education or formation.[6] What is needed is the formation necessary for a human being to reach true humanity and being, true freedom, a process which cannot happen without struggle and anguish, as Plato's famous myth of the Cave makes clear.[7] Using the insights of Greek philosophy, atonement doctrine in this classical form means far more than moral teaching or example, but is the means of enabling a human being, by *mimesis* (imitation) and *methexis* (participation) – as part of the process of divinization – to attain full human becoming and participation in divine life. The strength of this interpretation is to see the whole salvific drama of creation, incarnation, redemption and the divinization of humanity as a unity: creation and redemption are educative processes flowing into each other, and atonement is not seen in isolation from incarnation.

Despite its strength, this Eastern understanding eventually gave way to another interpretation. Apparently its categories were burst by essentially Christian correctives. Christianity, it is thought, wanted to stress the freedom and transcendence of God in the face of human nature and thus needed to portray atonement as something outside us, freely bestowed by God. Because Greek philosophy, caught as it was between the opposed categories of matter/spirit, could not simply identify the divine with human, it was necessary to break out of the Greek cosmological categories of atonement. (Not that its basic motifs would not endure – it was their interpretation which was in question.)[8] So the stage is set for the Latin, or Western, view of atonement.

THE LATIN DOCTRINE OF ATONEMENT

This is a very important interpretation of atonement for my theme: it is the version most frequently found in popular belief, worship and hymnology, principally through the form of atonement theory attributed to Anselm of Canterbury.[9] It is also that form of atonement doctrine to which feminist theologians are reacting – and usually in a hostile manner. Why has this theory provoked such strong reactions, both positive and negative? The crux of the difficulty, according to Gilbert Greshake, is that the theory is usually encountered in a negative light, principally, he thinks, because we have not understood the importance of relating its main theological stress to its sociological background.[10] Josef Ratzinger – now Cardinal Prefect of the Congregation for the Doctrine of the Faith – himself has succinctly summarized the difficulties we face when Anselm's view is distorted. The rigid logic of Anselm's view, he writes, can make the image of God appear in a sinister light.[11] We shrink, he continues, from such a concept of justice which makes the message of love incredible. Moreover he is aware that popular consciousness can – and continues to – distort the doctrine into seeing a wrathful deity demanding infinite expiation, and thus condemning his only Son to a violent death. British nineteenth-century theologians – mostly from an evangelical perspective – have certainly done this. Jonathan Edwards, for example, speaks of satisfaction for sin as the special fruit of the wrath of God: 'God let loose upon Christ the devil, who has the power of death, is God's executioner, and the roaring lion, that devours the doomed in Hell.'[12]

There are numerous negative understandings of Anselm's theory, and, as one writer concludes, 'no strictly penal theory can carry conviction in the twentieth century'.[13] Gustaf Aulen traces the origin of the theory far back to Tertullian and Cyprian in the third century, and sees its root idea to be that 'man must make an offering or payment to satisfy God's justice'.[14] It is how the notion of God's justice or honour is to be understood which is the crucial point. Popular understanding frequently relates this to the medieval situation of vassal and overlord. So Anselm is supposed to be thinking in terms of the repayment which is due to the slighted honour of humanity's overlord – a due so great that no human being could pay it.[15]

It is the very simplicity of this understanding and its supposed rationality which has gained it the most influence. Paul Tillich claims that the theory 'meets the burden of guilt, the experience of moral failure, and the impossibility of making up for what we have done'.[16] It was Tillich who pointed out the effect that it has had on popular piety, hymns and liturgies, as well as on Christian teaching and preaching: he attributed its firm grip on people's imagination as occurring because the theory speaks to the depth of contemporary guilt feelings: 'A system of symbols which gives the individual courage to accept himself, in spite of his awareness of being unacceptable, has every chance to be accepted itself.'[17] But Tillich never asked if it spoke to the guilt of women or faced the question which I face – that it might even have intensified those guilt feelings.

Even the nineteenth-century attempts to bring the popular account of the theory from its forensic setting to one of personal relationships had not begun to understand the full significance of the Latin view, or its place in the history of atonement interpretations.

Yet I believe there is a way to rescue Anselm's theory from its negative interpretations, although not necessarily from a feminist critique. For in the first place the real key to the Latin view, as Greshake argues, is not only how to interpret God's honour, but how the whole theory relates to its philosophical and sociological background. He asks whether differences between Eastern and Western thought have also influenced atonement doctrine and moved the theory forward. This would mean that, whereas the East always stressed the cosmic dimension, the West was interested in the political and juridical aspects of common life. Eventually Western medieval Christianity developed a new realization of God's judicial function with regard to human beings – the aspect of judgement which, we have seen, was an important aspect of God's passion for justice. Yet we should not need to see the order of justice as *opposed to* but *grounded in* the order of the cosmos. So the two models ought not to be in conflict.

Whereas the emphasis of the first model was on the restoration of corrupted human nature which needed to be set again within the process of deification (divinization) – or the unified creative/ redemptive process – the emphasis of the Latin model is on the restoration of the legal order through the forgiveness of sins. But both models, rightly understood, should include both meanings.

Now it can be seen why different Christologies are involved: in the East, Christ acts from the side of God, as an instrument of formation or education of humanity and therefore with an accent on his divinity; whereas in the West, it is the 'representative' side of Christ's action and his sacrifice which is stressed. So, yes, the idea of satisfaction is integral to this model, but the satisfaction is not that of the personal honour of an offended deity demanding compensation.[18] The reference is rather to the order and beauty of the world which have been defaced by sin. It is thus a question not of the reconciliation of a capricious deity but of the *world*, and it is the world, not God, which demands it be done in this way. God's honour is conceived by Anselm, more realistically, by analogy with that of the German medieval king, whose honour was guaranteed by the general justice, ordering and state of peace.

Interpreted like this, Anselm's model is said to manifest both subjective and objective aspects of atonement. For the individual it is one step in the process of 'advancing freedom history', as the inner pardon offered is a moment towards freedom and grace. It also links the individual in a sacramental and ecclesial way to Christ's objective, salvific work. Christ is representative of all humanity in giving God this honour: but he is not a scapegoat – nor a god against god – rather he is offering a window to freedom in which all humanity can participate. Nor does he render our own activity null and void: rather, 'the representative Christ invites participation in the trail he has blazed for us'.[19] 'Satisfaction' can then be seen as a moment of freedom in a much wider process of human becoming.

The way in which different types of atonement theories exhibit the same motifs is also shown by the fact of Christ as representative, as moral exemplar for the whole of humanity – which is quoted by Aulen as a special category.[20] Aulen uses Peter Abelard, the brilliant medieval theologian, famous for his controversies with Bernard of Clairvaux and for his ill-starred love affair with Héloise, and Friedrich Schleiermacher as examples. But this motif actually figures within all three types.

What is far more important is the way theologians have used this theme. I quote Abelard as an example of some of the difficulties of categorizing atonement theories and also because he prefigures the nineteenth-century move to see atonement within the context of loving relationship. Abelard clearly rejected the crude idea of Christ being offered to the devil as ransom price, seeing, by contrast, the purpose of incarnation and atonement as God enkindling the world to love of the Godhead:

> To whom then, does it not seem cruel and wicked, that one requires the blood of an innocent victim as a ransom price, or that in some other way the death of an innocent placates God? . . . To us it seems that we are justified nonetheless in the blood of Christ and reconciled to God in this: that by his extraordinary grace exhibited to us, in that his son assumed our nature, and by teaching us by word and example, persevered unto death, he draws us closer to himself through love . . . I think therefore that the purpose and cause of the incarnation was that he might illuminate the world with the light of his wisdom and kindle it to love of himself.'[21]

In his famous letter to Héloise, now Abbess of the Paraclete, in response to her letter showing how it would be impossible for her to repent of loving him, he shows the link between the suffering, sacrificial love of Jesus and its redemptive effects for the hearts of human beings:

> Come, too, my inseparable companion, and join me in thanksgiving, you were made my partner both in guilt and grace . . . Are you not moved to tears or remorse by the only-begotten Son of God, who for you and for all mankind, in his innocence was seized by the hands of impious men . . . to die a horrible and accursed form of death . . . Look at him going to be crucified for your sake, carrying his own cross . . . But he suffered truly for your salvation, on your behalf, of his own free will, and by his suffering he cures all sickness and removes all suffering.[22]

Abelard is cited at length to show how the theme of Christ as ethical moral exemplar cannot be separated as a distinct type of atonement theory, but is an element in all theories with a different significance for each. Within the Greek cosmic theory, for example, it is part of the educative process. In the Latin theory it forms a link between subjective and objective dimensions. In the eighteenth and nineteenth centuries the exemplary function of Christ would be recovered – but not so much as model of atonement as a pastoral-spiritual image. Eckhart's view of redemption, where Christ comes as reminder – 'in order that our instruction in divine, natural and moral matters *would be remembered*'[23] – is another illustration of this. At first sight this looks like the 'moral influence' theory, yet Eckhart was very influenced by Augustine and his Neoplatonic background, by the mystical tradition, and like Irenaeus he saw redemption as organically situated within the whole process of creation-divinization.

But before moving to a feminist critique of these theories one further type must be discussed.

ATONEMENT THEORIES OF MODERN TIMES[24]

If asked to sum up the core notion of this type of atonement theory, it would be the story of this moment of freedom – mentioned in connection with Anselm's theory – as it becomes increasingly radicalized in history. All atonement theories of the Enlightenment, rationalism, idealism and liberal theology will exhibit this as a prominent feature. The crucial question will be how to interpret the mediation of Christ between God and humanity in such a way that the *objective* character of the saving events is preserved, yet at the same time the individual's freedom and deepening subjectivity are respected, together with the *human* values of justice and solidarity.

Since freedom and the fulfilment of the ambitions of every human person are such important motifs for us today, this version of the theory is still popular. Yet there is still a feminist critique to be made.

According to Greshake, there are three principal forms of this version of atonement. The first is Christ as revelation, teaching and ethical ideal, not simply as moral influence, as was discussed earlier, nor as part of God's educative process, as in the first model, but Christ as ideal of true humanity, understood primarily as subject. So it is not so much the *person* but the *event* or *affair* of Christ which is redemptive, the ideal more than the bearer of the ideal. Thus the emphasis shifts from the person of Jesus Christ as the one who atones, to the *stimuli* (to justice, conversion, love and so on) which proceed from him. So these can be understood as they were in the Enlightenment era in a moralistic manner – as Immanuel Kant understood them – or, as it more often happens now, in a political or revolutionary manner.

The second type of modern theory is that of speculative idealism. Though on the face of it this would seem to be an acceptable theory to the contemporary mind, it presents dangers for women and any oppressed minority. For it sees atonement in terms of the developing consciousness of the unity of God and the human subject.[25] Freedom here appears to embrace a vision of totality. It is envisaged as a moment of highest intensity when subject and absolute are in mutual mediation: this is in fact how the Christ event can be interpreted. But how does it work for the ordinary individual? Christ's victory over sin and evil can either be seen as a historical event in the history of freedom – with its own uniqueness – or as a kind of ideal principle, a manifestation of a speculative concept, as the 'many' are forever in 'mediation' with the one. But the danger with this version is that atonement will remain at the level of an abstract principle, and that oppression and human misery will remain untouched by salvific events.

Schleiermacher is usually given as the classic example of the third type of modern theory. For Schleiermacher Jesus is the bearer of *absolute God-consciousness*: Christian community is the place where the believer experiences an empowering of God-consciousness:

> The Redeemer is like all men in virtue of the identity of human nature, but distinguished from them by all the constant potency of his God-consciousness, which was a veritable existence of God in him . . .
> The Redeemer assumes believers into the power of his God-consciousness and this is his redemptive activity.[26]

Yet Jesus is not an ideal, beyond history, but as human prototype he is an image, bestowed by God, with an actual causal function: death is the consequence for a person not touched by Jesus. So Schleiermacher links personal, freed consciousness with the person of Jesus, not as ethical influence, as in the first type, or as the consequence of a supra-historical ideal, as in the second type, but as the consequence of the influence of a historically factual person. What is more, there is an attempt here to link subjective and objective aspects of atonement, since Schleiermacher stands very firmly within a tradition where the believer's own developing God-consciousness is linked with the mediation of Christ, the God-man.

Unfortunately, Greshake's categories do not quite bring us into the twentieth century: nor do they embrace some of the nineteenth-century views of atonement in terms of personal relationships which I will use when constructing a relational model. Horace Bushnell would be an example of someone who bridged the gap between the older forensic view of atonement,[27] the moral influence theory and a more relational understanding. A third element of Bushnell's thought – important for my critique – is his use of the sacrificial lamb motif. He evokes the theme of the cross in God before the beginning of the world and the lamb slain before the foundation of the world.[28] In a sense he is a precursor of some process thinkers in the way he interprets the immutability of God as 'his ability to be sensitive to the feelings of finite creatures, and he is absolutely immutable in his capacity to always endure'.[29]

We have now seen atonement as Christ's victory over sin and evil, within God's formative activity, as the satisfaction of divine honour, and as part of the growth of human consciousness to freedom: many of these motifs are deep within our psyches as we reflect on the cross event. My task is to evaluate and re-image atonement from a new perspective.

CAN WOMEN ACCEPT ATONEMENT?

Women's experience has never yet been specifically brought to bear on atonement doctrines. Yet it is this belief in the intrinsic saving power of the cross which has presented the greatest paradox for the religious becoming of women. Identifying with the sufferings of Jesus on the cross, held up as essential for redemption, has contributed to women remaining transfixed as victim and scapegoat in society. But this matters not only for the socially sanctioned and punitive suffering of women. If atonement is seen as the capacity for suffering and endurance, then, exclaims the process thinker Daniel Day Williams, 'the question has too rarely been asked, "What is the meaning of atonement as *love* doing its distinctive work in dealing with guilt and self-destruction?" '[30]

It is this inspirational comment which forms the jumping-off point for a feminist alternative model – developed in the following Chapter 7. Could there be alternative symbols from those of 'satisfaction', 'sacrifice', 'victim' and 'expiation' which could provide an alternative basis for the 'how' of redemption?

First of all, it must be said in defence of traditional doctrines that because the Latin view of atonement is usually met in its distorted version, feminist reactions are frequently over-reactions to these distortions. But even with the distortions cleared out of the way, many difficulties still remain. For example, an exaggerated image of the satisfaction view of atonement is given by the late nineteenth-century Romantic poet, Christina Rossetti, in her poem, 'The Descent from the Cross':

> Is this the face that fills with awe
> Seraphs who veil their face above?
> Is this the face without a flaw,
> The face that is the face of love?
> Yea, this defaced, a lifeless clod,
> Hath all creation's love sufficed,
> Hath satisfied the love of God,
> This face, the face of Jesus Christ.[31]

Yet it must be admitted that Rossetti, although obsessed with religion, had a very narrow theology, which seemed to remove all joy from her life. The famous story of this writer at a tea-party – a shabby figure in black – suddenly leaping to her feet and crying, totally out of

118

the blue, 'I am Christina Rossetti!' – suggests she was in need of the process of 'redemption as self-affirmation' described in Chapter 4! As Virginia Woolf, in her critical essay on Rossetti, sums up;

> The pressure of a tremendous faith circles and clamps together these little songs. Perhaps they owe to it their solidity. Certainly they owe to it their sadness – your God was a harsh God, your heavenly crown was set with thorns. No sooner have you feasted on beauty with your eyes than your mind tells you that beauty is vain and beauty passes. Death, oblivion, and rest lap round your songs with their dark wave.[32]

Even if we dismiss Christina Rossetti as a poor theologian, it is still tragic to trace the connection between her belief in a God who demanded such satisfaction from his Son and her own joyless lack of self-image. Similar images fill contemporary women's fiction, which focus on blood, sacrifice, impalement and crucifixion, or on the image of Christ's crucifixion as appearing to accept and bless the suffering of women. The heroine in Margaret Atwood's *Surfacing* describes 'a roadside crucifix with a wooden Christ, the alien god, mysterious to me as ever'.[33] It is this Christ who seems either remote from the scene of suffering or even to encourage it. But, writes a recent author, when the theme is treated ironically, the Christ role and martyrdom it implies are transcended, 'and the protagonist is restored to human status. Where it is *not* ironic, the stereotyped image of woman as martyr and victim is reinforced – the image of the tree becomes that of the cross.'[34] Nor is the identification confined to novels. The novel mirrors the real-life situation. For so many wives of alcoholic husbands, violent husbands, or even of men who demand that the lives of their wives be poured out in financial and emotional dependency, find that the only comfort which religion offers is that their sufferings are united with those of the atoning Christ, who 'needs' this sacrifice for the continuing redemption of the world.[35]

So even though such writers have chosen to identify the martyred/victim situation of women with the atoning, crucified Christ, oblivious of more positive strands of the tradition, we still have to acknowledge the terrible damage done to women and ask *why* this particular aspect of atonement – especially if not theologically defensible – has been so influential. Just as serious is the absorption with a physicalist aspect of atonement, seen as actual expiatory bloodshedding, where this involved the notion of woman as scapegoat and victim, with the conclusion that this is her essential status.

Charles Williams, quoted earlier in connection with redemption as exchanged love, shows a very physicalist understanding of atonement

– and applies this specifically to women. Even though Williams holds together a unified creative-redemptive picture[36] – as I have tried to do – and believed in the redemptive mutuality of forgiveness, linking this with the sacramental action of the Eucharist,[37] and the idea of Christ's becoming forgiveness in the flesh, yet he still sees physical bloodshedding as essential to the atonement. In the character of Blanchefleur, his deepest symbol of exchange, he has given a figure of female redemption. She was portress of the convent, 'the contact of exchange', where she nurtured the infant Galahad. But this exchange is of a very crude nature. Blanchefleur has died because she came to a castle, where a lady lay sick and could only be saved by the blood of one who was both princess and virgin. Blanchefleur cut a vein, bled into a dish, and died that the other might live. The dead Blanchefleur becomes the symbol of all martyrdom and sustitution, through the bloodshedding as well as through her connection with Galahad, at whose coming the Grail-King will be healed:

> . . . a saffron pall
> over the bier and pale body of Blanchefleur,
> mother of the nature of lovers, creature of exchange;
> drained there of blood by the thighed wound,
> she died another's death, another lived her life.
> Where it was still tonight, in the last candles of Logres,
> a lady danced, to please the sight of her friends;
> her cheeks were stained from the arteries of Percivale's sister.
> Between them they trod the measure of heaven and earth, . . .[38]

It is not the idea of giving up life for others which is the issue here – clearly the practices of blood-doning, of donating a part of one's body for the saving of another, as well as giving one's life for a worth-while cause all belong to heroic aspects of human nature – but it is the continual emphasis on shedding women's blood as atoning which has such cruel consequences. But Williams does it to a worse degree elsewhere, where he even links the quest for the Holy Grail with the bodies of women – in the biological capacity for receptivity – the physical fact of menstruation with the bleeding of the atonement, and this, as I said earlier, provides him with the argument that women cannot serve on the altar as priests, because they are already on it in category of victim.

> I heard, as in a throb of stretched verse,
> the women everywhere throughout it throb with the curse
> and the altar of Christ everywhere offer the grails.
> Well are women everywhere warned from serving the altar
> who, by nature of their creature, from Caucasia to Carbonek,

> *share with the Sacrifice the victimization of blood,* . . .
> women's flesh lives the quest of the Grail . . .[39]

The reason for bothering with such distorted theology is that appreciation of the poetry frequently masks the truth that these ideas are rooted *psychically* rather than *rationally*, as the arguments against the ordination of women show. It is therefore at the subliminal level of image and symbol that the healing must begin.

Thirdly, there is a category of feminist theology which totally rejects atonement doctrines. I refer, of course, to Mary Daly's dismissal of the gospel as 'sado-masochistic',[40] and to Sheila Collins's criticism of sacrifice. Collins suggests that Christianity's core symbols are 'nekrophilic' and therefore the images of conversion which spring from such negativity are oppressive products of patriarchy. So, she writes,

> this concept of conversion with its adherence to a paradigm of life generating through death and sacrifice has functioned to preserve the oppressor status of patriarchal religion and institution by inhibiting the 'drive to search, the restless and creative power', which characterizes the life-force. With this understanding one gives up one's autonomy, one's restless drive for life and self-actualization, and becomes obedient to an image of God which demands constant self-denial.[41]

Collins thinks that the kind of self-denial extolled by the capitalist system makes possible the ultimate perversion of love. She calls for a consciousness-raising which operates on the principles of life-generating-life, an organic imagery, which is 'biophilic' rather than 'nekrophilic'.

Helga Sorge is another example of an extreme reaction to a distortion of cross theology.[42] She speaks, like Rosemary Ruether, of the deep psychic disturbance within the realm of loving, caused, she claims, by 'an erotic of power'. Sorge links the victimization of women and the glorification of suffering with the theology of the crucified God, choosing Jürgen Moltmann as her prime target. It is particularly Moltmann's idea of God the Father handing over his only Son to be crucified to which she takes violent exception,[43] and like Daly she sees the cross event as nekrophilic self-humiliation. Love of the cross throughout history is seen as reverence for death and equated with self-hate, as a school in 'love's impotence'.

All these writers will have nothing to do with atonement, seeing it purely as a justification for the scapegoating of women. But, whereas on the one hand I reject their interpretation as a trivialization of the cross event and an unconvincing dismissal of the concept of sacrifice, on the other hand the question must be faced: What is it about atonement doctrines that has facilitated the victimization of women?

The Latin theory, in the popular form usually encountered, is certainly not blameless in this respect. What Tillich has described as the psychological comfort of the theory (namely, the removal of punishment due to sin) does not always work for women, who, redeemed or not, are frequently left to bear the burden of society's guilt. There are still contemporary versions of medieval witch-hunts. For example, I have quoted the study by Susan Brooks Thistlethwaite of battered women who feel they have 'deserved it'; raped women are often assumed by society to 'have asked for it' and to have provoked the crime. If women stay at home to look after small children they are frequently classed as mindless, as second-class human beings, yet if they try to work, they are accused of upsetting the economic forces of the labour market, and are blamed for the problems of young people today. The blatant acceptance of pornographic exploitation of women, and the flagrant, organized prostitution of little girls in Thailand, the Philippines, Singapore and India manifest the contempt of society for the sexuality of women. It seems that woman cannot be redeemed from the guilt of being woman. For example, the exposure of girl babies, far from being merely a crime of ancient Sparta, still happens in China;[44] until very recently the mother of an illegitimate baby was unable to atone for the stigma of her 'sin'. Nineteenth-century fiction highlighted this in such novels as Thomas Hardy's *Tess of the D'Urbervilles*, George Eliot's *Adam Bede* and Mrs Gaskell's *Ruth*.[45] Even now there is evidence that women are more heavily penalized for so-called 'emotional crimes' like baby-snatching, regardless of the psychological sickness and deprivation which often lie behind such acts. Clearly, a double standard still prevails: women must 'atone' for acting contrary to their supposed feminine nature.

So even if the vassal-serf motif of the Latin theory is a misinterpretation, as Greshake argued, it has still, until very recently, meant for women that the man was the feudal lord to whom satisfaction had to be given, and the figure of Christ played a dual role: as Lord he was to be submitted to; as victim he was to be identified with.

Hence the symbol of Jesus as innocent victim, as the spotless lamb of popular iconography, with its pictorial link with the symbol of *virgo intacta* (spotless virgin), has intensified the victim identification for women. An intense condensation of theological motifs is present, from a positive scriptural image representing the willing self-offering of Jesus,[46] to the woman as innocent victim of sexual assault (the virgin martyrs), to the lamb as symbol of virginity seen as biological rather than spiritual integrity, with the connotation of the passive sexual role of woman and her victim state in society. When women are forced into passive-victim moulds the essential dimension of Jesus' self-offering is missing. And when we add the tremendous weight attached to the 'Immaculate Virgin' symbol of Mary, the trapped situation of women is all too evident.

Here I have to ask the question which has been posed by Ruether and others;[47] Can a male Saviour actually save women? It is the relation between the maleness of Christ and his redeeming qualities which is the frequently-discussed issue, with Mary Daly maintaining that this represents a repudiation of women. The question focuses on whether the redeemer symbol is *intrinsically* male. It is usually posed today in the context of the eligibility of woman for ordination to the priesthood, where an important strand of the argument has been whether there is something essential in the nature of women which makes it impossible for woman to represent Christ.[48] Two issues are being confused. The function of representing Christ, particularly in the liturgy of the Eucharist, is the burning issue with regard to the ordination of women. But the question of the redemptive meaning and effectiveness of the life and death of Christ and how this redemptive force is accessible today is the most significant single issue for Christian faith. It is easy to trivialize this question as one of gender. But the answer will lie, not in the gender of Christ, but in the christological interpretation given to these saving events, which the relational model of atonement will show.

Nonetheless, the criticism that atonement doctrines do not speak to the victimized situation of many women is justified. This is linked with the fact that they have not sufficiently addressed socio-political structures – or have not done so in a forceful and direct manner.

The Greek view of atonement also cannot escape criticism. We have seen that its strength was to embrace creation-redemption-deification as a unified movement, summed up in the metaphor of *paideia* (formation). The fact that this is seen, not individualistically, but as a social category, a social power which holds in bondage, linking notions of sin, sickness and death, is also a strength. But from a feminist point of view its lack of specificity is a deficiency. Why is sexism not recognized as a form of bondage or sin? The conflict for many women is fought precisely in terms of the bondage of sexism, so all talk of victory is meaningless unless the sin of sexism is named as an evil, rife in society's structures and symbols, and victory over sexism specified as the end of the process.

If this is not specified, then women, in so far as they have been scapegoated for sexual sin,[50] for example, in the Mary Magdalen tradition, more aptly symbolize humanity in bondage, enslaved by patriarchy, than humanity redeemed.

A further difficulty with the classical view is that, since the drama between good and evil is depicted in such cosmic terms, it is not clear how an individual is meant to appropriate its effects in ordinary life-experience. This is a psychological problem for women, who, until recently, have not been encouraged personally to affirm the reality of the redeemed self, but to seek salvation through motherhood, the religious life, and through self-negating service to others.

When we also consider that the victory over sin is depicted by Irenaeus as one of obedience over disobedience, its limitations are clear. For obedience is a dangerous societal concept, not only for women, locked into submissive roles, but also for soldiers and any individuals under obedience to unjust and tyrannical regimes, as the tragedy of the Holocaust shows. 'I was just obeying orders' has far too frequently been accepted as excuse for collaboration with unspeakable atrocities. What has to be proved is the integrity of the authority which demands obedience. What has to be respected above all is that the responsibility of the person is the priority. The very word 'obedience' itself now has a passive ring – in the context of the wedding vows it has all the overtones of patriarchal bondage. What should be pledged is the notion of a mutuality of commitment. In other contexts – such as religious life – it will be the total commitment to a shared ideal which is the required value.

Finally, to many people the model is abhorrent because it relies on victory through violent death. It seems to highlight Christianity's concentration on the death of Jesus as the content of redemption. As Hans Küng wrote, 'The Cross is not only the example and model, but also the ground, power and norm of Christian faith'.[51] I suggest that it is not the cross as such, but our inadequate interpretation of it, and fixation on death and violence which is the problem. Feminist spirituality offers alternative metaphors, with concentration on life-giving symbols, aware that it is often through the death of a *woman* that patriarchy derives its symbols and illustrates its values. For example, even the Old Testament, according to Phyllis Trible, uses the terrible story of the death of the concubine, whose body was divided into twelve parts and sent through the land of Israel (Judg. 19,20), as a story of escalating violence. No one denounces the action as a crime of violence against women.[52]

Even the attempts to save the Latin theory of Anselm ultimately fail. For if we are successful in reinterpreting the idea of divine honour as the disrupted order of peace and justice – and not as the wounded honour of a capricious deity demanding satisfaction – we still have to ask how closely the authority of God can be compared with the sovereignty of a German King. Not only are freedom, liberation and justice time-bound concepts, but we are in danger of defining what is possibly the most profound theological concept *in terms of* a political and sociological concept. As Francis Fiorenza has warned:

> Should not our experience of totalitarianism lead us to be cautious about using political sovereignty for understanding God's relation to the world? Does not the absence of traditional forms of sovereignty in our contemporary experience mean that we should no longer attempt to speak of God and redemption according to political patterns of sovereignty?[53]

To speak of God in such metaphors would prohibit the kind of divine-human mutual becoming for which the process model argues and ultimately the key images of love-as-breakthrough and the image of exchanged life as redemptive which I sketched in Chapter 5.

So after such criticisms, what is left? I think we take the insight that atonement doctrine is at the heart of 'advancing freedom history', in continuity with the 'modern' theories. In the theory which I develop, this continuity will manifest the organic unity between creative and redemptive movements. We will also hold in tension with creation the necessity for judgement and justice within the context of the individual person's journey to self-realization. From the subjective-idealist model I take as inspiration the stimuli which spring from the whole Christ event, which have in the past been interpreted morally, or subjectively, as the empowering of God-consciousness – but which must now realistically confront social and political reality.

So a Christian feminist interpretation looks not simply to the cross of Jesus but to the values this represents. It was because of his life and values that Jesus was executed. His death is not to be seen as the wrath of God against a guilty world, for which Jesus was punished, but is interpreted as the culmination of the great refusal and blockage of the dynamic of mutuality in relation, which was the outstanding feature of the way Jesus related to the world. So a feminist interpretation of atonement looks to this value as a hidden but overlooked strand within Christian tradition. From this standpoint in world history, after two World Wars and the threat of nuclear holocaust, the symbols of victory through violence have had their day. It is the *kairos* moment for an alternative: and, as was once said, 'There is nothing as powerful in the whole world as an idea whose time has come.'

7 'A passion to make and make again where such un-making reigns': Atonement from a Feminist Perspective

It is now time to face the biggest challenge of all. The capacity to operate from within the relational scene, to grasp the connected strands of interpersonal relatedness, to link interior and exterior dimensions of being and acting as well as the awareness of non-human aspects as sources of healing have been shown as strengths, emerging from women's experience. Whether or not historically all women have actually experienced this in their own lives at a conscious level, they have often been holding alive all humanity's yearning for deeper and more satisfying patterns of relating.

I have argued that this dynamic quality of mutuality-in-relating can be part of divine creative-redemptive energy in the process of world transformation. It has also been seen as the driving energy in the life praxis of Jesus. But whether it can function as a saving force, as soteriological, in the way the traditional atonement theories were meant to, needs to be discovered. Whether it can actually bear the weight of the guilt, evil and tragedy to which they spoke, is far from being proved. In this chapter I will delve for positive roots for this theory, before offering a new symbolism. Finally I will return to the central cross symbol, asking whether it can continue to hold such a powerful and unique position within contemporary Christianity.

But first of all, if we keep the very word *atonement* it must be re-imaged as *at-one-ment*, as a fundamental drive to unity and wholeness, which itself sparks off the creative-redemptive process. Not to do this would preserve the lingering aspects of guilt and expiation which cling, limpet-like, to the concept (with all the attendant difficulties already described). It would also encourage the criticism that all I am doing is dredging up doctrine from the silt of centuries and giving it a new coat of paint for the twentieth century and the feminist movement, so that feminist Christians can rest content in the Church, without questioning its symbol structure at the deepest level. *At-one-ment* itself is a metaphor which evokes the goal of mutuality and the process of achieving it.

But if my claim that this is a strand hidden within the tradition holds water, we should be able to glimpse other examples of mutuality-in-relation in Christian theology and living. I will bring three to light, and use them as building blocks for my theory.

ATONEMENT IN PROCESS THOUGHT

The argument unfolds within a relational world, the world of the systems theory of interlocking, mutually dependent eco-systems described in Chapter 2. It unfolds within a process world of the mutuality of divine and human becoming. So it follows that the first building block will be process thought on atonement. It is to the process thinkers that we owe the challenge to the traditional theories that their focus was on everything but the dynamics of love: 'What account would be given of atonement', wrote Daniel Day Williams, 'if we were to interpret it from the standpoint of the most realistic analogies we know to human love when it deals with broken relationships and the consequent suffering?'[1]

It is belief that the focus of creation/redemption/atonement processes should be on the healing of broken relationships which links the strength of the Greek theory of atonement with the critical-liberationist perspective developed here. The process thinkers provide a framework, even if a slightly woolly one, for they do not sufficiently develop their own insights against the politico-social structures.

But it was not Daniel Day Williams so much as Bernard Meland who strikingly drew attention to the unity of creation and redemption, insisting that to separate the two would appear to set Jesus Christ above the God of creation and to *particularize* faith in Jesus Christ to such an extent that the basic unity of God with all fellow-creatures is weakened.[2] (This is a theme dwelt on by feminist theologians and also by those who wrestle with the uniqueness of Jesus Christ in the context of ecumenism and world-faiths.) If we hold together this process, then atonement can be subsumed under the more-embracing, central concept of redemption, which is, Meland writes perceptively, 'the renewal of the creative act in human life by which the sensitive nature which is God is made formative and fulfilling in our purpose. *Whatever happens in life to open up our natures to the tendernesses of life which are of God is redemptive*' (my italics).[3]

Meland was particularly influenced by this idea of the tendernesses of God as redemptive, says Daniel Day Williams.[4] Whitehead's work itself inspired the theme: he saw that divine redemptive action '. . . dwells in the tender elements of the world, which, slowly and in

127

quietness, operate by love, and it finds purpose in the present immediacy of a kingdom not of this world . . . Yet, where is this tenderness? Converted into jurisdiction, authority, power-structures . . .'[5]

Within a view of life seen as relational, these pastorally-concerned men saw human becoming as response, redemption as being rescued from the structures of individualism through the graced experience – itself dependent on the sense of being forgiven – of entering the dynamics of the relational situation, which characterize every event.

The redemptive event, like the creative event which fashioned form from chaos, is a *form-giving process*, which will create meaning and purpose from the apparent hopelessness, failure and brokenness which threaten to overwhelm us in our personal and communal life. But it is not to be completely identified with the evolutionary process. It is rather an emergence at the level of human consciousness where there is a reaching out beyond egoistic satisfaction, or gratification, to a qualitative meaning of unity deeper than the principle of individual organization alone.

This emergent redemptive meaning cannot happen at the level of evolutionary growth alone because it can often be experienced as the very reversal of growth, as the 'shattering of the self' – an idea I have already questioned from the point of view of women's experience. Here Meland means not so much a shattering of the self as an attraction of the self towards a higher emergence of form. This is the higher plane to which George Eliot's Dorothea was attracted when she attempted to rise above her own pain in an effort to help others. In so doing she was co-operating with God in 'widening the skirts of light' – a mysticism of redemptive mutuality. In a way which anticipated the feminist critique, Meland believed it was a mistake to rely on Christ alone as mediator of grace, as this makes us totally dependent on Christology (thus failing to claim our own power in relation). We also tend to depreciate completely the structures of value contained in our own experience. For example, we fail to discern who in our own life and world is redemptive and liberating for us both as ideal and exemplar, and as subjectively empowering-in-mutuality. We are blind as to what resources are available to us here and now as we struggle to claim divine creative grace for today. Could we now rather look back to Christ, says Meland, as an irruption into history in which the good that is in God and the tendernesses of abundant life came into view? Thus the appeal to Christ as a source of faith in this grace he writes, 'is a return to the concrete depths of his own existence, to the aperture within our nature through which the good is made vivid and actual within ourselves'.[6]

128

With this interpretation we can see that the Pauline expression of living 'in Christ' does not really mean a *loss* of self but a *re-focusing of self-consciousness* around a higher centre of value. As we have seen, this is a vital point for women, for whom identity with another has frequently involved both a loss of and victimization of self. Just as female spirituality tries to find accord between inner and outer modes of experience, between bodily and spiritual dimensions, so redemption as Meland envisages it, only advances 'as we feel into the situation with our bodies such that our feeling self cries out in affection toward the right and the good, so that the feeling of our bodies accords with our conscious awareness in relation to ideas, facts, situations . . .'[7]

We can even find here the beginnings of a theory of power-in-relation, although Meland does not make the identification which Carter Heyward did with God as power-in-relation. He sees clearly that power is an ingredient in the relational situation, and can be misused for autonomous ends 'without concern for the fact of relatedness'. Yet in the Gospels power arises from an internal ordering of relationships and, presupposing sensitivity, assumes the magnitude of a great force. (This is what Carter Heyward had described as 'the power which drives to justice and makes it'.) In this combination of sensitivity plus power is the creative possibility of a novel condition of goodness in a particular relational encounter. This can then become – in process terms – a 'new society of occasions'. Meland calls for more awareness for this kind of power, which he calls – with great insight – a redemptive energy of faith which is the living force of the New Creation.

It might be objected at this point that such are Meland's insights – how does the theory I develop add anything new? Have feminist ideas of mutuality already been developed by process thinkers? But the problem with what Meland gives us -- with all its sensitivity and vision – is that he does not relate it to the concrete structures of society. He does not enter the process of the radical new naming of good and evil in their specificity. He has not seen *where* the divine tendernesses are being kept alive, nor what are the dynamics which crush them. Nor has he named, for example, the evil of sexism, which conceals the fact that divine tenderness is barred from society's structures as long as the myth of the eternal feminine sees tenderness as a personal and private feminine quality to be exercised within the confines of the home. If what Meland means by 'tenderness' involves replacing the ethic of individualistic egoism, the ethic of the success of a rich minority at the expense of an impoverished majority, by the values of compassion and justice and an *alternative* ethic of power, I can only concur. But this needs far more than tenderness: it will also demand protest, action and the raging of the stoic grandmothers!

Daniel Day Williams does take us further in his analysis of the human sin addressed by atonement doctrines, though he sees the latter as a crude hotchpotch of sacrificial and judicial analogies, no longer tenable today. Consistent with the analysis I have been presenting, he sees sin as the disruption of communion. He is aware of the two polarities of the becoming self – of self-affirmation and integration – but he sees them both as aspects of the will to communion. If the will to belong and to be in communion is the key to all human action and feeling, then sin is a blockage of this. He would even see the fury of hatred as born partly from the need to resist in the self what we really crave for in love and communion.

But what I find disappointing in his analysis is that, although he is aware of the feminist analysis of sin as passivity, he does not integrate this into his view of the differing nature of the conversion journeys and repentance which are needed. Conversion he sees – influenced apparently by Niebuhr – as 'a shattering of the self, particularly with regard to sexuality'.[8] What is wrong with sexuality as it is experienced by both men and women he does not tell us. Nor does he explain – although aware of the tensions between the polarities of autonomy and interdependence – what a detrimental effect the imbalance in society between men and women has had on the possibilities of mutuality between them. But as Williams writes, sin is not, as is often thought, the overstressing of autonomy to the detriment of relatedness but the assumption that our present state of selfhood is the total meaning of existence, so that we refuse the deeper meaning which is both within and beyond the present: here we are back again to sin as the great refusal, the blocking of the relational grain of existence: 'When that refusal becomes refusal to trust in the Giver of life, and the greater community He is creating, it is sin . . .'[9]

Williams's great strength is to see atonement as God's great task of reconciling love actually at work in the life and death of Jesus, so that his suffering is not viewed as penal and sacrificial, but as bound up with communication between persons. Jesus' suffering both disclosed and opposed evil, but also had a transforming power which enabled people to be changed, in its revelation of a God who suffers with suffering humanity. (If God does not suffer, Williams writes, then God is not involved with the profoundest experience of human love: yet we should speak with great restraint of the suffering God.)

It is his conviction that the Church continues this divine work of atoning and reconciling, which is at the same time the work of new creation. This prompts me to ask whether the contemporary experience of psychotherapy should be regarded as part of the process of at-one-ment which I am investigating.

ROOTS OF AT-ONE-MENT: THE PSYCHOTHERAPEUTIC PROCESS

At-one-ment based on the motif of the will to communion, or the dynamic of mutuality, has many similarities with the approach of psychotherapy: for example, it also respects the interdependence of many factors, and gives healing value to the quality of empathy.[10] As in the interpretation of Daniel Day Williams, the atonement is seen as God's work of reconciling love, so that, while what happened in Jesus Christ does bring about real redemption, this does not jeopardize God's basic order and activity in the world. Again, the traditional theories of atonement are found to be inadequate, and the essence of the therapeutic relationship is described as the cure and change (salvation/redemption) of brokenness in human relationship.[11]

The human situation of lack of mutuality is termed by psychotherapy 'incongruence', which can mean estrangement, death, bondage and idolatry. (Here the description of the bondage of sin can be viewed as similar to the Greek view of atonement/redemption which we have seen was typified by Irenaeus.)

The redemptive process according to this model is set in motion by the healing relationship between client and therapist. This will depend on the empathic acceptance of the client by the therapist. This vital factor is known as 'organismic experiencing': 'The essence of this hoped-for therapeutic change is the conscious experiencing and symbolizing of denied, distorted, rejected and disowned feelings.'[12]

The concept of healing empathic acceptance between therapist and client, analogical as it is of the larger structures of society, is appropriately symbolized by the cross and resurrection dynamic, which manifests God's feeling the depths of sin's destructiveness, God's love overcoming hostility by enduring it, but never losing the capacity to receive humanity into relationship. So again there is a similarity with the classical Greek cosmic view: this is because creative/redemptive processes are seen as unified – what is typical of *soteriological* activity is typical of *creative* activity. Also, sin, according to the psychotherapeutic view, is not so much viewed as guilt to be expiated (the Latin view), but as bondage or immaturity from which to be liberated. Browning even suggests that empathic acceptance should constitute the image of God in humanity: 'The mature man', he writes, '. . . would know and understand himself as

131

one whose end is to enter into increasingly larger circles of concourse with the events of the external world.'[13]

Clearly this view helps us to see how the relational process can be redemptive. It can also be understood as the key to the entire ministry of Jesus, who offered a dynamic process by which a person could come to the experience of healing and wholeness. The story of the healing of the blind man described in John's Gospel, chapter 9, would be an excellent example of this: Jesus responds to the immediate needs of the man by healing him of his blindness in such a way that his healing is at the same time a re-creation. (Anointing the man's eyes with clay appears to be a deliberate symbolic gesture evoking the creation story of Genesis.) The healing takes place in the context of other relational needs: the man's parents, the blindness of the Pharisees, the man's own spiritual needs. The climax of the story is the man's confession of faith in Jesus as the Son of God and the revelation that the truly blind are those who claim they can see, yet remain unflinching in their moral myopic stance.

From a feminist critical point of view it must first be said that empathic acceptance must be balanced by judgement which holds in tension both a social/political analysis[14] and a humility before the reality of God. For we cannot ignore the importance of authentic value judgements for God. The process model (particularly of a feminist thinker like Marjorie Suchocki) shows how that it is not only the acceptance by God of all our feelings and experiences – including those of lack of self-worth – which is redemptive in itself, but the redressing of the loss, and the transformation of these negative experiences into alternative possibilities. After all, if redemption means anything at all, it means the *overcoming* of these sinful structures which provoked the breakdown of mutuality. But awareness as to our acceptability, despite our failures and assurance of transformative possibilities, must involve condemnation of sexist institutions and practices which secured our bondage in the first place.

Another warning bell must be rung from a feminist point of view. The women's movement has alerted our attention to the difficulties of communication which many women experience with some male psychotherapists. Women's anxieties have often been interpreted as neurotic and unhealthy. Adequate language for their articulation of their fears has not been developed. Again, it is mostly contemporary fiction which has begun to explore the dilemma from a female point of view. For example, Marge Piercy in her novel *Women at the Edge of Time* focuses on an alternative definition of madness.[15] Doris Lessing, too, through the figure of Martha Quest exposes the superficial approach of psychiatry which frequently offers drugs and hospitalization instead of true healing:

Soon, probably in the next decade, the truth would have to be admitted. It would be admitted with a bad grace, be glossed over, softened. And just as we now say 'They burned and drowned witches for a couple of centuries out of a primitive and ignorant terror', soon we will be saying 'When they stopped torturing and killing witches, they locked people with certain capacities into lunatic asylums and told them they were freaks, and forced them into conformity by varieties of torture'.[16]

Thirdly, this discussion of what is normality raises the question whether the therapeutic process under consideration addresses itself to the deeper problems of the oppression of women. If the psychotherapist/counsellor/priest is himself part of the oppressive structure, how is it possible that he will release the subjugated knowledges referred to in Chapter 1, and the memories which will enkindle the healing processes?

This difficulty forces one to ask if atonement focusing solely on mutuality and the healing of personal relationships can work without a radical social analysis. This I will now investigate.

ROOTS OF AT-ONE-MENT: NINETEENTH- AND EARLY TWENTIETH-CENTURY THOUGHT

The real question now to be explored is how much we have actually progressed, by beginning to interpret atonement in terms of personal relationships. Historically speaking, the concern for mutuality at the heart of God's redemptive process is found earlier than the work of both process thinkers and psychotherapists. Pioneering work like that of Moberley,[17] Bushnell[18] and Scott Lidgett[19] were important in the Anglo-Saxon world in drawing attention away from the legal, forensic aspects of atonement to the realm of family relationships. H. H. Farmer developed the personal model of atonement as the polarization of the act which at the same time condemns and saves, judges and forgives, always within a personal context.[20] Because family relationships could now be reflected on in terms of reconciling love, because concepts of parenthood were changing, so the reciprocity of relationality and the mutuality of forgiveness became acceptable as an atonement model. Even the model of encounter became popular as an image of atonement.

But again we have to ring the warning bell. Bringing personal relationships to bear on the atonement doctrine may not make much difference to the redemptive possibilities for women. On the face of it, it seems very moving when a writer like Horace Bushnell compares

133

the atoning work of Christ to that of a mother who bears all her child's pain and sickness in her own feeling, and ta. :s every opportunity for sacrifice as her own opportunity.[21] But this trend towards feminization of nineteenth-century liberalism, says Ann Douglas, often represents sentimentalizing tendencies, and does nothing to challenge the stereotypical view of women: 'Strength, as essential to the genuine feminine as to genuinely masculine social structures, is absent, weakness itself, no matter how unintentionally, is finally extolled.'[22] This personalizing tendency itself had the consequence of pushing women further into the private sphere, re-emphasizing the qualities stressed by the myth of the eternal feminine, even justifying women's exclusion from the priesthood on the grounds of Christlikeness.[23]

On the face of it, then, this concern for mutuality and the dynamics of personal relationship seen as the work of reconciling love (as at-one-ment) may seem to be an enormous advance on the models described in Chapter 6; it has achieved much in redeeming the very image of God from punitive and vengeful features, and it touches the level of lived experience in its affective dimension. But since the emphasis is on *personal* healing and wholeness, it leaves untouched those structures of society and Church which prohibit the full becoming of women in the first place. In fact, it may even reinforce their inferior status, by emphasizing the healing value of relational strengths *in the private sphere.*

So a much more radical re-imaging of atonement images and symbols is required if we are to create a language which speaks to the conscious and unconscious levels which cry out for redemption.

FROM SUFFERING TO REDEMPTIVE WOMAN

Asher Lev's painting of his mother on a cross, the 'Christa' of Edwina Sandys, the murdered concubine of Judges 19 are all images of crucified and suffering women. The abused women who huddle today in the refuges for battered women know this reality only too well. Yet the crucifix in Christian iconography symbolizes victory over suffering and death. What I am trying to do here is to discover whether within Christian tradition there are any images of suffering, crucified woman as a *redemptive* figure, to be associated with the healing work of Christ. Can women bring forth redemption, Rosemary Ruether asks, from their sufferings on the cross of patriarchy?[24] Can they imitate and image Christ, in the sense of 'mimesis' and 'methexis' (participation) expressed by the Greek model of Atonement? If there are saving images to be discovered, they may be the key to the radical re-imaging of at-one-ment processes required here. To see women participating *actively* in the redemptive process, not as totally passive recipients, requires a new understanding of cross/resurrection within this process.

So my search is not at the level of the significance of the gender of Christ, but whether the cross/resurrection event can be illuminated from a feminist understanding of the dynamic of right relation, and whether, by embracing this dynamic, human beings can be co-agents and co-creators of their own redemption. I am not simply looking for examples of women in ministerial or disciple roles – of which there are many – but examples of women responding to the Christ event through redemptive mutuality, in a way which is both self-affirming, yet self-transcending, which enables the voluntary assumption of suffering for the sake of a higher ideal.

Many early Christian writers witness that in the first two centuries of Christianity men and women – even a woman slave – who became martyrs could be seen as other Christs, Christ could be seen 'in our sister'. There are two outstanding examples of this. The first is of Blandina, who, during the agony of her martyrdom, is described as *alter Christus*:

> Now Blandina, suspended on a stake, was exposed as food to wild beasts, which were let against her. Even to look on her, as she hung, cross-wise, in earnest prayer, wrought great eagerness in those who were contending, for in their conflict they beheld with their outward eyes *in the form of their sister, the One who was crucified for them* (my italics).[25]

The second example is interesting because it is the earliest Christian text of female authorship – or at least partially so.[26] It is a 'protest' account of third-century Christianity which dramatically tells the story of the persecution and martyrdom of Perpetua, daughter of a wealthy provincial of North Africa, her slave Felicitas (who was eight months pregnant), Satyrus – who was already baptized – and six others. The editors of this text see its significance in its portrayal of martyrdom as a powerful symbol of human liberation and self-fulfilment, and secondly, as demonstrating the emergence within the Church of a prophetic movement 'in which women assumed leadership roles indicative of a male/female equality unknown in later periods of Christian history'.[27]

It is termed a 'protest' account because it describes Perpetua's objections to restrictive elements within third-century Carthaginian society, which the editors take to mean her handing back her baby, so that she could endure prison more easily, and her assertion of independence over against the appeals of her old father. So, they say,

Perpetua's liberation was achieved through the transcending of the restrictions placed on female sexuality. Non-violent protests and liberation they see as the two themes characterizing her idealism. Similarly, they make great play out of the fact that Perpetua reconciled herself to God without the medium of a priest and generally seemed to be the instrument of her own salvation.

I think the authors are mistaken in imposing twentieth-century standards of what 'liberation' means on a third-century text. Even without this, the text speaks eloquently of the leadership qualities of Perpetua. A small group of newly-fledged Christians, in a prison situation, thrown back on their own resources, had no choice but to be reconciled to God without a priest. In any case, the distinction between cleric/lay was not so rigid, nor was the practice of private confession to a priest – in an *ecclesial* sense – as well developed as it became later.

The glory of Perpetua's achievement is the redemptive role she played in actively suffering for her chosen ideals. Perpetua's visions have authority within her community, she has sufficient intercessory power to release her brother from his sufferings, she enters into direct combat with the powers of evil, and – what is notable for my theme – is the way that mutuality-in-community is an outstanding motif of the story: 'Pudens, the official in charge of the prison . . . admitted many prisoners to our cell, so that we might *mutually encourage each other*' (my italics).[28]

They even managed to turn their final meal together into a Christian agape. Both Perpetua and Felicitas are identified with the redemptive action of Christ, and even in her last moments in the arena Perpetua is described as full of concern for Felicitas (who was bruised) and as exhorting her brother and another catechumen to remain strong in faith. Their death was thought of as a second baptism, ritually prepared for by the kiss of peace. In her hour of trial she is described as a true spouse of Christ, the darling of God.

Felicitas's hour of grace is also particularly moving, and illustrates, as does the story of Blandina, the powerful presence of Christ in the suffering Christian. Felicitas had prayed that her baby be born early: if not, she would not have been martyred with her companions, since the law forbade the execution of pregnant women, and she would have been forced to die later, with common criminals. In answer to prayer she found herself in labour:

Because of the additional pain of an early delivery she suffered greatly during the birth and one of the prison guards taunted her: 'If you're complaining now, what will you do when you're thrown to the wild beast?'

She answered, 'Now it is I who suffer, but then another shall be in me, since I am now suffering for him . . .'[29]

Surely this is an echo of the Damascus vision of Paul, when the voice of Jesus cried, 'Saul, Saul why persecutest thou *me*?' Felicitas in her suffering is surely actively 'bearing up God in the world', witnessing to the extraordinary identification of Christ with all who voluntarily engage in redemptive suffering. She is depicted as passing from one shedding of blood to another, from midwife to gladiator.

So, although in the twentieth century we see redemptive categories as needing to address socio-political categories, we do not achieve anything by imposing our contemporary demands on the second and third centuries.[30] Their witness carries its own power.

Other examples of woman in redemptive, leadership roles against patriarchy are the medieval saints such as Clare of Assisi who defied parents who wanted them to make suitable marriages in order to follow what they believed God wanted them to do. Catherine of Siena is an outstanding example of this. Not only did she repeatedly refuse marriage, she also refused its alternative as a consecrated virgin in a convent. For three years she lived out her chosen role in solitude at home, until at twenty-one she began an external life amid the poor and sick of Siena with a group called the 'mantellate', who wore habits but lived in their own homes.[31]

Elizabeth Moltmann-Wendel has also claimed that the redemptive role played by women in the early Christian community, in particular by Martha, Mary of Bethany and Mary Magdalen,[32] endures in the brutality suffered by the crucified woman as seen in medieval pictures. Said to have been married by her father to a pagan husband whom she did not love, she betrothed herself to Christ whom she asked to deform her by giving her a beard: whereupon her royal father had her crucified. But, says Elizabeth Moltmann, the interesting thing is that this figure with the beard and the long garment is remembered above all in the Eastern Alps not as victim, but '*liberatrix*, = female liberator, and even now is treated as a legendary, painful, artistic mistake'![33] What seems to block our appreciation of the liberating role of women in the Christian tradition is partly the artistic/literary/mythological canon that the hero/saviour/redeemer figure is automatically masculine, women appearing in the great myths only as 'goddess-ex-machina' figures, as temptress or earth-mother.[34] This is why the 'insurrection of the subjugated knowledges' becomes so important. This is why it is vital to listen to the hidden cry, when the sculpture 'Christa' evokes a new element, that Christ will come again, as a woman, a theme already part of Shaker belief:[35]

. . . Today, Christ will come again as a woman, and she will change the female image as a servant . . . If Christ will come again as a woman, she will work as a labourer, as a farmer, and as a housewife of a lower-class family. She will cry with all the women who are suffering under oppression politically, socially, economically, religiously . . . After she will resurrect she will appear to the oppressed children who could not leave from the Calvary of her Cross.[36]

It is this desperate plea from poor and oppressed women, who see themselves as outside the healing power of the redemptive process, who see themselves as un-affirmed by either Church or society – like the situation of black South Africans who call for a new Moses – which is the call for 'another voice', that of the subjugated knowledges, still concealed on the margins. What re-imaging of at-one-ment will call these into the light?

RE-IMAGING AT-ONE-MENT: 'TO HELP THE EARTH DELIVER'[37]

I have used the 'passion to make and make again' as inspirational for this view of the process of at-one-ment. The first symbol I propose within the re-imaging enterprise is that of the 'birthing of God', the creative energy for wholeness and transformation ceaselessly at work in creation, to which much of the experience of women bears witness.

The first point is that if we are in a position without power we have the possibility of developing a spirituality of devotion and care in the most ordinary of tasks, a sense of worth and reverence for the humblest of activities: the care of a child, cooking a meal for friends, growing vegetables, or simply a rootedness in the changing of the seasons. But we claim these activities not as a retreat into the private sphere, but as important human activities, with implications for the public, political sphere.

Yet where the reverencing and hallowing of creation has occurred in history – for example, quite recently, in Martin Buber's recovery of Hasidic mysticism – it has often been in an idealizing manner, without the recognition of the contribution which women are making.

Secondly, with this care for the humblest things, comes a spirituality of the awareness of their possibility for transformation – as we have already discussed – in, for example, the wisdom of herbal lore, the many arts of healing, cooking and growing plants, trees and flowers. The Findhörn Community in Scotland grows vegetables of immense size and quality on windswept sand-dunes. In the desert of the inner city people of vision transform bomb-sites into children's play-gardens.

But these are only part of what is meant by the great symbol of 'the birthing of God', which is at the same time the groaning of the universe in travail (Rom. 8.19–23). As Matthew Fox wrote, 'Birthing requires the refusal to be victim, and it will help to bring an end to our long living with violence.'[38] This is far from being a call for women to have more children to save the world. Nor is it an over-glorification of motherhood at the expense of fatherhood. What I am arguing is that as Christianity has now had two thousand years of death symbolism, it is at least *possible* that the slaughter perpetrated in the name of Christendom is related to its symbols of death, blood-guilt and sacrifice, and that an *alternative* way of encapsulating the redemptive events might stimulate more compassionate lifestyles. The slave-traders, with their ships full of dying Africans, prayed to the God of Christianity, as did the Crusaders on their way to sack the most revered shrines in Constantinople. More recently, both sides engaged in the struggle of two World Wars prayed for victory to the God of Jesus Christ. As long as we carry on over-glorifying violent death, and using the cross event to justify this, it is difficult to envisage any changed perceptions.

After all, how are people changed? Where are the cracks of consciousness which make people open to alternative values? Is it not possible, as Fox argues, that 'Eros has the power to wake us up, to see passion happen again, feeling return, hope and transcendence come alive . . . Here lie authentic conversions, changes of heart, and work, and lifestyle, so that one becomes committed to social transformation.'[39] Perhaps this could this be the shift of emphasis required from the overstressing of the cross event – mentioned earlier in the work of theologians like Küng and Moltmann – so that broader aspects of redemption have been overlooked.

Now it should be clear why I have consistently argued in the last two chapters for an interpretation of atonement which unifies the creative and redemptive moments. For if creation is about giving birth, then so is redemption, transformation and, ultimately, at-one-ment. It is also the symbol which unites divine and human activity. For creation is first of all about God giving birth to myriad forms of mutuality, which go far beyond the merely human personal categories. (Hence the insistence in Chapter 3 that 'Nature, too, mourns for a lost good' and is both subject and object of redemption.)

As contrasting with a theology of authoritative power, transcendence, absolute freedom and otherness, this birthing of God is an expression of God's fundamental being as interrelatedness. For in

the beginning is the interrelatedness. The idea has been given
liturgical expression by Carter Heyward:

> In the beginning was God,
> In the beginning was the source of all that is,
> God yearning,
> God moaning,
> God labouring,
> God giving birth,
> God rejoicing,
> And God loved what she had made.
> And God said,
> 'It is good'.
> And God, knowing that all that is good is shared,
> held the earth tenderly in her arms.
> God yearned for relationship.
> God longed to share the good earth,
> And humanity was born in the yearning of God,
> We were born to share the earth.[40]

By analogy, human birthing originates in the mutuality between
man and women, and itself creates new mutuality, between mother-
child, child-parents, family-*vis-à-vis* the wider community. But it is
the *woman* who is in travail for the new creation. The psychological
and spiritual implications of the birth-giving experiences of women
have never been explored as a resource for official theology.

Secondly, birthing is working, labouring. Thus the idea of divine
activity expressed in verbs rather than nouns – together with the
notion of the female self as relatedness[41] – is encapsulated by the
activity of giving birth to new forms of mutuality, as co-creating with
God in cosmic creativity, which Dorothee Soelle sees as the origin of
the call to holiness. As Meister Eckhart has written so expressively,
'From eternity to eternity God lies on a maternity-bed giving birth
. . . What does God do all day long? God gives birth . . .'[42]

Sara Maitland has pointed out – in a moving passage which links
creation, redemption and atonement with the experience of women –
that what is often missing from sentimentalizing accounts of
childbirth is that it is painful, messy and hard work:

> Birthing is the creating of new life through hard work (labour) and
> blood. Of course men do create life just as women do, and must be
> held to their responsibility for this . . .; but they do it differently –
> in joy and delight . . . But God also brought new life, Gospel life
> to birth, stretched out for hours on the Cross, autonomy removed
> by aggressive experts, the Eternal Word reduced to wordless cries,

bleeding down into the dark, overwhelmed by the sense of desolation . . . And afterwards the joy and the new life, the sense of mystery and distance. It seems that the creative birthing of God as expressed in Christ's passion . . . can be given a deeper relating if we can learn to hear as holy the bodily experiences of women, and *trust the metaphor of God the Mother* (my italics).[43]

But the metaphor of 'the birthing of God', far from being an invention of feminist theologians to make the experience of women more prominent, is in fact one of the hidden strands of our tradition which I am trying to reclaim.

Time and time again it is descriptive in the Old Testament of God's experience with God's child, Israel. Hosea (13.13) depicts the image of the sin of Ephraim (Israel) being that of missing the chance of birth to new hope, the failure of the delivery of the child. The prophet Micah uses the image of Israel, daughter of Sion, as the image of the woman in travail (Mic. 4.10). Isaiah, too, uses this image in the sense of the Day of the Lord, the day of destruction, when they will anguish like a woman in labour (Isa. 13.8). The same idea of labour pains brought on by the judgement of God is expressed by Jeremiah (4.31). But a more important aspect of the image is God's travail in bringing forth God's own people, a context of hope, even if also of labour and struggle (Isa. 42.14–16). We can also link the birth-giving and motherhood of God with that of women, using the metaphor of Jeremiah 31 (15–22):

> A voice is heard in Ramah,
> Lamentation and bitter weeping.
> Rachel is weeping for her children;
> She refuses to be comforted for her children,
> Because they are not.

This is the passage quoted by Matthew's Gospel (2.18) in the context of Herod's slaughter of the innocent children. The development of this metaphor has been traced by Phyllis Trible.[44] Here the motherhood of women is contrasted with that of God. Rachel is the ancestral human mother, lamenting from her grave the subsequent death of her children. 'Directed to no one in particular, and hence to all who may hear, the voice of Rachel travels across the land, and through the ages to permeate existence with a suffering that not even death can relieve', writes Phyllis Trible.[45] The suggestion is conveyed in v. 20 that Ephraim, the darling child of Jahweh, is also the child for whom Rachel weeps, and that God is sharing the mother's suffering. Remembering the child is the hope for Rachel's future. The triumphant climax of the story is where we move from the desolate lamentations of Rachel to the redemptive compassion of God. Male Israel becomes female Israel and there is an act of new creation:

> For the Lord has created a new thing on the earth:
> a woman protects a man. (Jer. 31.22b)[46]

Secondly, the image of motherhood[47] as linked with the birthing of new creation and the redemptive task of women is continued in the New Testament, in the context of hope and the breaking in of the Kingdom of God. It is most clearly seen in John 16.21–22, where Jesus explicitly makes use of the intertwining of the sorrow/joy motif as image of the birthing of the Kingdom, suggesting the theme of the present sufferings as the birth pangs of the new creation. If the birthing of the world issues from the compassion of God, then this is another dimension of the motherhood of God manifested by Jesus, a theme explored by many female writers from Julian of Norwich onward.[48]

Thirdly, one of the most startling images of the Book of Revelation is the woman in travail. The woman is depicted as delivering the divine child of the new creation – the anti-type of the harlot in the desert – who stands over against the forces of evil, symbolized by the dragon. But to whom does the woman refer? Frances Young asks whether any precise application should be sought: 'Is it Mary? Is it Jerusalem? Who is it? Maybe precision of that sort is not intended – maybe the emphasis is on the birth taking place, the fact of hope beyond the anguish, that judgement is not the end.'[49]

The woman of the Book of Revelation is a redemptive figure in two different ways. She gives birth to the child of new creation. But she is also in sympathy with nature, symbolizing the holy connectedness of all things. For the wilderness for the woman is not a place of desolation, but a place of nourishment and solace, prepared by God. The earth also comes to her rescue in swallowing the river which had issued from the dragon's mouth. (The theme of the affinity between woman and earth is reminiscent of the Psyche–Eros myth and has been given a new impetus by the feminist ecological movement.) That the woman does not need to slay the dragon is also interesting and has been commented on by Elizabeth Moltmann-Wendel in connection with the legend of Martha and the dragon of Tarascon in south west France.[50] Perhaps what women are showing is that it is possible to cope with evil forces without killing.

Taking all these images together we are confronted by a powerful symbol which takes us far beyond – yet includes – the physiological aspects, comprehending the vulnerability and letting-go of relationality, the basic organic interdependence of all forms of living, as well as a realistic confrontation with evil and suffering. But it is the creation of new forms of mutuality through *life-giving* processes, not through death and destruction, which is its strength. It is not an obsessive focus on mothering, or a re-identification of women with bodily roles.

But what is difficult to understand is why this symbol needed reclaiming from the Christian tradition. If we could understand why violence and death symbolism has always been more influential in Christendom, its imagery believed to have more saving potential, we might also understand much more why evil has such a powerful grip over human beings.

RE-IMAGING AT-ONE-MENT: THE LOSS OF A SYMBOL

Creative images of birth-giving seemed to have lacked influence in Christianity – apart from a kind of sentimentalizing crib-mystique at Christmas – while in symbols of military destruction ('Onward Christian soldiers') have always achieved prominence. This fact deserves consideration. It is easy to see that, once Christianity became accepted in the Roman Empire after the Edict of Milan in 314 AD, the emphasis on military conquest, and the continuing legitimization of the subordinate role of women, would mean that any imagery issuing from female experience would hardly be seen as significant. Also, the gradual loss on the part of women of any formative role in the mainstream Christian tradition or of influence in theologizing or ecclesial decision-making, with a few notable exceptions, would remove childbirth as a suitable symbol of faith. (The veneration of the Virgin Mary giving birth to Jesus has not helped the ordinary woman, since it was emphasized at an early date that this birth was miraculous, extraordinary and pain-free.[51] Yet the level of interest in the birth of Jesus has always remained high, at a popular level.)

It was precisely the physical, messy and laborious nature of childbirth which did not appeal to any spiritualizing tendency in theology. It belonged strictly to a woman's world, and was part of woman's socially-sanctioned subordination, vulnerability and pro-creative obligation – an inferior role compared with that of managing external affairs. The only exception to this was – and is – in royal circles, when a monarch, desperate for an heir to the throne, took excessive interest in his wife's pregnancy and childbirth.[52]

It is also true that in industrial and post-industrial countries the very experience of childbirth has frequently ceased to be a creative experience for women, because of the over-use of drugs and medication, and the reduction of the active participation of women owing to the control of childbirth by the medical 'experts', a problem which healthier attitudes are trying to redress.[53] Women have also suffered from the way the Church took over the legacy of the Old Testament as to the pollution of childbirth and consequent obligation for the ecclesiastical purification of the mother, which was the case in the Roman Catholic Church in England and Ireland before the Second Vatican Council, even when the cultural reason for it no longer existed. In how many homes did it happen, sadly, that a mother could not be present at her baby's baptism, because she had not been well enough to be 'churched', and the obligation for infant baptism meant there was no possibility of waiting?

Yet the Jewish practice of purification – based on Leviticus 12.2–4 – did not itself derive from any *moral* criticism of the experience of childbirth, or of sexual intercourse: the practice seems rather to stem from the fear and consequent taboo over loss of blood, which signified loss of vitality: 'The woman's vitality, linked with her blood, was diminished by childbirth, and by that token she was objectively separated from Jahweh, the source of life, until her integrity was restored.'[54]

While it may be true that the liturgical practice of 'churching' for women in Christianity was not based on the supposed uncleanness of childbirth, when coupled with the devaluing of women, and a certain exegesis of Genesis 3.16 – where the pains of childbirth are seen as punishment for the Fall – the effect has been to devalue both bringing-to-birth as a theological image and also the bodily experiences of women in general. Yet one cannot go to the extremes of Mary Daly and Adrienne Rich – 'The screams of the woman in childbirth were for the glory of God the Father'[55] – since a more careful reading of the biblical texts shows a shared responsibility for sin: 'Humanity brings the disaster of distorted relationships upon itself.'[56]

A more serious implication of the reclamation of the birthing image as central to theology is Mary Daly's criticism that this is in sharp conflict with Christianity's most important symbol, the death/rebirth symbol of baptism. Patriarchy, she claims, has robbed us of our birthing energies, and cultural rebirthing in a patriarchal sense involves death.[57] This would mean that Jesus' command, 'Unless one is born of water and the Spirit, he cannot enter the kingdom of God. That which is born of the flesh is flesh, and that which is born of the Spirit is spirit.' (John 3.5–6) was actually a despising of being-born-of-woman. For Daly the solution is not rebirth or baptism by the Father's surrogates, for it is this socialized rebirth which is the captivity from which we are trying to escape:

'Radical feminism is not reconciliation with the Father. It begins with saying "No" to the Father . . . Radical feminism means saying 'Yes' to our original birth.'[58]

Feminist writers often try to strengthen this case by appealing to primitive tribal customs, through initiation rites involving a death motif and a separation from the mother,[59] or with examples of ritual killing symbolizing initiation, rebirth or sacrificial ritual. Thus Nancy Jay has written:

> The only action that is as serious as giving birth which can act as a counterbalance to it, is killing. This is one way to interpret the common sacrificial metaphors of birth and rebirth, or birth done better, on purpose and on a more spiritual, more exalted level than mothers can do it.[60]

Patriarchy's insistence on the death-motif is seen by some – like Carol Gilligan – as illustrated by God's insistence on Abraham's killing of Isaac (Gen. 22.12), in spite of recent exegesis suggesting the story is Jahweh's *forbidding* of child-sacrifices, in contrast to the practices of other ancient Near Eastern tribes! The link has even been made by Mary Condren between the patriarchal death-motif and the Anselmian atonement theory as submission to the will of the Father:

> Submission is pushed so far . . . that we were taught we must be willing to be damned – for the glory of God! Why should so much mental activity have stopped there, and not inquired what glory there was in an omnipotent being torturing forever a puny little creature who could in no way defend himself? Would it be to the glory of man to fry ants?[61]

I have developed this point at length to show how it is so easy, when trying to redress an injustice, to go off at a tangent to the other extreme. In the first place, we cannot take on board, uncritically, analogies from other cultures, assuming they have a direct equivalence for Christianity's images and symbols. (Mircea Eliade himself has been criticized for over-identifying the Christian rites of initiation with, for example, the rites of Sioux Indians or Aborigines, where a ritual death element and a separation from the mother are involved.)

Clearly, Paul's theology of death and rebirth (seen in Romans 6) as the meaning of Christian baptism was influenced by the mystery religions of the time. But though Paul used the motifs taken from them, he did not identify baptism with them. Christianity was always seen as totally new and distinct. (In any case this was not his first image of baptism – and it remains one among many.)

Nor can Jesus be realistically accused of robbing women of birthing energies: he would hardly have used the image of childbirth as illustrative of the in-breaking of the Kingdom if this was the case. There has never been any suggestion in Christianity that there is something deficient about human birthing: on the contrary, the human birth of Jesus has been understood as a validation of humanity – this despite the tradition that it did not affect the virginity of his mother Mary. There is possibly some truth in the argument that it is women's involvement in childbirth which precludes them from ministerial roles at the altar: but this cannot be the whole truth, since there are so many celibate, theologically well-qualified women who – in the Catholic Church at least – are equally unjustifiably barred from the altar. I think the truth to which these accusations are pointing – though in Daly's case in a crude, exaggerated way – is that there is a widespread glorification of war-imagery, war-games, a tendency to settle all disputes through violence and retaliation, a general callousness over loss of human life, and Christianity has in fact been used to sanction this ethic of violence – as, for example, when Cardinal Cushing blessed the bombers which went off to Vietnam in the sixties.

It is to *reclaim* the rightful place for the creative image of birthing as link between women's experience and redemption that I explore further its relationship with conflict, suffering, death, and the cross.

RE-IMAGING AT-ONE-MENT: ALTERNATIVE MEANINGS OF DEATH

But the second reason for reclaiming the symbol of birthing from the tradition is that we are given alternative ways to experience conflict and even death. Female writers have often been able to grasp the pain and conflict at the heart of the creation process. Simone Weil, for example, rightly grasped the interwoven themes of creation and passion: 'God's creative love which maintains us in existence', she wrote,

> is not merely a super-abundance of generosity, it is also renunciation and sacrifice. Not only the Passion, but the creation itself is a renunciation and sacrifice on the part of God. The Passion itself is simply its consummation. God already devoids himself of his divinity by the Creation . . . Through love he abandons them to affliction and sin. For if he did not abandon them he would not exist. His presence would annul their existence as a flame kills a butterfly.[62]

Here Weil rightly grasps the suffering love of God for creation, even if there is a masochistic element in her spirituality. It is now well known that it was excessive, body-denying asceticism which attracted her: but the language of love is not the language of abandonment, and, as her biographer tells us, though Weil experienced the love of God in affliction, she manifested very ambiguous feelings with regard to creation.[63]

It is birthing as including these dimensions of painful, suffering love which is crucial here, for within it we have a paradigm of conflict which can be redemptive. Within the experience is given both joy and an acceptance of pain. So we have an alternative to victory through violence: as the medieval mystic, Hildegarde of Bingen, cried, 'God was able to conquer, without even using a warrior!'[64] If we push this image more deeply, we can see that through birthing as an image of creative mutuality there is the possibility of an honest coming to terms with the polarities of good and evil, light and darkness. God, on this interpretation of atonement, is, writes Frances Young, 'submitting to the pain and travail, so that by means of the labour a new world may be born'.[65]

There is also a recognition that in birth-giving and co-creation change is entailed for all concerned. A mother is changed by the birth of each child, as is the relationship of father and mother, and the wider groupings. It is not simply emotional changes, but changes of lifestyle which call for social organization. This points to a mutual change, growth and development of both God and world, through co-creating and co-suffering. Thus the kind and quality of relating will be the key to all change - for example, as to whether parents experience the leaving home of children as pain and loss, or as a means of moving to a new, qualitative kind of relationship.

Mutual change in relating is also explored by Dorothee Soelle, with reference to the consequences of choice for Adam and Eve in the creation myth:

> Adam and Eve are now confronted with the consequences of being workers and lovers. And because they have changed through their courageous step, God, the relational being also changes. God moves from parenthood to companionship . . . In spite of their failure to obey the commanding voice of the parental God . . . God supports them and makes clothes for them.[66]

But it is in the re-imaging of death that the symbol offers most hope. Because fear of death haunts most people, they cling to the image of Christ on the cross as model of endurance. But suppose there was another way to see this which used the images of birth, change, transformation. Instead of taking the image of victory over death, the 'Christus Victor' symbol of Jesus, innocent lamb, delivered up to slaughter as ransom payment, to be the predominant means of atonement, suppose we try to see if there are other transformative possibilities, based on the image of birth.[67]

Carol Ochs suggests the image of death as a disintegration, a falling-apart: 'We have felt the horror of falling apart, of a lack of a sense of self, of a fear that the centre will not hold – or that there may be no centre, no integrating pattern, no self.'[68] This disintegration is the opposite experience of 'being held' as an infant. It can be experienced physically, socially, psychologically, ethically or in other realms. Too often it is the psychological experience of women overwhelmed by patriarchal consciousness, literally by the sensation of being 'no-thing'. In Chapter 4 I discussed the feminist 'dark night' in this context, the disintegration experienced when all current values of society are experienced as empty and oppressive, there is alienation from the environment and only abandonment seems real. Yet Eckhart felt that the 'letting go' process *(Abgeschiedenheit)* was a vital part of the mystical journey.

In the birthing experience we are given a 'letting go' of self – in pain and struggle – for the creation of new being. We are given the sense of our physical bodies falling or even being torn apart. We have lost our 'centred self'. Nobody can reach us in this struggle, neither husband, lover, nor parent. We are in the dark, alone, in that primeval womb of chaos from which all life emerged. And yet, in that very darkness we can meet God as creative centre. We are held by that nurturing centre: from this being-torn-apart, this sense of loss, together You and I wordlessly create new life. And there will be integrity once more, and new sources of trust . . .

The second image of death is separation. It is a powerful symbol, with many expressions, ranging from the infant's separation from its mother, to the criminal's expulsion from the community, the physical experience of being separated by distance or imprisonment, the psychological experience of being estranged, alienated, even from all feeling (as was Atwood's protagonist) or sense of authentic self. This was the separation we discussed in Chapter 4 with the attempts of Martha Quest to recover, to 're-member', this lost self. It is the separation of death which is its greatest and most dreaded obstacle. To be separated from all that we love. Even to have to detach from the smallest physical joys of everyday – a cup of coffee, watching the night sky . . . Separation is a theme which is prominent in the myths. Hansel and Gretel tells the story of two children's attempts to leave their parents and face the conflicts of the world. Yet separation which threatens life is also essential for life. If Carol Gilligan's analysis is correct, because of the way we have constructed society, men develop through separation, women through relation and intimacy. But so much of the separation demanded by society – through boarding school and institution, for example – can be developmentally harmful for the young child. If the opposite of separation is a life-giving connection (a quality developed by women's spirituality), if the systems view that all things are interconnected is likewise true, then we are given tremendous hope. For holding together the pain of loss and separation is the deeply-felt experience of interdependence and community. The more we love and are interconnected, the more we suffer separation. Hence grief and mourning, given ritual expression at funerals, are a sign of how much we value the materiality of creation. Demeter mourns Persephone, Rachel weeps for her children – and it has been socially acceptable for women to grieve publicly in a way disapproved of for men. But to spiritualize away our grief by seeing ultimate reality in an otherworldly sense, death as welcome release from burdensome physical existence, seriously undervalues the whole created world.

I see the death of Jesus as being a tremendous affirmation of interconnection and presence. The separation was essential – 'If I go not, the Paraclete will not come to you' – because he had pushed his values to the limit which his present world would endure – but Jesus stresses connection and new forms of connectedness again and again, to be released in the very process of dying. He wanted to be remembered, cup in hand, celebrating: 'Do this in memory of me'. He will be with them to the end of the world, and his concern reaches out to those he leaves behind: 'Daughters of Jerusalem, weep not for me, but for yourselves and for your children.' Forgiveness and mutuality are the qualities of relating even as he hangs from the cross. Even that last terrible, desolate cry of separation from the very source of his being (Mark 15.34), was the means of releasing a new enduring form of relating to the world.

The third image is that of stasis – the stillness and changelessness of death, the absence of growth, change and development. People fear death because life is irreversibly cut off: they feel they have been cheated of old age, wealth, foreign travel . . . The masculine heroes of the myths achieve things – they win kingdoms, the hand of the beautiful princess, slay dragons, overcome obstacles . . . Or today they become directors of multi-nationals . . . Unemployment, illness and death are all dreaded as stasis, inactivity. But, says Robert Lifton, 'not all stillness is death. Some of it is quiet, deep centredness, a reaching down, instead of a thrashing around . . . The real distinction between the animate and the inanimate lies not in motion and stasis, but in the source of the motion.'[69]

Re-image the death of stasis as the stillness of 'waiting' – 'I said to my soul, be still' – the focused waiting and attentiveness discussed earlier. Re-image this as mythic time spent in the underworld, the work of winter, re-sourcing, re-covering roots, holding things together, awaiting the birth of a new idea, opportunity, without pre-empting its nature: as Adrienne Rich has said,

> Are we all in training for something we don't name?
> To exact reparation for things
> Done long ago to us and to those who did not
> survive what was done to them. . . .[70]

This is to confront death-in-life as change, loss, pain – but also as growth, connection and transformation. It is to experience death as part of the gracious process, because the creative becoming of God is intertwined with the process as relational source and ultimate destination.

RE-IMAGING THE LIFE-PRAXIS OF JESUS AS ATONEMENT

Instead of giving prominence to such traditional atonement symbols of Christ as victor, High Priest, Victim and Prime Exemplar, or replacing them with the 'androgynous Christ' of Mother Julian of Norwich or Mary Baker Eddy, because ultimately these too are ambivalent as the contribution of the female,[71] we begin by discerning and assuming responsibility for the evil of the present moment. If we see the truth of Jesus Christ as relational then the norm of love of neighbour assumes a priority in such a way as to make incarnate God's creative power.[72] And this *is* redemption. Christology, says David Shields, must be related to a dynamic, present, incarnational reality, 'as women name and create a new reality out of the tomb of patriarchy'.[73]

The symbol of Christ the Redeemer will now take its place among our chosen symbols and images of the divine – and these will be imagery drawn from female experience. This stress on present incarnational reality, though continually given prominence by feminist theologians, is also in keeping with the way many contemporary Christologies have reacted to insights from anthropology and human experience. This means giving up 'Christocentrism' because so many groups of people – women, Jews, ethnic minorities, the sexually alienated and other world faiths – are pushed to the margins by the Church's insistence that the actions of the historical Jesus are at the centre of all things. The danger with Christ's once-for-allness is that it has a tendency to 'stop history' and to undermine present relational responsibility, to disempower us from claiming power in relation. The pattern for a relational understanding is one where we are all caught up with God in a process of redemption. And this *was* the very pattern of the praxis of Jesus, a man who lived within the ambience of this relational power, deep in relationship with the creative source of that power, committed to the incarnating of this creative re-sourcing, which continually gave birth to the Kingdom of God. If this relational life-praxis is salvific it is because this is the basic pattern of the world, and because, through the passionate breakthrough we call resurrection, relational energy was released for those open to it.

But to say that the life-praxis of Jesus was purely *exemplary* as to what are the possibilities for power-in-relationship is both to draw us back to an impoverished understanding of an exemplary theory of atonement, as well as to underestimate the way a relational *Trinitarian* God is acting in the present. A feminist theology of interconnectedness makes it possible to hold together the relational being of God with human activity as co-creating, co-redeeming, together with the world's own inner healing resources, with which, in sensitivity, we can harmonize.

So the static image of Jesus as perfect man, ultimate symbol of redemption, gives way to the image of the Body of Christ, 'enfleshed by a relational Christology which opens us to recognize the way in which human connectedness brings God to the world'.[74] It could be that the feminist understanding of the relational self, the embodied and centred self, is adding a fresh understanding to the enfleshed nature of the Body of Christ (which I explore from a sacramental visionary point of view in the final chapter).

What, then, remains of the cross as central symbol of *at-one-ment* in such a relational understanding? If we move away from patriarchal preoccupation with death and destruction, alienation and estrangement, from images of the God who sends his Son to die, pointing the way to eternal life through crucifixion and death, replacing this with symbols of giving birth to new creation, of connection through separation, growth through stasis, integration through falling apart, healing through mutuality, compassion and solidarity, what need is there for cross as central symbol?

The cross of Jesus, with its arms extending as unifying the vertical with horizontal, the conscious with unconscious dimensions, the cross which for the Jewish painter Marc Chagall could symbolize the hope of the first Exodus and the tragedy of the Holocaust, will remain central. But its symbolic nexus will change. It will not be simply 'a reservoir for all pain', as Frances Young called it,[75] but a life-affirming protest against the injustice of all torture and crucifixions. We need this symbol to keep alive the memory of the redemptive, relational power at the heart of existence, enfleshed by the whole cross event. But it will also call to mind the forgotten stories – which Elizabeth

Schüssler-Fiorenza wished to reclaim – of all women and young girls who continue to be abused and battered under oppressive systems, the stories of all children, women and men whose suffering the world has not yet even begun to contemplate. To atone means to keep their memory alive, to mourn their sufferings, but also to see the crucified and risen Jesus as empowering hope that 'crucified woman' may yet be 'redemptive woman'. As long as we still struggle within alienated consciousness, with renewed creation as yet unborn, we need such a symbol.

Secondly, the cross as symbol of at-one-ment is a call to us to take up our responsibility to be co-sufferers, co-redeemers and co-creators – to stand in solidarity to prevent further crucifixions. The cross as sign of contradiction is an empowering symbol towards the at-one-ment of mutuality which is both the process and the end of the process. With this symbol of the Christ of mutuality and relationality we are enabled to name our human brokenness, the disintegration of the wounded earth, our deepest yearnings for healing and becoming whole. We are enabled to see the Body of Christ as the body of our mutuality. Images of pain become images of redeeming hope.

To remember the empowering actions of Jesus thrusts us both to the estranged relational scene of the present, and to the creative envisioning of a transformed future, when the travail of nature will know, with deep ecological wisdom, that the time is right, and, at last, the long labour is over and the earth can deliver.

8 Struggling to Birth: The Reclaiming of Redemption

This chapter looks at hard questions, in particular whether it actually *works* to speak of redemption either as the dynamic energy of mutuality or the making of right relation. I ask why this model should make any more impact on the sum total of human happiness than any other model from the tradition. I will also begin to explore this impact as inspiration in the field of sexual ethics, as a spirituality for education and as critique on the theology of sacraments.

REDEMPTION IN A SPIRITUALITY OF LIBERATION

Mutuality-in-relation, it will be objected, locks women firmly back into the same trap. Even if Gilligan *et al.* are right, and women operate from a broader relational basis, even if it could be proved that the world is fundamentally relational in character, so that we bear humanity's need for satisfying relational patterns, does not the evidence suggest it is precisely this vulnerability which has doomed women to perpetual subjection? Is not to reclaim this value as 'redemptive' simply flying (naively) in the face of facts?

This book has been an exercise in 'reclaiming' on many levels: in the first place I have been reclaiming religious language itself. 'Salvation' and 'redemption' (like other religious concepts) have small impact in a secular world, where 'saving' means investment and shareholding, 'redeeming' merely 'buying back'. The overtones of redemption and atonement – bleeding, guilt, expiation, vengeance and sacrifice – go against the grain of a world bent on material bliss, and at best, it could be objected, seem to belong to a mafia-style TV thriller.

Why try then to reclaim redemption from its traditional meaning of the historical action of a patriarchal God through his suffering Son, who 'atoned' for human evil in a once-for-all humiliating death, to be copied throughout the unwinding of history by the endurance of suffering and injustice by all who followed him? It is hard to see what advantage there is in plugging in once more to a theology where the 'merits' of his unique action – an infelicitous phrase – are 'applied' to us today by our own participation in such suffering.

My claim is that the word 'redemption' is neither a nostalgic borrowing from a rejected past, to be given a new secular garb, nor a forlorn attempt to make religious language 'relevant' to a capitalist culture; nor is it an attempt to be at the 'soft-centre' of the feminist movement, enabling me to keep safely within the Christian fold, rocking no boats, breaking no marriages, hanging on to the very doctrines which are the bastions of patriarchal theology, and cheering on the action at Greenham Common from the safe distance of a comfortable bed.

I believe that the new radical consciousness, the radical re-envisioning of life on earth of the Women's Movement, far from being dead,[1] has hardly even been tried. But like all other occasions in history when women have struggled to break free from subjection, the energy of the new consciousness can be diverted into backwaters where it can be 'harmlessly' channelled back into the dominating structures. Much of this book has been about the 'recovery of the subjugated knowledges'. It is the reclaiming of the memory, wisdom and knowledge lost to Christianity through the suppression of women and their experience as formative for Christian theology, which has been central to my concern.

As I look around the world I see one of the greatest obstacles to change as being the narrowness of the categories within which people can operate. The re-envisioning required has to be at the basic level of structures of consciousness and the symbols which emerge from this. The world sees the only answer to injustice and oppression as self-liberation, usually in some form of organized violence. For young people growing up in many parts of the world violence appears the only option available as an answer to tyranny. Yet the super-powers will reply with even more violence, power and might, bigger bombs and the consequent escalation of misery for poorer countries. Appeals for compassion – even from motives of self-interest – have little effect.

There has to be 'another voice', another ethic, to be called upon in order to break this cycle. There has to be another source of strength. It has to be the voice which cries in the wilderness for the rising-up of all the subjugated knowledges, not just for the oppressed women, but for the black South Africans, the Guatemalan Indians, and North American Indians and Aborigines marginalized by white settlers. It has to be the voice of the wounded earth, the water, air and soil ravished and polluted by the same ethic of dominance. But it is a 'different voice', because it offers other ways of effecting change than through warfare and violence. And this *is* the dangerous memory because it stands in opposition to the prevailing ethic. Although it is fully committed to the struggle for justice and right relation in the sphere of history, there is a deeper dimension which it touches.

And this is why we need the word 'redemption'. For this is a concept which includes the journey to self-realization and pushes further to making this real in society, through the communal struggle and the political struggle. It is self-realization, but from within the experience of the 'relational self', a particular contribution of women's experience, which has always sought to incarnate deeper levels of mutuality. Yet it is a path – as I have tried to show – trodden within the context of human limitation and finitude, the need to make sense of failure, to struggle with lost sense of self-worth and broken relation, the sense of waste and tragedy far beyond the experience of the lived moment. Christianity's mistake has often been to refer this back solely to the experience of Jesus – thus removing the urgency of the present moment (Jesus Christ has done it all for you) – instead of being empowered now by the dynamism which drove him, and living in the sphere of resurrection as relational power here-and-now.

It has fallen prey to spiritualizing tendencies, despised nature and made redemption an other-worldly concept. Reclaiming the lost wisdom of women's experience, together with the liberation spirituality of many groups of marginalized peoples, can redeem Christianity from layers of hypocritical self-justifying lifestyles, when the cross of Jesus, as Paul Oestreicher so movingly wrote, becomes a 'double-cross'.[2]

My concern is what happens when the revolution fails, as it so frequently does. Will redemption be for the loser or conqueror, and on which side of the political spectrum will it seem to fit? I seek for answers for Africa's continent of starving children, and for the generations of tortured, unremembered people who died for the sake of justice. We need to ask if this is a model of redemption which only works for the successful who achieve their own self-development, or if it actually offers any more hope, has any wider impact on the less fortunate than the model which offers divine compensation in another world. In this final chapter I begin to open up the unexplored territory which lies ahead.

The only hope-filled solution in the final analysis must lie in faith in a transcendental dimension, in the sense which transcends finitude, embracing God and world, which will lead us from our limited human abilities for meaning-making. For all our secular models of self-improvement and self-liberation fail if not caught up in this wider vision – as I explored through the five steps of the mystical path – and are but drops in the ocean of the huge forces of destructive energy which are all too visible. In Chapter 1 we saw

155

Sharon Welch, struggling with the limits of compassion and empathy, able to preserve sanity only by insensitivity: 'My sanity lay in my insensitivity'.[3]

A richer spirituality will not totally identify redemption with self-liberation, but, although committed to the passionate struggle for justice-making, will trust the transcendent source of relational power – which is God – even if at a given moment this is experienced as absence. For there must be a dimension of the creative-redemptive process which is beyond human control and conscious awareness. (This, we saw, was the meaning of the 'Dark Night' of the feminist mystics, Eckhart's 'letting-go', and the mythic time spent in the Underworld, diving deep to discover hidden resources . . .) So in order to allow vulnerability to be an effective empowering-to-justice, a 'bearing up God in the world', a feminist spirituality of liberation must seek for a voluntary commitment of passionate energy in love to courses of action which may involve suffering and death, because it sees the creation-redemption process as addressing the root forces of evil at a deeper level than its particular contemporary manifestation. But it will also see the life-giving, empowering forces of creativity as transcending personal existence; thus personal experience is contributing to a sense of cosmic redemption. Such a spirituality will not need to surrender sensitivity: according to the process model, it is possible that sensitivity, vulnerability, empathy may be the very preconditions of future occasions of novelty.[4] Redeeming grace will be seen as increasing depth of empowering sensitivity, which may offer new liberating possibilities in history.

This is why such a spirituality acquires a mystical dimension, which transcends any short-term political effectiveness. Watching at the gates of Peace Camps,[5] spilling blood on the steps of the Ministry of Defence, picking coffee with the Nicaraguan people: all these are actually giving biblical prophetic action a power for our time. And now it is plain why the lost stories need to be reclaimed and told: not because it is comforting to know that there were a few 'good' women in the Bible, capable of independent action. The real reason is a question of truth: How is redemption to be accomplished? When we see that women, too, were capable of liberating action, of claiming power-in-relation, this is an empowering source for us now. Remembering Miriam, dancing to liberation, remembering Esther, saviour of her people, remembering Deborah, prophetess and judge, remembering Hagar, the first mother of a promised child, flung into the desert – these are the lost knowledges. But we have to redeem the other stories too: the murdered concubine (Judg. 19), Hagar's final abandonment (Gen. 21.1–21), Jephthah's daughter (Judg. 11.29), and all the victims which patriarchy has claimed. They responded to mutuality-in-relating in the only way they could – and died for it. We 'redeem' them by building right relating here and now. But we do it in continuity with all fore-mothers and fore-sisters. For a spirituality of increasing depths of relatedness builds on the quality of solidarity, the sharing of experiences and bonding. But, finally, we know there will be victory, because redemptive mutuality is 'widening the skirts of light' in the face of darkness. And this is divine work, God ceaselessly at work in creation.

So the language of redeeming grace *is* the language of claiming power-in-relation, the power which reclaims passion and sexual energy for the making of right relation, which drives to justice, the power which *stands with* (withstands), protests, struggles, which bursts the bonds of unjust institutions – but also loves, remembers and grieves. It is a power, finally, which can unite the opposing polarities of affectivity and reason, of being and action. But in what kinds of relating will it find meaningful expression?

A PASSION FOR RELATING – BUT WHAT KIND?

I have suggested that there is a dynamic of relating which can be expressed politically as a redeeming force, as well as interpersonally between man and woman, within same-sex relating, in varying degrees of intensity, as well as an interconnectedness between the whole of creation. Now I seek to discover in what, precisely, lies the redemptive nature of the bonding, whether there are kinds of relational bonds which of their very nature inevitably preclude mutuality. Could it ever be 'reclaimed' in these cases? We need to envision the impact it would make on Church and society if, for example, heterosexual marriage could be free from patriarchal constraints and manifest an authentic dynamic of mutuality-in-relation.

That feminist spirituality is one of bonding and solidarity has been seen as its remarkable feature.[6] I have described one source of bonding in re-membering, re-claiming and identifying with lost stories – Elizabeth Fiorenza's hermeneutic of 'dangerous re-membrance'.[7] But a deeper source of bonding for Christian feminists is to see in Christian commitment a new way of relating, or, as Fiorenza says, 'a new set of relationships; the experience of God's presence among one another and through one another'.[8] This bonding is redeeming precisely in the sense (described in Chapter 4) of recovering a sense of becoming whole, of mutually ministering to each other in the process of self-affirmation. Nelle Morton has shown how it is precisely this 'ministering-in-mutuality' nature of the group which enabled its members to reach articulation:

157

One woman referred to her moment as a 'volcano erupting', another as a 'dam breaking loose' . . . sometimes incoherent and inarticulate sounds become audible. Once I saw a woman's throat open with a cry so great the cry could not come to sound – as in an old person who dies.[9]

Being *heard to speech*, being ministered to in mutuality has become an experience of liberating grace, enabling women to move from being victims to co-liberators of each other. It was been noted by the researchers of a remarkable book on *Women's Ways of Knowing*[10] how frequent is the experience of women that they are never listened-to, never heard, and if heard, never given validity. As Morton continued,

> Tasting a liberation they had never known before, they found it good. They began to appropriate a new kind of courage and to explore the future with no known history to inform, and a new ability to articulate that which has never before come to speech.[11]

This is truly a bringing-of-self to birth, the primal meaning of the birthing image, used in the last chapter as a model of atonement. The Christian inspiration for this kind of bonding is the vision of Jesus as healing presence, himself empowered by empowering others, and the redeemed community of men and women around him mutually ministering to each other and to the different groups of marginalized people around them: as Rita Brock has written:

> We redeem Christ when we recognize the images of Jesus that reflect our hunger for healing wholeness and claim those images as resources for hope because we belong to a community of transformation and empowerment . . . Christ is an image of shared power that works and is increased only in the sharing.[12]

In recognizing that the clarity of vision of ministry-through-mutuality has been lost down the centuries through ecclesial hierarchical structures which limited the contribution of lay people in general and women in particular, women are offering an alternative model for ministry for the Church as a whole. Reaching out to abused and battered women, creating new circles of hope: these are new models of ministry.

Yet, it will be asked, have not women *always* cared for the young, sick and dying? Women have always told the faith-stories, have been the carers and nurturers, have believed in sacrificial love. The difference now – from within a perspective which respects both the needs of self-development *and* relationality – is that it is a passion for justice which empowers the relating and sees the hallowing of

God, the God seeking justice for the oppressed, interconnected with the making of right relation.

Hence the dynamic of making right relation also forms the basis of a new feminist ethics.[13] Beverley Harrison, more than any other feminist theologian, has shown the interconnection of mutuality, sexuality, power in relationship and justice-making. She has shown how the recovery of the embodied self from the distorted, wounded expressions of sexuality in society restores a sense of connectedness with nature, the cosmos and each other – a discovery of the person as a richly-related being. Thus, she writes, our sexuality is our total, embodied connection to all things, our deeply-grounded relationship, is an

> intimately, inter-structured possibility. . . This means . . . that who I am in my 'power of relation' determines and is determined by my relationship and that my wellbeing and that of others to whom I am related depends foundationally on existing conditions of mutual respect between us or upon the lack thereof.[14]

But if bodily integrity is foundational for feminist ethics – and is essential for the concept of redemption I have developed – it is clear that women cannot feel 'redeemed' if their only bodily experience is of being 'objects' within power-dependent relationships, which preclude the possibility of genuine mutuality. It is the very character of these power-dependent relations which so often prevents any personal empowerment and even self-respect at the most basic of levels. Given this situation, frequently driven by guilt that it is their own fault that things fall apart, women pile more and more energy into a marriage, seeking a level of intimacy and intensity beyond what is possible.

Harrison accuses Christianity of increasing pressures on sexual relationships, especially in marriage, and of teaching people to expect too much of primary intimacy commitments. The Church has over-romanticized marriage, she feels, and has encouraged people to see their life partners as the mediating source of sexuality – and even of encouraging sexual repression. She calls for new paradigms of sexuality which evoke celebratory, creative, mutually-empowering and sensuous relationships, and accuses the Church of being out of touch with those who are discovering these forms, and thus of the vision of God which is being made incarnate in this struggle for justice.

Here is another area for listening to 'the different voice'. For it is not only a question of rejecting the injustices of patriarchal marriages, where women were – and frequently still are, even in a Western 'liberated' culture – objects of male power and control, their sexuality defined in terms of male pleasure or procreative necessity. The personalizing encounter movements popular since the sixties, and referred to in Chapter 2, responded to this by increasing the level of intimacy required for successful marriages, giving this theological meaning by analogy with the relationship between Christ and his Church (Eph. 5). Many people have undoubtedly been helped by this approach. But for others, as Harrison hinted, the level of expectation was increased to an impossible degree. But there is a much more profound issue at stake. Because sexuality has been defined in strictly heterosexual terms, on the model of heterosexual intercourse, largely from masculine norms of need and satisfaction, women have been blocked from *self-understanding* and from getting in touch with their own experience. They have been part of a world view already defined by this 'hetero-reality'. But the world might in fact offer totally other possibilities. Most people, in their fierce opposition to this rather frightening notion, do not realize that this is what lies behind the feminist lesbian movement, do not understand how the model of heterosexuality, frequently in distorted forms, has defined the limits of our total world view.

The problem can be seen on the level of language. What could this world be like, for example, if we did not speak of 'virgin snow', 'virgin territory', awaiting violation? If we speak of 'conquering' a mountain, 'assailing' its north face, 'mastering' a task, of the rape of the earth, we reflect the distorted sexuality which underlies our concepts. When sexuality itself is defined in terms of penetration, conquest and orgasm, we betray not only this distortion, but a conceptual impoverishment which has frozen our experience for centuries.

The transformation which is needed, as I have been arguing, is first at the level of our linguistic concepts, which are the gateway or window to how we perceive reality. We have for so long assumed that our very sentences must have a subject/object structure, in which the subject has control - 'does something to' - over the object. But suppose two entities were in a more mutual association or bonding, a totally different kind of linguistic structure might result. This could have enormous possibilities for the kind of relating which might ensue.

For Jungian analysts have long argued that women and men operated on a different type of consciousness. Irene Claremont de Castillejo, in *Knowing Woman: A Feminine Psychology*,[15] describes this as a difference between focused and diffuse awareness: 'Focused consciousness', she writes,

has emerged over thousands of years from the unconscious, and is still emerging. All our education is an attempt to produce and sharpen it in order to give us power to look at things and analyse them into their component parts. . . It is this focused consciousness which we are all using in the everyday world all the time. . . It is not however the only kind of consciousness. Most children are born with and retain, a diffuse awareness of the wholeness of nature, where everything is linked with everything else and they feel themselves to be part of an individual whole. Here lies the wisdom of the artist, and the words and parables of the prophets, spoken obliquely so that only those who have ears to hear can hear and the less mature will not be shattered.

Without loading this distinction with all the implications for the psyche which the Jungians do, and falling back to another version of the 'eternal feminine', it is still possible to see this kind of distinction present at the level of sexuality, once the blinkers of the male-defined heterosexual world are transcended and women are allowed freely to get in touch with their own experience.

For women have long known that their sexuality – and sexual pleasure – was experienced as issuing from a wider, more diffuse basis than that of men. Many women have felt guilty because childbirth was frequently for them a deeper and more thrilling experience than sexual intercourse – and they felt it should have been the other way around! Women experience sexual pleasure in breastfeeding and this diffuse sense of pleasure can be extended and deepened in the bonding with small children. But suppose this sexual energy could be deepened in other ways. Suppose it could be experienced in friendship based on tenderness and affectivity. Suppose it was part of the passion for justice, an energy which burnt for justice and freedom – and made it. Once penetrative genital intercourse is seen not to be the only possible model of sexuality, but one among many, there could be many enriching possibilities, as yet undiscovered, and all part of the creating/redeeming plan. Once it is recognized that our so-called permissive society has in fact *narrowed* the focus of human sexuality to one particular expression and concentrated an immense amount of human need on it, perhaps we will recognize the necessity for a change in consciousness.

Perhaps now it is also clear why feminist lesbians suffer from a dual oppression: for, writes Mary Hunt,

the cultural, economic and socio-political factors of patriarchy make female sexuality qualitatively different. Women begin from the oppression of women which is common in patriarchy, and then have the experience of lesbian women as yet another layer, not different in kind but degree from the oppression of all women.[16]

Most people do not realize that feminist lesbianism is radically re-envisioning sexuality in a qualitatively different way from a heterosexually-defined lesbianism and homosexuality. In the first place, it is the creating of safe spaces for relating – in both a literal and metaphoric sense – where, says Hunt, 'we aspire . . . for self and other . . . a sense of community for all women in a cultural context in which we can empower one another and our menfolk as whole human persons.'[17] This definition of lesbianism in such a relational sense brings her to describe the 'fierce tenderness' which can characterize this kind of loving: 'We can know something about the passion of women . . . for life and creativity, not simply for motherhood. We can appreciate something new about brokenness, emptiness and even sin which is revealed when separation, death or mistreatment end relationships.'[18] Both Mary Hunt and Isabel Carter Heyward assert the central place which lesbianism has for feminism: in lesbianism, they say, the feminist word is made flesh.

This is indeed an enormous challenge for Christian theology. It must first be put in the wider context of female friendship. No one can deny the way female friendship has been obscured, trivialized, dismantled, and destroyed by history, whereas in reality it is a powerful force in the lives of women. Mrs Noah in the medieval mystery plays has her 'Gossips', or women friends – men have business associates and colleagues, with attendant prestige in society. Yet in the Gospels it is the groups of women who follow Jesus and minister to him from their means (Luke 8.1) and who come together to the tomb on Easter morning to anoint him (Matthew 28.1; Mark 16.1; Luke 24.1), both very practical forms of ministry. But, when Jesus speaks explicitly of love and friendship, it is apparently to the male apostles (John 13). Here again are more redemptive stories to be reclaimed.

Yet at the same time the argument of some feminists that female friendship or 'gyn/affection' – the term coined by Janice Raymond[19] – should be restored as a force to replace disintegrating 'hetero-relations' or 'hetero-reality', cannot hold water in a full theology of mutuality-in-relating. For according to Janice Raymond, female friendship should create a women-centred existence, and although this is a wider concept than lesbian love, Raymond thinks it should translate into it. She argues that, unless 'gyn/affection' becomes an intrinsic part of the feminist political platform, feminism will not fulfil its basic goals of 'obliterating the mechanics, institutions and effects of female colonization in all its forms'.[20]

But a theology of redemption based on mutuality-in-relating must have the widest possible embrace if it is to be the vision of Shalom of the Kingdom of God. It is crucial to listen and learn from the critique which lesbianism makes of the unjust power-structuring of hetero-

162

sexual relations. More importantly, there must be action: too long has the cruel discrimination in terms of housing, jobs and exclusion from mainstream Church life been tolerated and positively encouraged. We have to be committed to the 'ongoing story of liberation', which means an exploration of the ethical and spiritual implications of the stance of feminist lesbians.

This is part of, but cannot be the last word for, the creation of relational, redemptive lifestyles within any ecclesially redemptive community. One of the striking features of the lifestyle of Jesus was that he tried to remove barriers, not create new ones, to reach out to the marginalized – not to leave them rejected, but rather to include them in his vision of the Kingdom. Thus the separatist bonding of sisterhood can be justified as a temporary form of relating – or as permanent, in cases where there has been extreme suffering, physical or psychological. The prophetic nature of such bonding can continue to challenge the wider groups. But the status of such a group cannot be raised to the essentialist category of primary definition of human nature.

The bonding of sisterhood is often presented in an idyllic and enticing manner, with a lyricism about its power and righteous indignation about its suppression in history, but the truth of human nature demands the recognition that we dwell not in a solely *woman-identified* universe, nor a solely *male-identified* one, but that authentic mutuality between the sexes creates a human universe. To create an entire cosmos of sisterhood, as Mary Daly would wish, ignores the fact that sisters have brothers, daughters have fathers, grandfathers and uncles – not to mention the marital relationship, or the many other sorts of bonding.

Just as patriarchy exalts motherhood for its own purposes, sisterhood too – despite its egalitarian basis – can be exalted out of all proportion. Furthermore, to eliminate men as the 'evil other' is to prolong the scapegoating process from which women themselves have continually suffered. It is to ignore the whole reality of evil, in which women have been involved and for which they must take their share of the responsibility. But it is also to allow that the power-subservience model has been the *only* hermeneutic of relationship in history. But there has been another story to be 'redeemed'. Whereas the power/subservience model has been the dominating key of interpretation, because of its effectiveness in controlling structures, institutions, admission to public office and the recording of history, yet even under the most unjust regime there have been occasions when the relational strengths of women – and those men who stood out against oppression – have kept faith with the theme of redemptive mutuality. To use Foucault's image, the subjugated knowledges have achieved prominence from time to time. There *have* been examples of just and creative loving. Even under a patriarchal system, which offers very little possibility, there are examples of self-affirming women-in-relationship – even if they have had to use the system to their own advantage, as well as self-affirming women in relationships of a mutual and healing nature. But it is true that those which are known to us, such as Perpetua, Teresa of Avila, Elizabeth of Hungary, or the great abbesses of the Middle Ages, are from wealthy or upper-class families, or are held up as models according to patriarchal values. The lives and relationships of poor women are, with few exceptions, lost to us.

It is as much a cruel distortion to say that men have *never* acted towards women in a genuine loving way, or that *all* heterosexual relationships are distorted by a power-subservience dynamic, as it is to claim that women alone are victims of war, massacre and starvation throughout history. If feminist lesbianism is defined as women developing mutual, loving and non-exploitative relationships, then surely a full theology or redemptive mutuality demands that both men and women, whether hetero- or homo-sexual (lesbian), develop these possibilities *together*. Just as Carter Heyward has written of the ongoing conscious of oppression and thus the ongoing story of liberation, so the story of redemptive mutuality has a history and a future. As Ursula King wrote, 'The struggle for a new integral spirituality to sustain our world and shape alternative, social, political and religious institutions, cannot be won by women alone, *but must be undertaken by women and men together.*'[21]

But does this mean that heterosexual marriage can be redeemed from patriarchal restrictions and institutionally-tolerated cruelty? The question is whether the differences in the way sexuality is experienced by women and men allow for lifelong, mutually-satisfying, committed unions. So much has been written about the sufferings of women cross-culturally and throughout history because of patriarchal marriage, and it does not need repetition here. What *is* needed is much more discerning work to determine under what conditions genuine, just and redemptive mutuality can take place in marriage. Feminism has placed monogamous marriage under attack for its ideology: twentieth-century society has placed its all-too-precarious existence in jeopardy through new forms of social deprivation.

Within a new awareness of the many-faceted expressions of sexuality, the hope is that we will work towards realistic, honest forms of life-long bonding which will not delude or cheat us by promising too much, or make us believe we have been crying for the moon. A relational world does not mean that all our intensity of emotion must be focused on to one person – what a burden to uphold! Nor am I arguing for infidelity and extra-marital affairs, which seem to have provided the only alternative to marital boredom. There will be a wholeness, a beauty and a justice to be striven for in any relationship, and monogamous marriage will always have something precious to offer humanity, in its covenanted basis – which Scripture has made so much use of – and in the risk taken of promising life-long commitment: this in a society which needs *more* not less images of commitment. But the *mutuality* of the covenanted basis is far from being a real option for many. Just forms of bonding in marriage for women are still to be struggled for, attained and witnessed to in law, in financial arrangements and in the way society sees the responsibility for child-care. But the *meaning* of the commitment will have many variations: for some, the stability and security in which to work will be its most important value. The *sacramental* value will be in the values shared, worked at and made tangible for society.

Once we have re-interpreted the married commitment in terms other than possessiveness, control, exclusivity and sexual rights, and more in terms of a bonding based on shared values, commitment to the full becoming of each other, justice and mutuality, there is still relational energy to be focused and channelled in many directions. Throughout this book I have been trying to open up the many redemptive possibilities of the relational scene, the affectivity and tenderness between men, women and children, which may not have an explicit sexual expression – and certainly not a genital one – but has its origin in diffuse sexual energy.

The alternatives to heterosexual relating suggested by separatist lesbian feminists are one-sided options. Not only do they explicitly exclude half the human race, but they do not responsibly address the vital issue: What kind of redeeming, mutual relationships should be responsible for the well-being of the next generation? Feminists cannot ignore the question of future life on earth, the issue of the ideal conditions in which to bring up children. To say that in lesbianism 'the feminist word is made flesh' is woefully one-sided, if by it is meant that it can be made flesh in no other way. We need more relational patterns of mutuality, not less. But unless the Church will listen and hear the woman's point of view, unless she will heed the cry that in many traditional marriages there is no justice for women, the journey to self-affirmation may never even begin, and the trend to separatism will only grow more pronounced.

REDEMPTIVE MUTUALITY AND EDUCATION

Another area where the model of mutuality-in-relating which issues from the creative re-envisioning of feminist theology is sorely needed is in education. We live in a time of tremendous disenchantment in this field. The under-resourcing of so many areas in education has brought low morale for teachers and sometimes impossible working conditions. From the side of pupils, no longer is education regarded as a golden gate to an interesting job and comfortable life. Fewer and fewer subjects are regarded as vital – the criterion is a short-sighted utility – and research possibilities have dwindled. The very activity and enterprise of education itself needs redeeming.

Thus my focus is not on theological or moral education as such, on the issue of gender discrimination, or on a particular area of curriculum development, but on the kind of spirituality needed for 'redeeming' education today. I try to see if the image of redemption as right relation developed here could offer transformative possibilities.

When the critique which feminist theology makes has been applied to education it has already been seen to have a prophetic dimension. Yet this is not startling: women have always been pioneers on the educational scene. Mary Ward, who founded the Institute of the Blessed Virgin Mary, Angela Merici who founded the Ursulines, Cornelia Connelly who founded the Holy Child order are just a few examples of women, motivated by concern for the basic needs of girls for education, who successfully overcame the severe barriers of the time against the advancement of women. The orders they founded are all examples of educational orders which in the present day are remarkable in being able to adapt, renew and reform according to the demands of social justice. From the days of the great Abbesses Radegunde (AD 518–87) and Hilda of Whitby (AD 614–80) women have been consistently involved in educational endeavours of creativity and variety.

From the perspective of liberation theology social justice must be the responsibility of the school as a whole, and this of course means tackling issues such as the justice of wage structures, admission policies, staff appointments, the justice of work-load distribution, punishment systems, the fairness of resource allocations, constructing anti-racism policies, and so on. The perspective of relationality will ask what model of relationship is operative within a particular school. Until very recently there was not much variety possible in the monastic-ascetic model of school. The pioneering work of education-alists like Maria Montessori and Rudolph Steiner has greatly changed the opportunities for creative models of education. Yet many of the creative enterprises in education fail because of the prevailing ethic of competitiveness, because of lack of resources, or a lack of the right kind of support.[22] In any case the creative experiments in schooling more frequently confine themselves to the private, independent system, and the poorest section of the populace

– who must be the Church's particular concern – remain unaffected. Or, worse still, they suffer because talent and resources are siphoned-off elsewhere.

A feminist perspective of redemptive mutuality offers, first of all, a perspective of wholeness, that is, in its efforts to overcome body/mind dualisms it addresses the whole person – with implications for method, content, setting and style of interrelating. The aim of mutuality will require teacher-pupil dialogue, with much more 'listening-to' than 'talking-at' as a first step to learning experience. (Nelle Morton's urging of the importance of being 'heard to speech' is relevant here). The unhappy experience of girls in the classroom situation finding themselves totally cut off from the prevailing language of learning is still all too common.

The spirituality of 'focused attention' so beloved of Simone Weil will be important here:

Not only does the love of God have attention for its substance, the love of neighbour, which we know to be the same love, is made of the same substance. *Those who are unhappy have no need for anything in this world but people giving them attention.* The capacity to give one's attention to a sufferer is a rare and difficult thing: it is almost a miracle; it is a miracle.'[23]

But 'focused attention' is not merely a spiritual notion; it can be a facilitator of action. As Iris Murdoch observed: 'I have used the word 'attention', which I borrow from Simone Weil, to express the idea of a just and loving gaze directed upon an individual reality. I believe this to be the characteristic and proper mark of the moral agent.'[24]

This brings into play the tension between mutuality and reciprocity which underlies this book. Mutuality considered as ethic of redemption is a far deeper concern than reciprocity. Relationships in the classroom are, unfortunately, far from egalitarian – teachers are paid, pupils generally do not want to be there – but by focusing on the value of mutuality, the dynamic of relatedness which is called into being, both teacher and pupil can participate in a profound creative enterprise.

But what I am discussing is a process much wider than the classroom. This is not just because of the fact that many adults are illiterate – and many people, particularly third-world women have had no access to education – but because education is a lifetime process, and there are many areas of living for which education will be appropriate at a later time, for example, pre-marital counselling, bereavement therapy and in-service training.

For all these the style and setting will greatly determine the kind of learning experience which takes place. 'Wholeness' refers not just to body/mind wholeness, to a concern for a person's whole-life situation – family, language, sex and religion – but to the style and philosophy which will reach out to the whole person. So a concept of holistic learning will recognize the multiple stimuli by which a person learns and will include poetry, images and symbols on a cross-cultural level, and an understanding of the power of images to issue forth in action and decision-making. Images, wrote Nelle Morton, 'bring little children to attitudes of superiority and inferiority long before they are able to conceptualize. . . . Images are woven into the language of the world and our religious language so that we educate children and ourselves to speak to our own destruction. . .'[25]

Holistic learning also sees memory, imagination and story-telling as powerful tools, particularly in the recovery of the 'subjugated knowledges', for re-connecting and establishing a 'genealogy' even if this is discontinuous with the dominant tradition. By this I mean the specific history and experience of a particular ethnic group, but, secondly, the particularity of girls' experience, especially the strengths of relationality and empathy which have never been part of the educational scene.

Yet recently we have begun to see the possibilities which arise from understanding the gender-specific ways and modes of coming-to-know. In the final chapter of *Women's Ways of Knowing* mentioned above, the writers describe – in a way which develops the image of atonement as bringing-to-birth – the role of teacher as midwife: the teacher, they say, will participate in the thinking of the students and will encourage the students to speak in their own active voices.[26] Building on Sara Ruddick's article on 'Maternal Thinking',[27] they stress the primary concern of teaching as the preservation of the vulnerable child: 'The midwife teacher's first concern is to preserve the student's fragile, newborn thoughts.'[28] Midwife teachers will focus on the students' growth and will be clear that 'the baby' will not be theirs but the student's.

Such a holistic approach to education will relate to students' alienated attitudes and responses to the social sickness from which they spring, and understand the learning process as having social and political responsibilities. So it is not just a question of eliminating patriarchal symbols and images, of transforming the capitalist success-oriented ethic in education, or balancing an over-intellec-tualized discipline with experiential content. It is a question of discovering, through education, a method which permeates the entirety of curriculum and ethos,

> The passion to make and make again
> where such un-making reigns,[29]

168

of making justice and liberation incarnate by enabling and empowering those groups which are on the bottom of society's ladder, through a holistic learning process which includes the discovering and naming of symbols for human brokenness.

But it is also redemptive, because in and through the procedures of nurturing the processes of coming-to-know, God's creative power-in-mutual relation enables disadvantaged children and disenchanted, alienated adults to 'touch their strength', and claim what wholeness is theirs in the midst of brokenness and finitude.

So what could seem an abstruse theological concept – the idea of atonement in feminist process theology – now is seen as contributing to an educational method. For in the educational process there is a creative coalescing of the ideas of novelty, the God who suffers with, yet offers new possibilities, for whom tragedy is not the last word; the recovery of the past is seen as both judgement and empowering of the present. Within the metaphor of interrelating this will draw consistent inspiration from the Christ event as challenge to discovery of juster forms of coming to self-knowledge within a community and political context.

For the method to be effective, 'connectedness' must be respected. This means connectedness with the environment and with the socio-political situation, bodily well-being and integrity, and above all, the necessity of the 'attentiveness' of the process to issue forth in action. And only thus shall we heal the dualistic divisiveness between life and learning.

This is the agenda not only for schools, but for parish educational programmes and for for peace and justice groups. It is the reason for the success of so many women's learning projects: where learning respects the 'situatedness' of women, and touches the strengths of interrelating, the innate trust of 'bringing to birth' something new, there is a possibility of breaking free from the bondage of the past. Ivan Illich, Paulo Freire, Leonardo Boff and now feminist theology have all stressed the urgency of working with groups for the transform-ation of society,[30] of empowering the 'victim' to become part of the redeeming process, thus making the liberation of the spirit an integral part of the educational venture for the coming of the new creation.

REDEMPTIVE MUTUALITY AND THE SACRAMENTS

To ask what influence the making of right relation, or the model of redemptive mutuality would have on the sacraments is to enter uncharted territory. For even though liberation theologians have begun to make a political-social critique of sacramental theology[31] this has not taken on board the insights of feminist theology except in very general terms. Feminist theology itself has not given the theme much attention, probably because it is an area of great pain and the cause of many women both refusing communion and even leaving the Church. The writing of women in the area of sacramental theology seems to be confined to the use of inclusive language in the liturgy and the exclusion of women from the priesthood.

The theme of redemptive mutuality in the area of the sacraments brings much richness, but for women it also brings much pain. And this needs to be brought to the light of day. For so much of the value of relational experience is just not acknowledged as sacramental and in fact can be specifically destroyed by sacramental ritual. For example, I have been focusing on the image of birth-giving as model of at-one-ment. For women this is frequently a joyous experience: the new baby is a precious, loved and beautiful creation – and yet, until recently, as I discussed in Chapter 7, a woman in the Catholic Church had to go to a purification ceremony after childbirth, and the liturgy of baptism stressed the sinfulness of the child – even if, theologically, it did not impute sinfulness to the baby – from which baptism would deliver him/her. How bewildering this was for many women, detracting from natural joy. Moreover, it was often reinforced by insisting on its necessity as a sort of insurance ticket for heaven. Fortunately a renewed theology of baptism – in the context of the Rite of Christian Initiation of Adults – now stresses infant baptism as incorporation within the Christian community, which goes some way towards meeting this problem.

Secondly, the present practice of sacramental confession within the Catholic, Anglican and Orthodox Churches takes no account of the feminist analysis of sin. Where sin is understood as pride, disobedience and the egoistic concentration on self, there is no space or understanding shown for women who have a poor sense of self or none at all – largely because Christianity has told them to find it through identification with another, through obedience to the will and wishes of another, and through the sacrifice of any incipient independence of their own. Precisely through individual confession have women's relational strengths been harnessed into reinforced victimhood. Yet these two examples only nibble at the fringe: I do not even need to mention the suffering which continues to be inflicted on women through exclusion from the ordained ministry – although there are signs of great hope in the Anglican Church – by the patriarchal interpretation of sacramental marriage, and by exclusion from the ministry of healing.

It is popular today to speak in terms of models or root metaphors with an anthropological base when describing the sacraments. In order to show how redemptive relationality affects sacramental spirituality, I will explain how just such an attempt falls short in terms of the model which I develop. This is George Worgul's root metaphor of 'celebration'.[32] I have chosen this because Worgul is at pains to take the best of the insights from anthropology and developmental psychology, to respect the human need for ritual and the notion of personal encounter, and in some ways represents the best of contemporary sacramental theology. 'Celebration' is chosen by Worgul as a fundamental root metaphor of the sacraments because it is a human reality, a reality of community and because it links past, present and future. It connects interior and exterior dimensions and unfolding deepening possibilities of human meaning. I recognize this as a valuable contribution. What Worgul does not explore is the link between the celebration of the sacraments and social justice.

Enrique Dussel, the liberation theologian, for example, has asked if it is always possible to celebrate the Eucharist in conditions of oppression and injustice,[33] Tissa Balasuriya links the celebration of Eucharist with a consistent church commitment to social justice,[34] while Monica Hellwig and Thomas Cullinan have developed the symbolism of bread and wine to include economic and political considerations.[35] Women too can pose the question as to how the Eucharist can claim to be a full expression of the Christian Church, when the symbols of sharing, the bread and wine of a life given to redemptive mutuality, expressly exclude women as celebrants, as well as failing to make the connection with the suffering of women throughout the world.

A theology which sees redemption as linking relational energy with a passion for justice sees social justice as the heart of the Eucharist, the sacraments as a whole and therefore ecclesiology. Baptism will be seen as entry to the redeemed and redeeming community, where the struggle against the structures of injustice – the original sin of the world – is seen as the community's central task. If the central sacramental symbols are located in a socio-political setting, if sacramental grace is the grace which liberates from the multi-layered oppressions and afflictions, then we cannot be selective as to *which* oppressions are relevant. Christ came to redeem from all situations of slavery and sin, including the sin of sexism.

This is precisely where a feminist spirituality of relationality challenges the sacraments. First, it specifically highlights the lack of mutuality, the distorted relationality in all forms of contemporary life. The Church must respond to this by being 'redeemed community' in the sense of offering a redeemed way of being together as people. This is the ultimate meaning of the symbol of at-one-ment or reconciliation – not merely as a symbol of once-for-all victory achieved by Jesus, with cosmic significance, but as empowering symbol, to create still further forms of redemptive mutuality: as Ruether says, '. . . Redemptive humanity goes ahead of us, calling us to yet incompleted dimensions of human liberation'.[36]

This is also the vision of an inclusive and process Christology. Because the model of redemptive relationality protests at any notion of community presenting distorted relationality, it criticizes structures of dominance/subservience inside and outside the Church. It uses the slogan 'the personal is political' as cutting-edge for criticizing sacramental and ecclesial symbols. For in the euphoric days after the Second Vatican Council, when the Church was viewed from the perspectives of sacrament, community and People of God, the economic and political dimensions of these symbols went unnoticed. There was little awareness – in a Western setting at least – that it was a mockery or even a counter-symbol to share the eucharistic bread with those who were hungry or oppressed, unless the community committed itself to action for social justice. For how could the Church herself call to conversion as a 'light to the nations' unless she too was prepared to repent of the wrongs done to women, and to all marginalized peoples though the centuries, as well as committing herself to build right relation?

These difficulties come to a head with the central ecclesial symbol of the 'Body of Christ'.[37] A feminist theology of mutuality will try to dismantle false icons of mutuality and offer its own visions enfleshed in terms of the 'Woman-Church' movement. But it will see the Body of Christ image primarily as a sign of contradiction: as Elizabeth Fiorenza puts it: 'A feminist Christian spirituality is rooted in the ecclesia of women as the "Body of Christ". Body as image and model for our being Church. As long as women's bodies are battered how can we claim "mutuality with men" in the Body of Christ?'[38]

A spirituality of redemptive mutuality has been inspired by the life, death and resurrection of Jesus, a person who incarnated in his own life the divine, creative power of just and redemptive relationality, empowered and empowering. Christ lived so utterly and completely in the reality of exchanged life and love, of just relating, that his death, far from causing this flow to cease, unleashed a flood of creative and transforming power into history, to be an empowering force to all who respond to its relational strength. To be authentically the 'Body of Christ' the Church must be empowered by the same dynamic.

Not only will such a spirituality of mutuality continue its prophetic role of denouncing injustice in ecclesial structures, in androcentric and misogynist texts, exclusive language in the liturgy, but it must also raise up counter-symbols of women as redemptive, power as liberating and shared, lifestyles based on egalitarian principles. And it will enflesh the Body of Christ in new ways.

For if its emphasis is on redemptive mutuality, then the dimension of redeemed bodiliness must become accepted as sacramental material. Reclaiming the sacrality and depth of intimacy of eating together, including those who have prepared the food, of shared life and work performed in just conditions, of sexuality in its many dimensions rediscovered as joy, and liberated from its degraded and exploitative expressions, brings new meaning to the Body of Christ as ecclesial image.

The very words 'Body of Christ' proclaim the power and significance of interrelationality and the salvific value of the connectedness for which I have been arguing. But their power as a root sacramental and ecclesial image is not simply in their mirroring of the connectedness of all things. Their power is that Christ points to God, the divine source of connectedness, as holding all things together. And herein lies the whole source of redemption, of sacramental outpouring of grace, of hope in the midst of human brokenness. For God, the creative source of relationality, does not buy sanity at the expense of sensitivity. However successful are our present and future liberation movements, nothing will undo or bring back the raped, tortured and mutilated bodies of innocent women, children and men, victims of human sin, past and present. But the Body of mutuality of Christ will hold alive the memory of suffering, not for mourning alone, but for God's redemption, for the point at which all human efforts at self-liberation become taken up and unified with the redeeming forces of life itself.

So the specificity of the contribution which women's spirituality makes to the Body of Christ image is, in part, the particular bonding of the 'Woman-Church' movements which are in search of more authentic ways of being Christian: for women, they offer the space to discover being created as *imago Dei*, whole, with sexuality as redeeming strength and not as humiliation. For the Church as a whole, 'Woman-Church' basic communities offer a prophetic image of what Church could be, without the distortions or corruptions of patriarchy. The women who belong to such 'Woman-Church' groups in many instances are feeding back into the wider church structures the fruits of their insights and experiences. But women's spirituality will also enflesh the Body of Christ by the hallowing and reverencing of the different ways of being human, which women do as a normal part of living – such as the tasks of nourishing and nurturing, which have been discussed in connection with the divine imaged as female.

For all these reasons Worgul's root metaphor of celebration – and others like it – is inadequate if we are to reach a sacramental understanding in a secular world, which will grasp the need to see our central symbols as a cry to make social and political justice incarnate, and as reflecting the way in which men and women actually relate to one another. Words like 'celebration', 'festivity', 'communion', 'reconciliation' cannot be left floating in an imaginary heaven, focusing attention away from present oppression. They should be means of rousing our passionate energy to make things different here and now, beginning – in an ecclesial context – with the way we pray and worship together.

With the feminist vision of the self as relational and embodied – with all the potential this implies for empathy and compassion – the sacramental vision challenges to make right relation as a redemptive lifestyle. It will be redemptive, because it will plunge deeper than levels of protest and struggle, beyond levels of experienced affectivity and sexuality – yet will be all the more powerful for claiming both of these – and because it plunges deeper than mere reciprocity, since inter-relationality must claim power and strength, even when it clashes with the refusal of relationality. It is at this bedrock point that it is possible to see where the language of grace, prayer and worship are important. The whole redemption process – and I include self-liberation, self-realization and struggles for freedom within the process, seeing all these as co-extensive – has been a graced process from the very beginning. To pray, as Marjorie Suchocki has written, 'is to change the way the world is by adding that prayer to the reality of the world'.[39]

If spirituality is depth of relatedness, then redemption as making right relation includes prayer as a dimension. Any spirituality which struggles with threatening dualisms to identify means of overcoming the split between flesh/spirit, being/doing, and so on, will articulate its own prayer language.

So a spirituality focusing on right relation will see the language of prayer creating new forms. Prayer can be seen as sensitivity, as tenderness and increasing depth of relatedness, both among persons, our connectedness with creation, and God. Feminist process thought has only just begun to articulate the way in which prayer, as bringing novel and healing forms of relationality to consciousness from the unconscious, is a way of changing the world, of creating mutuality and bonding, of bringing to articulation the unspoken feelings of anguish and brokenness, of experiencing the tangibility of healing, and focusing on the symbols which bring it to birth: 'healing', writes Rita Brock, 'requires calling up the depths of cold pain in ourselves and in each other until the warmth of our own

174

tenderness and yearning for each other makes us alive again'.[40]

So the language of grace which such a redemptive spirituality engenders is no nebulous promise. Grace is the sensitive awareness of one's own bodiliness, personal strengths and strengths in relationship. It is the imaginative empathy to reach out to both the happiness and pain of another – 'to be is to respond', as Daniel Day Williams has said. This will build on relational strengths and empathetic gifts, and the quality of compassion already referred to. So women's circles of imaginative empathy reach out beyond the immediate experience of the pain of oppression and exclusion from Church or society, to the deeper, tragic situations of brutalized women at a world-wide level, to the pain of women throughout history. From there it reaches out to the suffering of all marginalized groups, women and men, the interweaving of all oppressions, and from there to the root of all suffering in the evil which grips the world and cries for redemption.

Sam Keen, a contemporary American writer, recognized the redemptive value of this imaginative empathy, although he has not seen that it is the particular contribution of woman, nor that it can be used by society to victimize her. He writes:

> The capacity for radical empathy, which is the essence of agape, is universal. The human imagination can inhabit any conceivable being. We are all Protean creatures. . . A mother watches a doctor as he prepares to give her child an injection. As the needle touches the child she winces. At this moment she has broken her identity with her own body and entered the body of her child. . . The more feelingful, undefended our bodies becomes, the wider the range of our knowing.[41]

Secondly, the language of grace is the language of claiming power-in-relation, the power which drives to the making of justice, which *stands with*, in solidarity with suffering humanity. This is grace as power-in-relation which in Christian theology is encapsulated by the mystery of Jesus' outpouring of the Spirit in history, the Spirit which drives to right relation. In a sacramental spirituality the language of redeeming grace which creates right relation will envision the sacramental moments as *both* the celebration of mutual loving actually experienced, and the celebration-in-hope of authentic conversions to mutuality, where the reality of the present moment is far from the case. Many of the celebrations of 'Woman-Church' are of this nature: that the Church be recalled to the true sense of mutuality.

Finally, it is the language of grace, or graced relationality, because it respects not just the dimension of self-affirmation, independence and autonomy, which is also open to the divine source of grace, but the integrative dimension which pushes further, beyond the level of experienced reciprocity, to new sources of redemptive relationality, to the point where clinging to sanity threatens to drown sensitivity. It is at this point that redemptive mutuality can take on the language of self-sacrifice, surrender and self-giving love. Mutuality becomes understood not merely as a self-created reality, totally under human control, but as the givenness, the giftedness of a many-layered universe which is both gift (creation), and yet to be fashioned (redemption).

This is the insight of feminist spirituality of our particular age: that the full becoming of the universe will reach fruition not through an ethic of domination, competitiveness, individualism and military strength, but through the living out of increasing depth of redemptive relatedness.

Notes

Chapter 1: Feminist Redemption: Reclaiming the Symbol

1 Adrienne Rich, 'Natural Resources', in *The Dream of a Common Language* (New York and London, W. & W. Norton, 1978), p. 64.
2 This is part of the wider discussion in philosophy of religion as to the nature of religious language. Feminist theologians take a variety of positions, from Mary Daly's rejection of traditional religious terminology in favour of a 'radical new naming' to an exploration, like that of Sallie McFague, of new models and metaphors, while still remaining within the Christian and biblical framework. See *Metaphorical Theology; Models of God in Religious Language*, London, SCM, 1975; *Models of God*, London, SCM, 1986.
3 A phrase made famous by Nelle Morton, 'Beloved Image', in *The Journey is Home* (Boston, Beacon, 1985), pp. 127-8.
4 ibid., p. 127.
5 *The Underside of History: A View of Women through Time* is the title of the book by Elise Boulding, Boulder, CO, Westview Press 1898, 2nd edn 1981.
6 Euripides, *Medea*, tr. Rex Warner (University of Chicago Press 1970), lines 410-20.
7 C. M. Halkes, *Zoekend naar wat verloren ging* (Ten Have, Baarn, 1985), p. 29.
8 Adrienne Rich, 'Natural Resources', in *The Dream of a Common Language*, op. cit., p. 67.
9 I am aware of the complexity of this issue and the morality of the armed struggle. For an official statement of the Catholic Church's position on liberation movements, śee the Congregation for the Doctrine of the Faith's document, *Christian Freedom and Liberation*, London, Catholic Truth Society 1987. My point here is to analyse the limits of the human experiences to which 'liberation' and 'redemption' point.
10 Catholic Institute of International Relations, Regent's Park College, London, May 1988, on Vigilantes and Death Squads in El Salvador, South Africa and the Philippines.
11 E. Schillebeeckx, *Gerechtigheid en Liefde, Genade en Bevrijding*, Bloemendaal, Uitgeverij H. Nelissen BV, 1977; London, SCM, 1980, tr. J. Bowden as *Jesus: An Experiment in Christology*.
12 Sharon Welch, *Communities of Resistance and Solidarity: A Feminist Theology of Liberation* (Maryknoll, NY, Orbis 1985), p. 89.
13 Here I am specifically challenging Paul Tillich's 'method of correlation', that is, the correlation between human experience and biblical revelation. I see a much clearer unity between human experience and 'religious' experience. There is a deeper problem - alluded to above, in

the quotation from 'Beloved Image', namely, that of articulating and naming 'raw' experience, when the necessary concepts do not exist.

14 Matthew Fox, ed., *Western Spirituality, Historical Roots, Ecumenical Routes* (Santa Fe, NM, Bear and Co, 1981) p. 4. Fox's work is important in encouraging us to develop a new theology of creation. But he is in danger of idealizing, and, by not engaging in any serious social analysis, of not being sensitive enough to vicious circles of deprivation in which people find themselves. See also *Original Blessing, A Primer in Creation Spirituality*, Santa Fe, NM, Bear and Co, 1981; *A Spirituality named Compassion: the Healing of the Global Village: Humpty Dumpty and Us*, San Francisco, Harper and Row, 1979.

15 This is particularly important for developing a theology of the cross, which I attempt in a later chapter.

16 The answer is, of course, Yes, as feminist theologians engage in this activity. See Elizabeth Moltmann-Wendel, *The Women around Jesus*, London, SCM, 1982, tr. J. Bowden; Rosemary Radford Ruether, *Mary, the Feminine Face of the Church*, London, SCM, 1977; Marina Warner, *Alone of All Her Sex*, London, Weidenfeld and Nicolson, 1976.

17 This slogan is from *Redstocking*, April 1969, reprinted in *Feminist Review* (New York, Random House 1975), p. 205.

18 Elizabeth Schüssler-Fiorenza, 'Feminist Theology as a critical study of Liberation', in *Theological Studies*, 36/4, pp. 605–6. See also 'Claiming the Centre: a critical feminist theology of liberation', in *Womanspirit Bonding*, eds. Janet Kalven and Mary I. Buckley (New York, Pilgrim 1984), pp. 293–309.

19 Rosemary Radford Ruether is one of the feminist theologians who is most prolific in her writings, with about twenty books and over 200 articles to her name. She is also an example of someone who puts into practice the theology she believes in. She is tireless in her condemnation of oppression and has personally involved herself in issues ranging from sexual politics, civil rights, anti-semitism, nuclear power, ecological issues, and lately, the rights of Palestinians. She, too, is concerned about the fact that white, middle-class feminists often lack sensitivity towards black women and even towards poor white women.

20 Letty Russell, *Human Liberation in a Feminist Perspective*, Philadelphia, Westminster, 1974.

21 Isabel Carter Heyward, 'An Unfinished Symphony of Liberation', in *Journey of Feminist Studies in Religion*, 1 January 1985, pp. 25–32.

22 'Womanist' is a term coined from the writings of the novelist Alice Walker. One of the leaders of the movement is the black theologian and Episcopalian priest, Kelly Brown.

23 Rosemary Ruether, *Sexism and God-talk* (London, SCM, 1983), pp. 18–19: 'the critical principle of feminist theology is the promotion of the full humanity of women. Whatever denies, distorts or diminishes the full humanity of women is therefore appraised as not redemptive. Theologically speaking, whatever diminishes or denies the full humanity of women must be presumed not to reflect the divine, or to reflect the authentic nature of things.'

24 Michel Foucault, *Power/Knowledge: Selected Interviews and Other*

Writings 1972–1977, New York and London, Pantheon, 1980; tr. C. Gordon, L. Marshall, J. Mepham and K. Soper.

25 Foucault, ibid., p. 81.

26 Sharon Welch, *Communities of Resistance and Solidarity: A Feminist Theology of Liberation*, Maryknoll, NY, Orbis, 1985: I feel Sharon Welch's despairing conclusion is because she has taken on board Foucault's premisses too uncritically. I argue that the standpoint of liberation theology is firmer than she realizes, and that it contains other dimensions than revolt and protest.

27 John-Baptist Metz, *Faith in History and Society: Towards a Practical Fundamental Theology* (New York, Crossroads, 1980), pp. 66–7.

28 Foucault, op. cit., p. 193.

29 For example, in Dale Spender's book, *Women of Ideas (and What Men Have Done to Them)*, London, Melbourne and Boston, Methuen, 1982.

30 Here I follow the dating proposed by Sheila Collins, *A Different Heaven and Earth* (Valley Forge, PA, Judson Press, 1974), p. 107: pre-patriarchal period – c. 4,500BC, early patriarchy – 4,500–600BC, patriarchy triumphant – 600BC to the present.

31 Mary Daly, *Pure Lust: Elemental Feminist Philosophy* (Boston, Beacon, 1984), pp. 171–3.

32 Schillebeeckx, op cit., p. 676.

33 This is not to assert that Paul himself obeyed this injunction. We know from texts such as Rom. 16.1 Cor. 16.19 Phil. 4.3; Col. 4.15, that women were Paul's co-workers and teachers. The text of Gal. 3.28 – 'In Christ there is neither Jew nor Greek, male nor female, slave nor free' – has been particularly inspirational for feminist writers.

34 See Rosemary Ruether, 'Misogynism and Virginal Feminism in the Fathers of the Church', in *Religion and Sexism: Images of Women in the Jewish and Christian Tradition*, ed. Ruether (New York, Simon and Schuster, 1974), pp. 150–83.

35 Ruether, *Sexism and God-Talk*, p. 97.

36 Martin Luther, *Lectures on Genesis 2.18*, in *Luther's Works*, Vol. 1, ed. Pelikan (St Louis, Concordia, 1958), p. 111.

37 Rosemary Ruether, 'Feminist Theology in the Academy: how not to re-invent the wheel', in *Christianity and Crisis*, 4 March 1985, pp. 57–62.

38 Dell Martin, *Battered Wives* (New York, Volcano Press, 1970), p. 2.

39 Hesiod, *Works and Days* (Harmondsworth, Penguin, 1973), tr. Dorothea Wender, lines 47–105.

40 Here I argue against the extreme stance taken by some feminist theologians who reject the cross and attitude of self-sacrifice completely. Mary Daly, for example (quoting Helen Diner), asserts that 'in Christianity the Tree of Life becomes the torture cross of the world' (*Gyn/ecology: the Metaethics of Radical Feminism*, Boston, Beacon, 1978, p. 79). This will be pursued further in a later chapter.

41 Edwina Hunter, 'Reflections on the Christa from a Christian Theologian', in 'Reflections on the Christa', in *Journal of Women in Religion*, 4 February 1985, p. 30.

42 Chaim Potok, *My Name is Asher Lev* (New York, Heinemann, 1972), p. 329.

Chapter 2: Seeking New Structures: Building New Foundations

1 Margaret Atwood, *Surfacing* (London, Virago Press, 1979), p. 191.
2 Here I speak only of the recent surfacing of the Women's Movement of the sixties. What must never be forgotten is the breakthrough work of the nineteenth-century feminists and novelists, such as the Brontë sisters, George Eliot (Mary Ann Evans) and Mrs Gaskell.
3 Eric Erikson, *Childhood and Society*, London, Penguin, 1950.
4 The figures often cited for the number of women burnt as witches – 11 million – could be exaggerated, it is said, so that the number is equivalent to the number of Jews killed in the Holocaust.
5 Mary Daly, *Gyn/ecology: the Metaethics of Radical Feminism* (Boston, Beacon, 1978), p. 190.
6 Adrienne Rich, *Of Women Born* (New York, Bantam, 1976), p. 168, cited by Daly in op cit., p. 258.
7 The idea that God demanded the murder of the Beloved Son, Jesus, and thus sanctioned child-abuse, is contained in an unpublished paper, by Joann Carlson Brown and Rebecca Parker, *For God so Loved the World*, September, 1986. I consider this to be the lunatic fringe of feminist redemption theology.
8 See Jon Sobrino, *Christology at the Crossroads* (London, SCM, 1978), p. 225 (acknowledging a debt to Jürgen Moltmann, *The Crucified God*, Munich, Kaiser Verlag, 1973; London, SCM, 1974, tr. R. A. Wilson & J. Bowden).
9 S. Kierkegaard, *The Sickness unto Death* (Copenhagen 1854; New York, Doubleday, 1951, tr. V. Lowne), pp. 183–4.
10 Reinhold Niebuhr, *The Nature and Destiny of Man*, vols i, ii, New York, Scribner, 1964.
11 Judith Plaskow, in her doctoral thesis, *Sex, Sin and Grace, Women's Experience and the Theologies of Reinhold Niebuhr and Paul Tillich*, Yale University, 1975, has carefully examined the concepts of sin and grace in the work of these two theologians, finding their work inadequate from the point of view of women's experience.
12 Valerie Saiving Goldstein, 'The Human Situation – A Feminine View', in *Journal of Religion*, 40, 1960, pp. 100–112.
13 ibid., p. 108.
14 Erich Neumann, quoted by Judith Plaskow, op cit., p. 40. Eric Erikson makes the same point, namely that women harbour an 'inner space', which destines them biologically and ethically to care for infants. See 'Inner and Outer Space: Reflection on Womanhood', in *The Woman in America*, ed. R. Lifton (Boston, Greenwood, 1967), p. 6.
15 Carolyn Osiek, *Beyond Anger: On Being a Feminist in the Church* (Dublin, Gill and Macmillan, 1986), p. 69. She admits a debt to the research of Jean Majewski, *Without a Self to Deny: Called to Discipleship when We Were Yet Un-Persons*, Chicago, MTS Project, 1984.
16 Paul Tillich, *Systematic Theology*, vol. III, p. 144. Tillich's theology is suspect as regards women, judging from his wife's biography. See Hannah Tillich, *From Time to Time*, New York, Stein & Day, 1973.

17 Dorothy Dinnerstein, *The Mermaid and the Minotaur: Sexual Arrangements and the Human Malaise* (San Francisco, Harper & Row, 1976), p. 191.

18 ibid., p. 176.

19 This point is developed forcefully by Carolyn Heilbrunn, *Reinventing Womanhood* (London, Gollancz, 1979), pp. 125–170.

20 Sigmund Freud, in *The Ego and the Id,* in standard ed. of *Works* (SE), vol. 19, London, The Hogarth Press, 1923, ed. James Strachey.

21 Simone de Beauvoir, *The Second Sex* (Paris, 1949, 2 vols; London, Penguin, 1972, tr. H. M. Parshley), p. 16.

22 For criticism from a feminist point of view of Freud on sexuality, see Luce Irrigaray, *Speculum of the Other Woman*, New York, Cornell University Press, 1985, tr. Gillian E. Gill.

23 For example, the authoritative work of E. E. Maccoby and C. N. Jacklin, *The Psychology of Sex Differences*, Stanford, CA, Stanford University Press, 1974, in 634 pages of research produced only four fairly well empirically-established differences, namely, that girls, aged about 11, have a greater verbal ability, that boys in early adolescence have a greater visual-spatial ability, a greater mathematical quickness about the ages 12–13, and that boys of 2–2½ years old have greater aggressive tendencies. No other tendency was shown to have serious empirical backing.

24 Ruether, *Sexism and God-Talk*, (London, SCM, 1983), p. 111.

25 See André Guindon's article, 'L'Être-Femme', in *Église et Théologie*, 9 January 1979, pp. 103–68: 'La fémininité aussi bien que la masculinité est une version intégrale d'une existence finie de l'être humaine'.

26 Mary Daly, *The Church and the Second Sex* (Boston, Beacon, 1985, 3rd edn)., pp. 147–65.

27 Gertrud Von le Fort, *The Eternal Woman*, Germany, 1934; Milwaukee, 1962, tr. Placid Jordan, OSB.

28 ibid., p. 149. I omit from the discussion a more recent work, E. Danniels and B. Oliver, *Woman is the Glory of Man*, Maryland, 1966, tr. Angeline Bouchard, because it is an example of both pseudo-biology and pseudo-psychology, containing such statements as 'her brain is generally simpler and lighter than men's, which may explain her lesser capacity for deduction' (p. 162).

29 See Paul Evdokimov, 'Le Devenir du Féminin selon Nicolas Berdiaev', in *Contacts*, 29/100 (1977), pp. 265–73.

30 Thus Teilhard du Chardin, *Genèse d'une Pensée* (Paris, 1964), pp. 154–5.

31 Sheila Rowbotham, *Woman's Consciousness, Man's World* (Harmondsworth, Penguin, 1973), pp. 38–9.

32 This is developed by Paul Evdokimov, *La Femme et Le Salut du Monde*, (Paris, Desclée de Brouwer, 1978), p. 156.

33 'La tendresse du Dieu', ibid., p. 167.

34 Evdokimov, *Le Devenir du Féminin*, op cit; elsewhere Berdiaev opposes the masculine personal to the feminine cosmic and communal, in *De la Destination de l'homme; essai d'éthique paradoxale*, Paris, Je Sers, 1935.

35 Helena Deutsch (a disciple of Freud), *The Psychology of Women*, vols i and ii, New York, Grune, 1944–5.

36 F. J. Buytendijk, *La Femme, ses modes d'être, de paraître, d'exister*, Essai de Psychologie existentielle, Bruges, 1954.

37 G. Lombroso, *L'Âme de la Femme*, Paris, 1937, tr. L. Le Henaff.

38 K. Stern, *Refus de la Femme*, Essai, Editions HMH, Montreal, 1968.

39 C. J. Jung, 'On the Anima', and 'On the Mother Archetype', in *Archetypes and Collective Unconscious*, Collected Works, vol. 9, Princeton, New Jersey, Princeton University Press, 1969. Extended discussion about the effect of Jung's personality types on feminist theory is beyond the scope of this book. See Rosemary Ruether, *New Woman, New Earth* (New York, Harper and Row, 1975), ch. 6, pp. 37–61, and for a radical critique of the theory of archetypes, Naomi Goldenberg, 'Jung after Feminism', in *Beyond Androcentrism*, New Essays on Women in Religion, ed. Rita M. Gross (Montana, Scholars' Press, 1979), pp. 53–7.

40 For a discussion on the difficulties of the theories of androgynous being, see James Nelson, *Embodiment: An Approach to Sexuality and Christian Theology* (London, SCM, 1979) pp. 98–103. Again, the Russian Orthodox tradition is fond of the notion and sees the restoration of the lost integration of the human being as taking place within marriage.

41 Ann Belford Ulanov, *The Feminine in Jungian Psychology and Christian Theology*, Evanston, Northwestern University Press, 1971; *Receiving Woman: Studies in the Psychology and Theology of the Feminine*, Philadelphia, Westminster, 1981.

42 E. Whitmont, *The Return of the Goddess*, New York, Crossroads, 1984. See Part 4, 'A Myth For Our Times'.

43 A beginning is made by Demeris S. Wehr, *Jung and Feminism: Liberating Archetypes* (Beacon, Boston, 1987: London, Routledge, 1988).

44 Here I use the insights of Carol Gilligan, *In a Different Voice: Psychological Theory and Women's Development*, Cambridge, MA, Harvard University Press, 1982; also 'In a Different Voice: Visions of Maturity' in *Women's Spirituality* (ed. Joann Wolski Conn, New Jersey, Paulist 1986), pp. 63–87. Much of Gilligan's psychological inspiration derives from Jean Baker Miller, *Towards a New Psychology of Women* (Boston, Beacon, 1976; London, Pelican, 1978), and the research of the sociologist, Nancy Chodorow, *The Reproduction of Mothering: Psychoanalysis and the Sociology of Gender*, Berkeley and Los Angeles, University of California Press, 1978.

45 Carol Gilligan's criticisms of the developmental psychologists are mainly directed against her colleague, the late Lawrence Kohlberg, and his six-stage moral development theory. The particular polemic lies beyond the scope of this book: her real objection is that Kohlberg's schema grounds ethics in justice and fairness. This, says Gilligan, fits better the development of boys. Girls develop an ethical system based on care and responsibility.

46 Gilligan, op. cit., p. 6.

47 There is now a large amount of research on this topic. See Michelle Z. Rozaldo, and Louise Lamphere, eds., *Women, Culture and Society*, Stanford, 1974; Adrienne Rich, *Of Woman Born – Motherhood as Experience and Institution*, New York, Bantam, 1976; London, 1977.

48 Jean Baker Miller, *A New Psychology*, op cit., pp. 76–7.

49 Gilligan, *In a Different Voice*, op. cit., p. 173.

50 See Bruno Bettelheim, *The Uses of Enchantment – the Meaning and Importance of Fairy Tales*, New York, Random, 1975, for how myth can be used for the illumination of the child's psychological growth to maturity: again, his work is tinged with patriarchal thinking.

51 For an interesting investigation of the *female* hero, see Carol Pearson and Katherine Pope, *The Female Hero in American and British Literature*, New York, Bowker, 1981.

52 Bettelheim, op. cit., p. 195.

53 For an important study of the myth of Demeter and Persephone see Mara Lynn Keller, 'The Eleusinian Mysteries of Demeter and Persephone: Fertility, Sexuality and Rebirth', in *Journal of Feminist Studies in Religion*, 4/1/Spring 1988, pp. 27–54.

54 ibid., pp. 39–40. For further attempts to trace pre-patriarchal layers of myth, see Starhawk, *Truth or Dare: Encounters with Power, Authority and Mystery*, New York, Harper and Row, 1987.

55 George Eliot, *The Mill on the Floss*, London, Penguin, 1965.

56 ibid., p. 365.

57 loc. cit.

58 Martin Buber, *I and Thou* (Leipzig, 1923; London, 1970, ed. and tr. W. Kaufmann, T. & T. Clark), p. 69.

59 Dorothee Soelle, *To Work and To Love – A Theology of Creation* (Philadelphia, Fortress, 1984), p. 8.

60 Matthew Fox, *Original Blessing: A Primer in Creation Spirituality* (Santa Fe, NM, Bear and Co, 1981), p. 40.

61 For the systems theory, see E. Lazlo, *The Systems View of the World*, Oxford, Oxford University Press, 1957; *Introduction to Systems Philosophy*, London, Merrill, 1972; also L. Von Bertalanffy, *General Systems Theory*, London, Allen Lane, 1972.

62 See A. Koestler, *Janus*, London, Hutchinson, 1978.

63 Paul Davies of the University of Newcastle quoted by W. Schwarz, *The Guardian*, 6 April 1987.

64 This is also done by Fritjof Capra, *The Turning-Point: Science, Society and the Rising Culture* (New York, Simon and Schuster, 1982).

65 ibid, p. 29.

66 The key text on process thought is A. N. Whitehead, *Process and Reality*, Cambridge, Macmillan, 1929, corrected edn, New York, The Free Press, 1978. For an introduction to process thought, see J. Cobb Jr and D. Griffin, *Process Theology – an Introductory Exposition*, Philadelphia, Westminster, 1976.

67 Marjorie Hewitt Suchocki has written most on Whiteheadian process thought. See *God, Christ and Church*, New York, Crossroads, 1985. See also *Feminism and Process Thought*, ed. Sheila Greeve Davaney, New York and Toronto, E. Mellen, 1981.

68 J. Cobb and D. Griffin, *Process Theology*, op. cit., p. 14.

69 Doris Lessing, *The Four-Gated City* (London, Grafton, 1972), p. 588. This is the last novel in Lessing's five-novel sequence, *The Children of Violence*. I will follow the redemptive path of Martha Quest in chapter 4.

70 Marjorie Hewitt Suchocki, 'Openness and Mutuality in Feminist Thought and Action', in *Feminism and Process Thought*, op. cit., p. 63.
71 Whitehead, *Process and Reality*, op. cit., pp. 525–6.
72 ibid., p. 496.
73 Elizabeth Kraus, *The Metaphysics of Experience: A Companion to Process and Reality* (New York, Fordham, 1979), p. 162.
74 Feminist criticism – for example, Mary Daly, *Beyond God the Father* (Boston, Beacon, 1973), p. 188 – tends to accuse Whitehead of ignoring the process as it affects women, but warms to his focus on aesthetics. There is considerable anxiety lest Whitehead – in his di-polar concept of God – may in fact be smuggling in the old 'absolutes' of classical theism under a different guise.

Chapter 3: Women and Nature: A Redeeming Connectedness

1   Susan Griffin, *Women and Nature: the Roaring Inside Her* (New York, Harper and Row, 1978). p. 219.
2   See for example, Jack Dominian, *Marriage, Faith and Love*, London, Darton, Longman & Todd, 1984.
3   Paul Tillich, 'Nature mourns for a lost good,' in *The Shaking of the Foundations* (London, Penguin, 1963), pp. 82–92.
4   W. Wordsworth, 'On Westminster Bridge', in *Poems*, London, Penguin, 1977.
5   For a careful study of the Christian theological tradition towards nature, see Paul Santmire, *The Travail of Nature: The Ambiguity and Ecological Promise of Christian Theology*, Philadelphia, Fortress, 1985.
6   Gerard Manley Hopkins, 'God's Grandeur', in *Poems* (London, Penguin, 1953), p. 27.
7   Matthew Fox, talk given at St James's Church, Piccadilly, London, May 1987.
8   From 'The Unforked Message of Chief Seattle', in *Flesh and Spirit: A Religious View of Bi-Centennial America* (Gamaliel, Washington DC, Community for Creative Non-Violence 1976), p. 73.
9   Charlene Spretnak and Fritzjof Capra, *Green Politics: The Global Promise* (London, Grafton 1985), p. 233.
    The term 'deep ecology' was invented by the Norwegian ecologist, Arne Naess in the 1970s.
10 T. S. Eliot, *The Waste Land*, in *Poems* (London, Faber and Faber, 1963), pp. 61–80.
11 See *Parzifal* by Wolfram von Eschenbach, New York, Random, 1961.
12 See Edward Whitmont, *Return of the Goddess*, New York, Crossroads, 1982, especially Part 4, 'A Myth for our Times', pp. 149ff.
13 Original source unknown. I found it in Joan Chittester, *Winds of Change: Women Challenge the Church* (London, Sheed and Ward, 1986), p. 15.
14 Friedrich Schleiermacher, *Speeches on Religion to its Cultured Despisers*, New York, Harper and Row, 1958, tr. John Oman from 3rd German edn.

15 Rudolph Otto, *The Idea of the Holy*, Oxford, Oxford University Press, 1958, tr. John W. Harvey.

16 The words of Elizabeth Moltmann-Wendel from a talk given to Women in Theology (WIT), London, 1984.

17 John Cobb, 'Feminism and Process Thought: A Two-Way Relationship', in *Feminism and Process Thought*, ed. Sheila Greeve Davaney (New York and Toronto, The Edwin Mellen Press, 1987), pp. 32–61.

18 Thus Merlin Stone (in 'The Great Goddess – Who Was She?' in *The Politics of Women's Spirituality*, ed. Charlene Spretnak, New York, Doubleday, 1982), in her arguments for the historical reality of matriarchy, when the Goddess reigned supreme, is opposed by Sally Binford ('Are Goddesses and Matriarchies Merely Figments of Feminist Imagination?' in *The Politics of Women's Spirituality*, op cit., pp. 541–9), on the grounds that the historical basis is extremely shaky and that she has confused matriarchy with matrilineality. The latter channels the power held by males through female descent – therefore the supposed superiority makes no difference to the situation of women.

19 Rosemary Ruether, *Sexism and God-Talk* (London, SCM, 1983), p. 52.

20 Carol Ochs, *Behind the Sex of God: Towards a New Consciousness Transcending Matriarchy and Patriarchy*, Boston, Beacon, 1977.

21 ibid., p. 4.

22 Thus Carol Ochs, op. cit., pp. 47–50, quoting E. Neumann, *The Great Mother: An Analysis of the Archetype* (Princeton, NJ, Princeton University Press, 1955, 2nd edn 1963, tr. R. Mannheim), pp. 55–63.

23 Adrienne Rich, 'Natural Resources', in *The Dream of a Common Language* (New York and London, W. & W. Norton, 1978), pp. 65–6.

24 See Paul Santmire, *The Travail of Nature*, Philadelphia, Fortress, 1985. The theme is also tackled by Harvey Cox in terms of the opposition between nature and artefact throughout history, in *The Seduction of the Spirit: The Use and Abuse of People's Religion* (London, Wildwood House, 1974), pp. 280–301: 'It has re-appeared in various forms . . . in the medieval conflict between the Cathedral and the Desert . . . in today's life-style images projected by the astronauts and the rural communards. . . The biblical tradition never sanctifies one at the expense of the other. It supports both nature and artefact when they are appreciated as the provisional, limited creations that they are. It condemns both insofar as we escalate them into the sources of salvation' (p. 300).

25 Anne Conway's philosophy was known as 'monistic vitalism'. The Latin translation of her work appeared anonymously in a collection of three works, apparently written by Francis Mercury Von Helmont, Amsterdam, 1690. The English re-translation, with Anne Conway as supposed author, was *The Principles of the Most Ancient and Modern Philosophy, concerning God, Christ and the Creatures*, viz. of spirit and matter in general, whereby may be resolved all those problems or difficulties which neither by the School nor common modern philosophy, nor by the Cartesian, Hobbesian or Spinosian could be discussed. . . Printed in Latin at Amsterdam by M. Brown, Amsterdam, 1690, reprinted London, 1692. Preface to the English translation of 1692 states that the book is the work

of 'a certain English countess, a woman learned beyond her sex, being very skilled in the Latin and Greek tongues, and exceedingly versed in all kinds of philosophy'. See Carolyn Merchant, *The Death of Nature: Women, Ecology and the Scientific Revolution*, (San Francisco, Harper and Row, 1980), pp. 253–74. As she concludes, 'Anne Conway's philosophy ultimately did not go beyond the limits of the categories of substance philosophy within which she worked. Her monistic resolution of the mind-body problem, although more parsimonious than the dualism of Descartes, was simply a reduction of all reality to the idealist category of spirit' (p. 263).

26 Carolyn Merchant, op cit., pp. 261–2.
27 E. Neumann: *Amor and Psyche: The Psychological Development of the Feminine*, a commentary on the tale by Apuleius, Princeton, NJ, Princeton University Press, 1956, tr. Ralph Manheim.
28 Charlotte Brontë, *Jane Eyre* (Harmondsworth, Penguin, 1971), p. 346.
29 Elizabeth Barrett Browning, 'Aurora Leigh', in *Poems*, London, 1898, lines 883ff.
30 Emily Brontë, *Wuthering Heights* (London, Penguin, 1970), ch. 16.
31 This is the opinion of Emily's biographer, Winifred Guerin, *Emily Brontë*, Oxford, Oxford University Press, 1971.
32 'No Coward Soul is Mine', Emily Brontë, 2 January 1846, in *The Complete Poems of Emily Jane Brontë*, ed. from MSS by C. W. Hatfield, 1941, p. 191.
33 E. Brontë, *Wuthering Heights*, op. cit., ch. 16, p. 166.
34 ibid., ch. 9, p. 80.
35 ibid., ch. 9, p. 78.
36 For the new quest genre in feminist literature, see Annis Pratt, 'Women and Nature in Modern Fiction', in *Contemporary Literature*, XIII/4/ (1972), pp. 476–90.
37 Annie Dillard, *Pilgrim at Tinker Creek*, London, Picador, 1975.
38 Margaret Atwood, *Surfacing*, London, Virago Press, 1973.
39 ibid., p. 15.
40 ibid., p. 191.
41 Hildegarde of Bingen, *Scivias*, Eng. tr. from critical Latin edn by Bruce Hozeski, Santa Fe, Bear and Co, 1986, pp. 48ff.
42 Ntosake Shange, *For Coloured Girls who Commit Suicide when the Rainbow is not Enuf*, New York, Macmillan 1975.
43 Important sources for Goddess religion are: Carol Christ: 'Why Women Need the Goddess: Phenomenological Psychological and Political Reflections', in *Woman Spirit Rising*, eds. Christ and Plaskow (San Francisco, Harper and Row, 1979), pp. 273–89; Naomi Goldenberg, *The Changing of the Gods*, Boston, Beacon, 1979; Starhawk, *The Spiral Dance: The Rebirth of the Ancient Religion of the Goddess* and *Truth and Dare: Encounter with Power, Authority and Mystery*, San Francisco, Harper and Row 1979, 1987; Zsusannah Budapest, *The Holy Book of Womens' Mysteries*, I and II, Los Angeles, Susan B. Anthony Coven 1, 1979, 1980; Merlin Stone, 'The Great Goddess – Who Was She?' in *The Politics of Women's Spirituality*, ed. Charlene Spretnak, New York, Doubleday, 1982; 'The Three Faces of Goddess Spirituality', in ibid., pp. 64–70.

44 Rosemary Ruether, *Sexism and God-Talk* (London, SCM, 1983), p. 48.

45 For female divine biblical imagery, see Virginia Ramey Mollenkott, *The Divine Feminine: the Biblical Imagery of God as Female*, New York, Crossroads, 1983. Liturgical texts using divine female imagery include Janet Morley, *All Desires Known*, London, Women in Theology, 1988.

46 This is the Redstocking slogan referred to in Chapter 1.

47 This is a vital question posing many contemporary problems. If an openness to other positions is not preserved a narrow separatism is produced which will exclude all except an elitist few whose views are 'ideologically sound' on every issue.

48 Starhawk, 'Witchcraft as Goddess Religion', pp. 49–56, in *The Politics of Women's Spirituality*, op. cit. A detailed discussion on the Wicca Movement is beyond the scope of this book: suffice it to say that it is a craft, 'the craft of the wise', which is being re-discovered, re-claimed, with a basic orientation to the earth, whose great symbol, discovered in a rich diversity, is the Goddess, and whose only law is 'love all beings'. The coven is the basic unit of the craft, and covens generally meet in full moons and the major festivals. It usually contains thirteen members, bonded with considerable trust, and displays enormous diversity, both in membership and ritual. (A paraphrase of Starhawk, op. cit.)

49 Starhawk, op. cit., p. 51.

50 Starhawk, 'Ethics and Justice in Goddess Religion, in *The Politics of Women's Spirituality*, pp. 415–22.

51 Carol Christ, 'Why Women Need the Goddess', in *Woman Spirit Rising*. eds. Christ and Plaskow (San Francisco, Harper & Row, 1979), p. 277.

52 Adrienne Rich, *Of Woman Born* (New York, Bantam, 1976) pp. 93–4.

53 The story of Cassandra from a feminist point of view within the legends of the fall of Troy is attempted by Marion Zimmer Bradley, in *Firebrand*, London, Michael Joseph, 1988. Her creative reinterpretation of the legends is brilliant, though her character development is rather weak.

54 Mary Daly, *Beyond God the Father* (Boston, Beacon, 1973), p. 8.

55 Mary Daly, *Why Speak about God?* in *Woman Spirit Rising*, op. cit., p. 212.

56 Mary Daly, 'The Qualitative Leap beyond Patriarchal Religion', in *Quest*, 1 April 1975, p. 36.

57 ibid., p. 51.

58 The problem of the dark night of the soul, when it appears that God is absent, I develop in the following chapter.

59 A reinterpretation of death-images will be discussed in Chapter 6.

60 George Eliot, *Middlemarch*, ed. Gordon S. Haughton (Boston, Houghton Miflin, 1956), p. 287. First published in 8 parts, 1871–2.

61 ibid., p. 576.

62 ibid., p. 577.

63 ibid., p. 578.

Chapter 4: Affirming Self-Redeeming Self

1 F. Dostoevsky, *Crime and Punishment*, London, Heinemann, 1955, tr. Constance Garnett.

2 George Eliot, *Adam Bede*, London and Edinburgh, William Blackwood, 1859. I use the writings of Mary Ann Evans frequently: she is one of the best examples of a theologically educated literary woman with insights into the importance of relationships which drew her to battle with the restrictive framework of society in which she lived.

3 ibid., p. 442.

4 ibid., p. 457. The question as to why George Eliot felt unable to give her heroines the freedom she herself enjoyed is beyond my topic here. See *George Eliot* by Jennifer Uglow, London, Virago, 1987.

5 See Mary Grey, 'Reclaiming Mary', in *The Way*, October 1989.

6 Elizabeth Schüssler-Fiorenza, *In Memory of Her* (London, SCM, 1983), Introduction, p. xiv.

7 See, for example, Phyllis Trible, *Texts of Terror: Literary-feminist Readings of Biblical Narratives*, Philadelphia, Fortress, 1984; Carol Ochs, *Women and Spirituality*, New Jersey, Rowman and Allanheld, 1983, pp. 33–40 (Hagar), pp. 40–44 (Leah).

8 ibid., p. 33.

9 Evelyn Underhill, *Mysticism* (London and New York, 1907, 12th edn, New York, E. P. Dutton, 1961), pp. 169–70. The five movements to be explored are: awakening, purgation, illumination, dark night of the soul, and the unitive life. This is a slightly extended version of the ancient Christian mystical way of St Bonaventure, *De Triplici Via, The Works of St Bonaventure, Opuscula* vol i, London, 1960–70. This consisted of three movements: Via Purgativa, Via Illuminativa and Via Unitiva.

10 Teresa of Avila, *A Life*, from *The Complete Works of St Teresa of Avila*, ed. and tr. by E. A. Peers (London, Burns and Oates, 1951), vol i, p. 80.

11 Doris Lessing, *Martha Quest* (London, Collins, 1952); *A Proper Marriage*, 1954; *A Ripple from the Storm*, 1958; *Landlocked*, 1962; *The Four Gated City*, 1972. I acknowledge a great debt to Carol P. Christ's work on the quest theme – many of the ideas here are inspired by her writing. See *Diving Deep and Surfacing*, Boston, Beacon, 1980; 'Explorations with Doris Lessing in Quest of the Four Gated City', in *Women and Religion*, eds. Judith Plaskow and Joan Arnold Romero (Indiana University Press, 1974), pp. 31–61; Spiritual Quest and Women's Experience', in *Anima*, 1 February 1975, pp. 4–15. Also to Margaret Atwood, 'The Surfacing of Women's Spiritual Quest and Vision', in *Signs*, 11 February 1976, pp. 316–20.

12 Carol Christ, 'Spiritual Quest and Women's Experience', op. cit., pp. 11–12.

13 Doris Lessing, *The Four Gated City*, op. cit., p. 505.

14 Doris Lessing, *Martha Quest*, p. 53.

15 M. Proust *Remembrance of Things Past (À la Recherche du Temps Perdu)*, tr. C. K. Scott-Moncrieff, New York, Random, 1982.

16 Quoted by Mary Daly, *Pure Lust* (Boston, Beacon, 1984), pp. 171–3. The quotation comes from Virginia Woolf, *Moments of Being: Unpublished Autobiographical Writings*, ed. and introduced by Jeanne Schulkind (New York, Harcourt Brace Janovich, 1970), p. 70. Daly stresses the power of writing for remembering, and speaks of tidal memory which

restores interconnectedness with the cosmos. This is 'the tidal power of empowering memory', Daly, ibid., p. 175.

17 See M. and D. Linn, *The Healing of Memories: Prayer and Confessional Steps to Inner Healing*, New York, Paulist Press, 1974.

18 Carol Christ, *Spiritual Quest*, op. cit., p. 8.

19 This is the phrase of Adrienne Rich, in 'Natural Resources', in *The Dream of a Common Language*, New York and London, W. & W. Norton, 1978.

20 I develop some of Charles Williams's ideas in the following chapter because of his influence on the writer, Rosemary Haughton. See, in particular, his poems *Taliessin Through Logres*, London, Oxford University Press, 1938; *The Religion of the Summer Stars*, 1939; quotation from *The Region of the Summer Stars* (London, Editions Poetry, 1944), pp. 26–7. (Italics are mine.)

21 ibid. (my italics)

22 See Sandol Stoddard, *The Hospice Movement*, New York, Random, 1979. Victor and Rosemary Zorza, *A Way to Die*, New York, Knopf, 1980.

23 Elizabeth Kubler-Ross, *On Death and Dying*, London, Tavistock Publications.

24 This is a solution offered by Joann Wolski Conn and W. E. Conn, 'Self-Transcendence in the Spiritual Life', in *The Pedagogy of God's Image: Essays on Symbol and the Religious Imagination* (California, University of California, 1980), pp. 137–52: 'In the simplest terms, without a transcending self, there is no self-transcendence'.

25 See Chapter 3.

26 Mary Craig, *Blessings*, London, Hodder and Stoughton, 1975. Here I am in no way condoning evil or attempting to solve the problem. The focus is on self-transcendence.

27 Carol Christ, *Explorations with Doris Lessing*, op. cit., p. 58.

28 Doris Lessing, *The Four Gated City*, op. cit. pp. 38–39.

29 ibid., p. 236.

30 Carol Christ, *Explorations with Doris Lessing*, op. cit., p. 58.

31 Simone Weil, *Waiting on God*, London, Fontana, 1951, tr. Emma Crawford.

32 From *Simone Weil*, by Simone Petrément (London and Oxford, Mowbray, 1976), tr. Raymond Rosenthal, p. 422.

33 See Angela West, 'Watching at the Gates of Greenham: A Women's Theological Initiative', in *New Blackfriars*, 67/789/(1986), pp. 125–37.

34 Doris Lessing, *Martha Quest*, op. cit., p. 11.

35 Doris Lessing. *A Ripple in the Storm*, op. cit., p. 27.

36 Doris Lessing, *Landlocked*, op. cit., p. 275.

37 Kate Chopin, *The Awakening*, first published 1899, London, The Women's Press, 1978. This novel appeared shocking at the time, as it portrayed a woman's desperation in a meaningless marriage. Yet, like the women novelists I have already quoted, Kate Chopin appeared not to be able to create a positive solution for her heroine.

38 This point is discussed by Matthew Fox, 'Meister Eckhart on the Fourfold Path of a Creation-Centred Spiritual Journey,' in *Western Spirituality, Historical Roots, Ecumenical Routes*, op. cit., pp. 218–220.

Fox's discussion is of course centred within the polemic between creation and redemption centred spirituality. This quotation is from Eckhart's *Latin Works*, (Stuttgart, Koch and Kohlhammer, 1898), p. 156.

39 Teresa of Avila, *A Life*, vol i, from Peers, ed., and tr., *The Complete Works of St Teresa of Avila*, vol i, p. 16.

40 Carol Ochs, *Women and Spirituality* (New Jersey, Rowman and Allanheld, 1983), p. 127.

41 Matthew Fox, 'Meister Eckhart on the Fourfold Path', op. cit., pp. 224–9.

42 Carolyn Osiek, *Beyond Anger* (Dublin, Gill and Macmillan, 1986), p. 79.

43 Simone Weil, *Waiting on God* (London, Fontana, 1951), p. 34.

44 George Eliot, *Romola*, London, Smith, Elder and Co, 3 vols, 1863.

45 Doris Lessing, *The Four Gated City*, p. 491.

46 Carol Christ, *Explorations with Doris Lessing*, p. 153, quoting *The Four Gated City*, pp. 538–9.

47 Doris Lessing, *The Four Gated City*, p. 59. I leave aside Carol Christ's discussion on Martha Quest's prophetic-visionary powers in connection with Sufi mysticism, as here my focus is the redemptive path within the Christian mystical tradition.

48 Matthew Fox, *A Spirituality named Compassion: the Healing of the Global Village*, Minneapolis, Harper and Row, 1979.

49 Useful resources for this section, apart from works already cited, have been Constance Fitzgerald, 'Impasse and the Dark Night', in *Women's Spirituality: Resources for Christian Development*, ed. Joann Wolski Conn (New Jersey, Paulist Press, 1986), pp. 287–311; Mary E. Giles, 'Take Back the Night', in *The Feminist Mystic*, ed. Mary E. Giles (New York, Crossroads, 1982), pp. 39–70.

50 T. S. Eliot, 'East Coker', in *Poems* (London, Faber and Faber, 1963), p. 201.

51 St John of the Cross, *The Collected Works of St John of the Cross*, tr. Kieran Kavanaugh and Otilio Rodriguez, Washington DC, Institute of Carmelite Studies, 1973.

52 Constance Fitzgerald, 'Impasse and the Dark Night', op. cit., p. 291.

53 Mary E. Giles, 'Take Back the Night, op. cit., p. 39.

54 Carol Ochs, *Women and Spirituality*, op. cit., p. 131, uses the experience to explain the pain of mothers who must learn that their children need to develop alone and that they must let go of all love-as-possessive.

55 Alice Walker, *The Colour Purple* (New York, Harcourt Brace Jovanovich, 1982), pp. 164–8.

56 Adrienne Rich, 'The Spirit of Place', in *A Wild Patience Has Taken Me Thus Far* (New York, W. & W. Norton, 1981), p. 44.

57 Quoted from Simone Petrement, *Simone Weil* (London and Oxford, Mowbray, 1976, tr. Raymond Rosenthal, p. 516, from *A Letter to Schumann*.

58 Marjorie Suchocki, 'Anxiety and Trust in Feminist Experience', in *Journal and Religion*, 60/4(1980), pp. 459–71.

59 As D. S. Browning, in *The Atonement and Psychotherapy* (Philadelphia Fortress Press, 1966), p. 109, writes, 'When the tension between conditions of worth and denied experience becomes too great, the gestalt of the self may collapse and a psychotic break may occur.'

60 The phrase is that of Bernard Meland, a process philosopher, in *Fallible Forms and Symbols*, Philadelphia, 1976, discussed by Suchocki in 'Anxiety and Trust', op. cit., p. 462.

61 Constance Fitzgerald, 'Impasse and the Dark Night', op. cit., p. 290.

62 T. S. Eliot, *'Little Gidding'*, in *Poems*, p. 222.

63 ibid., *'East Coker'*, p. 202.

64 ibid., p. 200.

65 R. Kegan, 'The Evolving Self', in *Women's Spirituality: Resources for Christian Development*, New York, Paulist Press, 1986, pp. 88–106.

66 T. S. Eliot, *Ash Wednesday*, in *Poems*, p. 105.

67 Alice Walker, *In Search of our Mothers' Gardens* (New York, 1983; London, The Women's Press, 1984), p. 240.

Chapter 5: 'With you . . . the fires can burn again'

1 M. Buber, *I and Thou*, op. cit. (Edinburgh, T. & T. Clark, 2nd edn 1958), p. 18.

2 Daniel Day Williams, *The Spirit and the Forms of Love* (Welwyn, Herts, James Nisbet, 1968), p. 136.

3 ibid., p. 36.

4 C. Hartshorne, 'Introduction: the Development of Process Philosophy', in *The Philosophy of Process*, ed. D. Browning (New York, Harper and Row, 1965), p. xix.

5 Nikos Kazantzakis, *Report to Greco* (London, Cassirer, 1965), tr. P. A. Bien, p. 292: 'Blowing through heaven and earth, and in our hearts, and in the heart of every living thing, is a gigantic breath – a great Cry – which we call God. Plant life wished to continue its motionless sleep. . . But the Cry leapt within it and violently shook its roots: "Away! Let go of the earth, walk!". . . It shouted this way for thousands of eons; and lo! as a result of desire and struggle, life escaped the motionless tree and was liberated. . .'

6 John Taylor, *The Go-Between God* (London, Collins, 1974), ch. 1, 'Annunciation'.

7 Edwin Muir, *Collected Poems* (New York, Harper and Row, 1960), pp. 223–4.

8 Isabel Carter Heyward, *The Redemption of God: a Theology of Mutual Relation* (Washington DC, University Press of America, 1982), p. 162.

9 ibid., p. 9.

10 Carter Heyward, *Our Passion for Justice, Images of Power, Sexuality and Liberation* (New York, Pilgrim Press, 1984), p. 206.

11 ibid.

12 Carter Heyward, *The Redemption of God*, op. cit., p. 172.

13 Heyward, ibid., p. 80. For many American feminist theologians – like Carter Heyward and Carol Christ – Wiesel's novels, especially *Night* and *The Gates of the Forest*, were an introduction to the horrors of the Holocaust.

14 Eli Wiesel, *Night* (Les Editions de Minuit, 1958; London, Penguin, 1980), tr. Stella Rodway, p. 77.

15 J. Moltmann, *The Crucified God*, Munich, Kaiser Verlag, 1973; London, SCM. 1974.

16 Kwok Lui Pan, 'God Weeps with our Pain', in *New Voices for Reading*, eds. Pobee and Wartenburg-Potter (Geneva, World Council of Churches, 1986), pp. 90–5.

17 Debra Seidman, *The Voices of Women surviving the Holocaust: Women and Resistance*, quoted in Janice Raymond, *A Passion for Friends: Towards a Philosophy of Female Affection* (Boston and London, The Women's Press, 1986), p. 40.

18 Elizabeth Macalister, 'Women: Witnesses to the Resurrection – a Garden in a Cracked Soil', in *Sojourner*, 16 April 1987, pp. 15–17.

19 J. B. Metz, 'The Future in the Memory of Suffering', in *Concilium*, 8/6/1972, pp. 9–25; *Faith in History and Society: Toward a Practical, Fundamental, Theology* (New York, Crossroads, 1980).

20 E. Schillebeeckx, *Gerechtigheid en Liefde, Genade en Bevrijding*, (Bloemendaal, Uitgevery H. Nelissen BV, 1977; London, SCM, 1980), p. 697. Schillebeeckx also finds that he has failed to give a theological interpretation of the 'memoria passionis' of Jesus Christ.

21 Carter Heyward, 'Till Now We Had not Touched our Strength', in *Our Passion For Justice*, op. cit., p. 124.

22 Here I am building on the achievements of contemporary Christology in getting us at last to take seriously the humanity of Jesus and the journey by which he moved to divine self-consciousness. I am very influenced by the Christology of Jon Sobrino, who sees the crucified Jesus at the heart of liberation struggles, as well as by that of Dorothee Soelle, and the more recent relational Christology of Tom Driver, *Christ in a Changing World*, New York, Crossroads, 1980.

23 Gerd Theissen, *The Shadow of the Galilean*, London, SCM, 1987, tr. John Bowden. This highly imaginative historical novel explores the meaning of the appeal of the Zealot movement in first-century Palestine, and the reasons for its rejection by Jesus.

24 Marjorie Suchocki, 'Openness and Mutuality in Process Thought and Feminist Action', in *Feminism and Process Thought*, ed. Sheila Greeve Daveney (New York and Toronto, E. Mellen, 1981), p. 69.

25 Elizabeth Moltmann-Wendel, *A Land Flowing*, op. cit., pp. 137–48.

26 This is except for the third anointing story, where she is named by John as Mary of Bethany (John 12.1–8).

27 The significance of this is nowhere better described than by Elizabeth Schüssler-Fiorenza, *In Memory of Her* (London, SCM, 1983), pp. xiii–xiv.

28 That is, until feminist theology began to uncover other traditions. See Elizabeth Moltmann-Wendel, *The Women Around Jesus* (London, SCM, 1982), tr. John Bowden, pp. 15–48, where alternative Martha traditions are discussed.

29 Ilse Joseph, *Playing for Peace: A Survivor's Mission*, Lewes, Sussex, Book Guild, 1987.

30 Charles Péguy, quoted by M. Novak, *A Theology for Radical Politics*, New York, 1969.

31 See, for example, Raymond Brown's commentary, *Anchor Bible*, vol. 29, New York, Doubleday 1966.

32 Charles Williams, *The Figure of Beatrice*, London, Faber and Faber, 1950. The 'Beatrician moment' is when Dante first set eyes on Beatrice, a moment which determined the significance of his whole life.

33 Carter Heyward, with great insight, distinguishes between *relational* power (*dunamis*), and institutionally-conferred power (*exousia*).

34 Beverley Harrison, 'Keeping Faith in a Sexist Church', in *Making the Connections: Essays in Feminist Socialist Ethics*, ed. Carol R. Robb (Boston, Beacon, 1985), p. 263.

35 See Tom Driver, *Christ in a Changing World*, New York, Crossroads, 1981.

36 For example, the story of the Roman centurion, Luke 7.9: 'I tell you, not even in Israel, have I found such faith.'

37 Audre Lord, *Use of the Erotic: the Erotic as Power*, Brooklyn, Out and Out Books, 1978, quoted in Rita Nakashima Brock, 'The Feminist Redemption of Christ', in *Visions of Christian Feminism*, San Francisco, Harper and Row, 1984), p. 64.

38 Audre Lord, ibid.

39 Sally Gearhart, 'Energy Resourcement', in *Women and Values; Readings in Recent Feminist Philosophy*, ed. Marilyn Pearson (Belmont, CA, Wadsroth, 1986), pp. 220–30.

40 The notion of the co-inherence between all levels of existence was developed by poet and novelist Charles Williams. From a feminist and process point of view he is much too rigid in his categories. He saw the categories of divine/human as inter-penetrating but definitely as polarities. Williams had no concept of the divine as a category immanent within the human experience: there has rather to be an invasion from without.

41 Rosemary Haughton, *The Passionate God* (London, Darton, Longman & Todd, 1979). The idea of 'exchange' permeates the whole book.

42 ibid., p. 47.

43 Carter Heyward, *The Redemption of God* (Washington DC, University Press of America, 1982), p. 162.

44 Rosemary Haughton, op. cit., p. 153.

45 Charles Williams, 'Bors to Elayne: On the King's Coins', in *Taliessin Through Logres*, (Oxford, Oxford University Press, 1938), pp. 42–5.

46 Williams, *The Region of the Summer Stars*, London, Editions Poetry, 1944.

47 Heyward, 'Must Jesus be a Holy Terror?' in *Our Passion for Justice* (New York, Pilgrim Press, 1984), p. 216.

48 Rita Brock, 'The Feminist Redemption of Christ', in *Visions of Christian Feminism* (San Francisco, Harper and Row, 1984), pp. 54–74.

Chapter 6: The Placating of the Deity?

1 Marjorie Suchocki. 'The Challenge of Mary Daly', in *Encounter*, vol. 41, no. 4, 1980), p. 314.

2 I use as a basis for this reflection the three classifications of Gilbert Greshake, in 'Der Wandel der Erlösungsvorstellungen in der Theologie

Geschichte', in L. Scheffczyk ed., *Erlösung und Emancipatie*, Quaestiones Disputatae 61 (Freiburg, 1973), pp. 61–101. See also Greshake, 'Erlösung und Freiheit: Zur Neuinterpretation des Erlösungslehre Anselms von Canterbury' *Theologische Quartalschrift*, vol. 153, no. 4, 1973, pp. 323–45. In Anglo-Saxon circles the classification of Gustaf Aulen, in *Christus Victor: An Historical Study of the 3 Main Types of Atonement*, London, 1931, remains popular.

3 See T. Gorringe, *Redeeming Time: Atonement through Education*, London, Darton, Longman & Todd, 1986.

4 Irenaeus, *Adversus Haereses*, eds. Robertson and Donaldson, Translations of the Writings of the Fathers, vol. v, Edinburgh, 1968. Irenaeus first places the atonement within the context of incarnation and then shows how through Christ, God entered the world, so that Christ's victory is God's victory. Christ's 'recapitulation' meant the summing up of all things, illustrating the fulness of the meaning of the divine plan.

5 See Don S. Browning, *The Atonement and Psychotherapy*, Philadelphia, Fortress Press, 1966.

6 Greshake sees this early Greek notion of *paideia* or formation as the key idea summing up this notion of atonement.

7 Plato's myth of the cave, says Greshake, involves a liberating moment, when the philosopher, touched by God, brings people to conversion and responsibility for others.

8 Emil Brunner, *Christian Doctrine of Creation and Redemption*, Dogmatics, vol. 2 tr. Olive Wyon (Philadelphia and London, Westminster), pp. 283–5, has classified the basic motifs of atonement as (1) sacrifice, (2) penal suffering, (3) ransom payment, (4) victory over the powers of darkness, (5) Jesus as the Passover lamb through whom new communion with God is created. Daniel Day Williams has added a sixth: 'the god who dies and rises again, that his followers might have immortality'. See *The Spirit and the Forms of Love*, Welwyn, Herts, James Nisbet and Co.; 1968. Dillistone, in *The Christian Understanding of Atonement* (Welwyn, Herts. James Nisbet, 1968), broadens the theme to include tragedy, passion and integration.

9 See Anselm, *Cur Deus Homo?* tr. S. N. Deane, in *St Anselm: Basic Writings*, Introd. by C. Hartshorne (La Salle, IL, 2nd edn, 1962), pp. 191–302.

10 Greshake seems unaware of the similar approach of Shailer Matthews, *The Atonement and the Social Process*, New York, 1930, and 'Social Patterns and the Idea of God', in *The Journal of Religion*, vol. xi, 1931, pp. 158–78. Matthews stressed the interrelation between cultural, religious and political patterns and the way the death and atonement of Jesus is interpreted.

11 J. Ratzinger, *Introduction to Christianity* (Munich, 1968; tr. J. R. Foster, New York, Crossroads, 1969), p. 174.

12 Jonathan Edwards, *Works*, vol 11 (Edinburgh, 1796, 1806, 1834; New Haven, CT, Yale University Press, 1977), p. 575.

13 F. W. Dillistone, *The Christian Understanding of Atonement*, op. cit., p. 214.

14 G. Aulen, *Christus Victor* (London, 1931), p. 83.

15 Thus F. W. Barry, *The Atonement* (London, Hodder and Stoughton, 1968), p. 140.

16 Quoted by Daniel Day Williams, *The Spirit and the Forms of Love*, op. cit., p. 176.

17 Paul Tillich, *Systematic Theology*, vol ii (Chicago, James Nesbitt, 1957), p. 172. This was one of Tillich's great pastoral concerns. See his sermon 'You are accepted', in *The Shaking of the Foundations* (London, Penguin, 1963), pp. 155–65.

18 See J. Scott Lidgett, *The Spiritual Principle of the Atonement* (London, Charles Kelly, 1897), who had interpreted the atonement totally as satisfaction made to God for the sins of the world.

19 Greshake, *Erlösung und Freiheit*, op. cit., p. 344.

20 Aulen, *Christus Victor*, op. cit., pp. 133ff. But it is a mistake, Greshake claims, to play off Abelard and Anselm against each other, as liberal theology has tended to do. Abelard was trying to link subjective and objective aspects of atonement by showing that Jesus' death should arouse a corresponding love in our hearts: 'So our redemption is that supreme love produced in us by the passion of Christ, which not only frees us from slavery to sin, but acquires for us the true liberty of the sons of God.' (P. Abelard, *Commentary to the Romans*, 11, 3, 26, ed. E. M. Buytaert, *Corpus Christianorum* XI (Turnholt, 1969), tr. Frances Young, p. 118.

21 loc. cit.

22 Peter Abelard, *The Letters of Héloise and Abelard*, tr. Betty Radice (London, Penguin, 1974), pp. 149–50.

23 Eckhart, *Lateinische Werke*, quoted by Matthew Fox, '*Meister Eckhart on the Fourfold Path*', op. cit., p. 219.

24 I have omitted the 'forensic' or 'penal' theory of atonement of the Reformers as a special category (mentioned, for example, by Vincent Taylor, *The Cross of Christ* (London, Macmillan, 1957), pp. 72–3). This is because Greshake does not see this as a separate type, but rather blames nominalism, the Reformers, and liberal theologians for the distortion of 'satisfaction' teaching, particularly for erecting and maintaining the polarity '*aut* misericordia *aut* iustitia Dei' (*either* mercy *or* the justice of God). Greshake, *Erlösungsvorstellungen*, p. 88.

25 The theology of F. C. Baur is usually quoted as an example of this. (*Die Christliche Lehre von der Versöhnung in ihrer Geschichtlichen Entwicklung*, Tübingen, 1838).

26 Friedrich Schleiermacher, *The Christian Faith*, Eng. tr. of 2nd German edn (Berlin, 1830), eds. H. R. Mackintosh and J. S. Stewart (Edinburgh, T. & T. Clark, 1928), titles to section 94, p. 385, section 100, p. 425.

27 Horace Bushnell, *God in Christ* (New York, AMS Press, 1850), pp. 119–81; *The Vicarious Sacrifice*, vols i and ii (London and New York, 1866). Bushnell used the analogy of three types of law to classify atonement theories: (1) criminal – Christ bears the punishment for our sins; (2) civil – Christ offers himself as ransom payment for us; (3) ceremonial – Christ is the propitiatory offering which obtains remission of sin.

28 This motif was very influential for J. Moltmann, in *The Crucified God*,

Munich, Kaiser Verlag, 1973; London, SCM, 1974, and *The Trinity and the Kingdom of God* (Munich, 1980; London, SCM, 1981, tr. J. Bowden), and, as far as I can discover, can be traced back in the Russian Orthodox tradition before Berdyaev, to Boukharev, who was overwhelmed by the idea of the eternal immolation of the lamb before the foundation of the world. (See P. Evdokimov, *Le Christ dans la Pensée Russe* (Paris, Les Éditions du Cerf, 1970), p. 87.)

29 D. S. Browning, *The Atonement and Psychotherapy* (Philadelphia, Fortress Press, 1966), p. 73.

30 D. D. Williams, *The Spirit and the Forms of Love* (Welwyn, Herts, James Nisbet, 1968), p. 176.

31 Christina Rossetti, 'The Descent from the Cross', in *Poems* (London, 1918), p. 119.

32 Virginia Woolf, in *The Common Reader Second Series*, 'I am Christina Rossetti' (London, The Hogarth Press, 1932, 1986), p. 243.

33 M. Atwood, *Surfacing* (London, Virago Press, 1979), p. 14.

34 Barbara Hill Rigney, *Lilith's Daughters: Women and Religion in Contemporary Fiction* (Wisconsin, University of Wisconsin Press, 1982), p. 7.

35 See Robin Norwood, *Women who Love Too Much*, London, Arrow Books 1986.

36 'God in flesh was to maintain both Incarnation and creation: he must then be the victim of the choice of man. . . Creator and Victim then: the third function went with those two. He would not only endure, he would renew; that is, accepting their act, he would set up relations with them on the basis of that act. . . Creator, Victim, Redeemer, then. . .' Charles Williams, *The Forgiveness of Sins* (London, Faber and Faber, 1950), p. 131.

37 This mutuality of forgiveness, 'a mutuality between God and man which is also expressed between man and man' (Williams, ibid., p. 182), is beautifully described as 'a state of being into which we grow and not a series of acts which we exercise'.

38 Williams, 'The Last Voyage', in *Taliessin through Logres* (London, Oxford University Press, 1938), p. 86.

39 Williams, *The Region of the Summer Stars*, (London, Editions Poetry, 1944), pp. 26–7 italics are mine. Elsewhere Charles Williams has linked this with the bloodshedding of the Eucharist.

40 Daly does this especially in *Gyn/ecology* (Boston, Beacon, 1978; London, The Women's Press, 1979), pp. 79ff, where she describes what she sees as the harmful effects of cross theology for women. See my discussion, ch. 2, 'The Female Sin, choosing to be Victim'.

41 See Sheila Collins, *A Different Heaven and Earth?* (Valley Forge, PA, Judson Press, 1974), p. 203.

42 Helga Sorge, 'Wer leiden will muss lieben: Feministische Gedenken über die Liebe der Christliche Vorstellung vom gekreuzigte Gott', in *Feministiche Studien*, 11/1 (1983), pp. 54–69.

43 Yet she ignores the fact that Moltmann begins his book, *The Crucified God* (Munich, Kaiser Verlag, 1973; London, SCM, 1974) with a critique of false or unworthy interpretations of cross theology throughout history (ch. 1). It is known that he was following the insights of W. Popkes,

Christus Traditus (Zurich, 1967), and he has been well criticized for his views by, for example, Dorothee Soelle, who says, in *Suffering* (Stuttgart, 1973; Philadelphia, Fortress, 1975), p. 72, 'This author is fascinated by his God's brutality'.

44 See Kwok Lui Pan, 'God Weeps with our Pain', in *New Voices for Reading*, eds. Pobee and Wartenburg-Potter (Geneva, World Council of Churches, 1986).

45 Thomas Hardy, *Tess of the D'Urbervilles*, London, Dent, Everyman, 1984; George Eliot, *Adam Bede*, London and Edinburgh, William Blackwood, 1859; Mrs Gaskell, *Ruth*, London, Everyman, 1982.

46 Isaiah 53.7: '. . . like a lamb that is led to the slaughter and like a sheep that before the shearers is dumb'.

47 Rosemary Ruether, 'Can a Male Saviour Save Women?' in *Sexism and God-talk* (London, SCM, 1983), pp. 115–38; *If a Woman cannot represent Christ, Can Christ be said to represent women?* Guest lecture at Heythrop College, June, 1986.

48 This controversy lies beyond the scope of the book. That the incarnation is intrinsically linked with the male gender is the conservative position taken by The Vatican's Declaration on the Ordination of Women, *Inter Insigniores*, London, Catholic Truth Society, 1977. A similar essentialist position from an Anglican point of view is taken by J. Saward, *Christ and His Bride*, London, Church Literature Association, 1977. For a more balanced position, see Monica Furlong, ed., *Being Feminine in the Church*, London, SPCK, 1984.

49 This criticism is made by Francis Fiorenza, 'Critical Social Theory and Christology: Towards an Understanding of Atonement and Redemption as Emancipatory Solidarity', in *Proceedings of the Catholic Society of America*, 30 (1975), pp. 63–110.

50 See Elizabeth Moltmann-Wendel, *The Women around Jesus* (London, SCM, 1982), pp. 61–90.

51 Hans Küng, *Christ-Sein* (Munich, Piper Verlag, 1974), p. 400.

52 Phyllis Trible, 'An Unnamed Woman: The Extravagence of Violence' in *Texts of Terror*, (Fortress, Philadelphia, 1984), pp. 65–91.

53 Francis Fiorenza, op. cit., p. 101.

Chapter 7: 'A Passion to make and make again'

1 Daniel Day Williams, *The Spirit and the Forms of Love* (Welwyn, Herts, James Nisbet, 1968), p. 40. The value of Williams' thought is the depth of his pastoral experience and thus the depth of analysis he gives to the model of reconciling love, as well as his constant adherence to the process model, though willing to transcend it where necessary. His rootedness within the biblical tradition and his refusal to underestimate the problem of evil are also notable. These points are made by J. McQuarrie, 'Process and Faith: An American Testimony', in *Thinking about God* London, SCM, 1975), pp. 213–20. To this I would add, the sensitivity and concern with which Williams writes.

2 B. E. Meland, 'Analogy and Myth in Post-Liberal Theology', in *Process Philosophy and Christian Thought*, eds. Delwin Brown, Ralph E. James Jr, and Gene Reeves (Indianapolis, Bobbs Merrill Co, 1971), pp. 116–27.

3 Meland, *Faith and Culture* (Chicago, Illinois Univ. Press, 1955), p. 176.

4 D. D. Williams, 'Time, Progress and the Kingdom of God', in *God's Grace and Man's Hope*, San Francisco, Harper and Row, 1949.

5 A. N. Whitehead, *Process and Reality*, (Cambridge, Macmillan, 1929), p. 520. See also *Adventures of Ideas* (New York, Macmillan, 1933), p. 133.

6 B. Meland, *Faith and Culture* (Chicago, Illinois University Press, 1955), p. 184.

7 ibid., p. 187.

8 D. D. Williams, *The Spirit and the Forms of Love*, op. cit., p. 240.

9 ibid., p. 207.

10 See, for example, the systems theory of Murray Bowen, *Family Therapy in a Clinical Practice*, New York, Aronson, 1978. This is related to the atonement doctrine of Leander S. Harding, 'The Atonement and Psychotherapy', in *Anglican Theological Review*, vol. lxvii, no. 1 (1985), pp. 46–57.

11 Here I follow the thematic analysis of Don. S. Browning, *The Atonement and Psychotherapy*, Philadelphia, Fortress Press, 1966. He is very influenced by Carl Rogers, *Client-centred Therapy*, London, Constable and Co., 1951, with its insistence on the importance of four factors. These are the actualization tendency, the organismic valuing process, congruence, and the need for positive regard.

12 Browning, op. cit., p. 121. Rogers gives fifteen outcomes of the therapeutic process, ranging from the liberation from the self of deeper actualization tendencies of the organism, to the increase of positive response and acceptance of others (ibid., p. 128).

13 Browning, op. cit., p. 197.

14 This criticism is also made by other process thinkers, including Lewis Ford, *The Lure of God: A Biblical Background to Process Theism* (Philadelphia, University Press of America, 1978), pp. 87ff. I have omitted both Freudian and Jungian perspectives from this section because (1) these analyses are already very well-known, and (2) Browning's model fits very well with the process model and the model of mutuality which I develop. A recent work which attempts to link the psychotherapeutic process with the Christian healing and redemptive process is Scott Peck, *People of the Lie – the Hope for Healing Human Evil*, New York, Touchstone, 1983.

15 Marge Piercy, *Women at the Edge of Time*, New York, Fawcett, 1976.

16 Doris Lessing, *The Four Gated City* (London, Grafton Books, 1972), p. 516. There are beginning to be contemporary explorations and questionings of the boundaries of madness. For example, R. D. Laing, *The Divided Self: An Existential Study of Madness*, London, Pelican, 1972; and, from a feminist point of view, Elaine Showalter, *The Female Malady, Women, Madness and the English Culture*, 1830–1980, London, Virago, 1987.

17 R. C. Moberley, *Atonement and Personality*, London, Longmans, Green and Co., 1901.

18 H. Bushnell, *The Vicarious Sacrifice*, 2 vols, London and New York, 1866.

19 J. Scott-Lidgett, *The Spiritual Principle of the Atonement*, London, 1897.

20 H. H. Farmer, *The World and God*, Welwyn, Herts, James Nisbet, 1955.

21 H. S. Smith, ed., *Horace Bushnell*, New York, 1965.

22 Ann Douglas, *The Feminization of American Culture*, New York, Knopf, 1977.

23 See H. Bushnell, *Women's Suffrage: Reform against Nature* (New York, Charles Scribner, 1869), p. 66. The same argument, as was pointed out by Susan Brooks Thistlethwaite, *Metaphors for Contemporary Church* (New York, Pilgrim Press, 1983), p. 85, also restricts the *Church itself* to operating on a private sphere.

24 Rosemary Ruether, *Woman-Guides* (Boston, Beacon, 1985), p. 104.

25 H. Musurillo, ed., 'Acts of the Martyrs of Lyons and Vienne', in *The Acts of the Christian Martyrs* (Oxford, 1912), p. 75.

26 See P. Wilson-Kastner and G. R. Kastner *et al.* eds, 'The Martyrdom of Perpetua: A Protest Account of Early Christianity', in *A Lost Tradition: Women Writers of the Early Church* (Washington DC, University Press of America, 1981), pp. 1–32.

27 ibid., p. 3.

28 ibid., p. 27.

29 ibid., p. 27.

30 Unfortunately, Rosemary Ruether does this, in describing the relationship between Christianity and the establishment. She argues (*Woman-Guides*, p. 109), that the unity of creation/redemption itself carries a danger – for Christ needs to be set over-against the oppressive structures of society, otherwise Christology would be sucked back into a world view which sacralizes sexism, imperialism and slavery, seeing them as the 'order of creation'. Yet, in the argument I develop, I see the identity between creation and redemption not as sacralizing secular structures, but as *transforming* them.

31 Mary E. Giles, ed., *The Feminist Mystic* (New York, Crossroads, 1982), p. 7.

32 See Eizabeth Moltmann-Wendel, *The Women around Jesus* (London, SCM, 1982).

33 Elizabeth Moltmann-Wendel, *A Land Flowing*, op. cit., p. 132.

34 This has been well argued by Carol Pearson and Katherine Pope, *The Female Hero in American and British Literature*, New York, Bowker, 1981.

35 See *The Testimony of Christ's Second Coming* (1856), quoted in Rosemary Ruether, *Woman-Guides*, op. cit., pp. 127–31.

36 The words of Chung Sook Ja, a feminist minister from Korea, 'Reflections on the Christa from a Theological Educator', in *Reflections on the Christa*, ed. Edwina Hunter, in *Journal of Women in Religion*, 4 February 1985, p. 48.

37 Adrienne Rich, 'Natural Resources', in *The Dream of a Common Language* (New York and London, W. & W. Norton, 1978), pp. 65–66.

38 Matthew Fox, *Original Blessing* (Santa Fe, NM, Bear and Co., 1981), p. 195.

39 ibid., pp. 286–92.

40 Isabel Carter Heyward, 'Blessing the Bread: A Litany', in *Our Passion for Justice* (New York, Pilgrim Press, 1984), pp. 49–51.

41 The idea of the being of God as relatedness is developed by Dorothee Soelle, *To Work and To Love*, Philadelphia, Fortress, 1984. See p. 46: 'I am struck by the fact that verbs, not nouns, spring to mind. I need to wonder, to be amazed, to be in awe, to renew myself in the rhythm of creation, to perceive its beauty, to rejoice in creation and to praise the source of life. Listing these verbs reminds me of people who believe that God has created them and all creatures who trust in the goodness of creation.'

42 Quoted by Matthew Fox, 'The Spiritual Journal of the Homosexual and just about Everyone Else', in *A Challenge to Love: Gay and Lesbian Catholics in the Church*, ed. R. Nugent (New York, Crossroads, 1983), pp. 189–204.

43 Sara Maitland, 'Ways of Relating', in *The Way*, 26 Feb. 1986, pp. 124–33.

44 Phyllis Trible, *God and the Rhetoric of Sexuality* (Philadelphia, Fortress, 1978), especially 'Journey of a Metaphor', pp. 31–59. The linguistic basis of comparison is the link between *rah mim* (compassion), and *rehem*, (womb): 'Our metaphor lies in the semantic movement from a physical organ of the female body to a psychic mode of being. . . To the responsive imagination this suggests the metaphor of love as selfless participation in life. The womb protects and nourishes but does not possess and control. It yields its treasure in order that wholeness and well-being may happen.' (p. 33).

45 Phyllis Trible, ibid., p. 40.

46 The Hebrew text suggests the redemptive task of women specifically as participating in God's motherhood. Yet this is frequently obliterated from the commentaries by alternative translations or even emendations of the text.

47 The metaphor is also found in Isaiah 2.49, where again the focus is on the motherly, uterine-based compassion of Jesus: even if the compassion of earthly mothers fails (as it did in Lamentations 4.10), the womb-love for the child of Jahweh will not fail.

48 See Caroline Bynum, *Jesus as Mother: Studies in the Spirituality of the High Middle Ages*, Berkeley and Los Angeles, University Press of California, 1982.

49 Frances Young, *Can These Dry Bones Live?* (London, SCM, 1984), p. 50.

50 Elizabeth Moltmann-Wendel, *The Women around Jesus* (London, SCM, 1982), pp. 37–48.

51 For example, in the *Liber de Ortu Beatae Virginis Mariae*, ch. 13, in *Les Évangiles Apocryphes*, textes et documents, eds. Herne et Lejas, (Paris, 1911), pp. 96ff.

52 Such was the joy of Henry VIII of England in 1537, when the baby Edward VIII was born, that the boy's mother, Queen Jane, died almost unnoticed (J. J. Scarisbrick, *Henry VIII*, London, Eyre and Spottiswoode, 1968), p. 353.

53 See Ann Oakley, *Women Confined: Towards a Sociology of Childbirth* (Oxford, Martin Robinson, 1980); Adrienne Rich, *Of Woman Born*, New

York, Bantam, 1976. Positive attitudes are developed by – among others – Sheila Kitzinger, *The Experience of Natural Childbirth*, London, Penguin, 1978.

54 Thus R. Brown, J. A. Fitzmyer, R. E. Murphy, *Jerome Biblical Commentary*, vol. i, (London Geoffrey Chapman, 1968), p. 75.

55 Quoted by Mary Daly, *Gyn/Ecology* (Boston, Beacon, 1978), p. 258: source is Adrienne Rich, *Of Woman Born* (New York, W. W. Norton, 1976), p. 168.

56 Thus Mary Hayter, *The New Eve in Christ: The Use and Abuse of the Bible in the Debate about Women in the Church* (London, SPCK, 1987), p. 114.

57 Mary Daly, 'The Qualitative Leap', in *Quest*, 1 April 1975, p. 126.

58 ibid.

59 Mary Condren, 'Patriarchy and Death', in *Womanspirit Bonding*, eds. Janet Kalven and Mary Buckley (New York, Pilgrim Press, 1984), p. 10, quoting M. Eliade, *The Rites and Symbols of Initiation* (New York, Harper and Row, 1975), p. 30.

60 Nancy Jay, 'Sacrifice as Remedy for Having Been born as Woman', in *Immaculate and Powerful: The Female in Sacred Image and Saving Reality*, eds. Clarissa W. Atkinson, Constance R. Buchanan and Margaret R. Miles (Boston, Beacon, 1985), pp. 283–301.

61 Charlotte Perkins Gilman, *His Religion and Hers: The Faith of our Fathers and the Work of our Mothers* (London, 1924), p. 160.

62 Simone Weil, *Some Reflections on the Love of God*, in *Gateway to God*, op. cit., p. 80.

63 Simone Petrement, *Simone Weil*, tr. R. Rosenthal (London and Oxford, Mowbrays, 1976). For her asceticism and attitude to eating, see Judith Van Herik, 'Simone Weil's Religious Imagery: How Looking Becomes Eating', in *Immaculate and Powerful*, op. cit., pp. 260–82; also Ann Loades, *Searching For Lost Coins: Explorations in Christian Feminism* (London, SPCK, 1987), pp. 43–57.

64 Hildegarde of Bingen, in *Scivias* (Santa Fe, NM, Bear and Co. 1986), pp. 13–14.

65 Frances Young, *Can these Dry Bones Live?* (London, SCM, 1984), p. 58.

66 D. Soelle, *To work and To Love* (Philadelphia, Fortress, 1984), p. 75.

67 The theme is explored by Carol Ochs, *An Ascent To Joy: Transforming Deadness of Spirit* (Indiana, University of Notre Dame Press, 1986). She touches on the theme in *Women and Spirituality* (New Jersey, Rowman and Allaheld, 1983) p. 82, as well as in *Symbols of Death and Life*, in *Crosscurrents*, vol. 33, no. 4 (1985), pp. 387–92. She uses the symbols of death developed by Robert Lifton, *The Broken Connection: on Death and the Continuity of Life*, New York, Basic, 1980.

68 Carol Ochs, *An Ascent to Joy*, op. cit., p. 37.

69 ibid., pp. 45–6.

70 Adrienne Rich, 'The Spirit of Place', in *A Wild Patience Has Taken Me Thus Far* (New York, W. & W. Norton, 1981).

71 So says Susan Brooks Thistlewaite, *Metaphors for the Contemporary Church* (New York, Pilgrim Press, 1983), pp. 93–100.

72 Carter Heyward, *The Redemption of God* (Washington DC, University Press of America, 1982), p. 15.

73 David Shields, 'Christ: A Male Feminist View', in *Encounter*, vol. 45, no. 3 (1984), pp. 221–32.

74 Susan Brooks Thistlethwaite, *Metaphors*, p. 100.

75 Frances Young, *Can These Dry Bones Live?* op. cit., p. 21, quoting John Steinbeck, *To a God Unknown*, New York, 1935.

Chapter 8: Struggling to Birth: The Reclaiming of Redemption

1 'The Death of Feminism' was the title of a leader in *The Times Educational Supplement*, December 1987, where it was claimed that feminism in the sense of a struggle for equal rights was over, because the battle was won (!?) and also in the sense of offering an alternative ethic, because no such ethic had emerged.

2 Paul Oestreicher, *The Double-Cross*, London, Darton, Longman & Todd, 1986.

3 Sharon Welch, *Communities of Resistance*, (Maryknoll, NY, Orbis 1985), p. 89.

4 The idea of power, imagination and sensitivity as Christian virtues is developed by Evelyn E. Whitehead and J. D. Whitehead, *Seasons of Strength, New Visions of Adult Christian Maturing* (New York, Doubleday, 1986), pp. 75–147.

5 See Angela West, 'The Greenham Vigil: A Women's Theological Initiative for Peace', in *New Blackfriars*, vol. 67, no. 789 (1986), pp. 125–37.

6 See, among other works, Mary E. Hunt, 'Women Ministering in Mutuality: the Real Connections', in *Sisters Today*, no. 51 (1979), pp. 35–43; Elizabeth Schüssler-Fiorenza, *Gather Together in my Name – Towards a Christian Feminist Spirituality*, Women Moving Church Conference Proceedings, eds. Diann Neu, Maria Riley, Washington, 1982.

7 Elizabeth Schüssler-Fiorenza, *Bread not Stone: The Challenge of Feminist Biblical Scholarship* (Boston, Beacon, 1984), p. 19.

8 Elizabeth Schüssler-Fiorenza, *In Memory of Her* (London, SCM, 1983), p. 345.

9 Nelle Morton, 'The Rising Woman Consciousness in a Male Language Structure', in *The Journey is Home* (Boston, Beacon, 1985), p. 17.

10 Mary Field Belenky, Blythe McVicker Clinchy, Nancy Rule Goldberger, Jill Mattock Tarule, *Women's Ways of Knowing*, New York, Basic Books, 1986.

11 Morton, op. cit., p. 10.

12 Rita Nakashima Brock, 'The Feminist Redemption of Christ', in *Visions of Christian Feminism*, p. 74. (San Francisco, Harper and Row), p. 74. As Carter Heyward wrote (*The Redemption of God*, Washington, DC, University Press of America, 1986, p. 33): 'I draw attention to Jesus because I believe that what he did may be instructive in our understanding of the power in relational experience. . . I see in what he did the human capacity to make God incarnate in the world.'

13 This is one of the most important areas being currently developed. I cite

here only key works which build on the metaphor of mutuality, omitting works on specific issues like race, ecology and education. See Mary Daly, *Gyn/Ecology*, Boston, Deacon, 1978; Beverley Wildung Harrison, *Making the Connections: Our Right to Choose: Towards a New Ethic of Abortion*, Boston, Beacon, 1983; Mary E. Hunt, 'Transforming Moral Theology – A Feminist Ethical Challenge', in *Concilium* vol. 182, no. 6 (1985) pp. 84–90; Barbara Hilkert Andolson, Christine E. Gudorf, Mary E. Pellauer, eds., *Women's Consciousness, Women's Conscience: A Reader in Feminist Ethics*, Minneapolis, Harper and Row, 1985.

14 Beverley Harrison, 'Human Sexuality and Mutuality', in *Visions of Christian Feminism*, p. 148. Harper and Row, 1984.

15 Irene Claremont de Castellejo, *Knowing Woman – A Feminine Psychology*, San Francisco, Harper and Row, 1973.

16 Mary Hunt, 'Transforming Moral Theology', *Concilium* vol. 182, 6 (1985), p. 88.

17 ibid.

18 ibid. Yet it must be remembered that defining lesbianism in these terms is still controversial and is not the only feminist position. For example, Letha Dawson Scanzoni, in 'Lesbianism and Homophobia: A Discussion', in *Woman-Spirit Bonding*, Janet Kalven and Mary I. Buckley, eds. (New York, Pilgrim, 1984), p. 261, does not define lesbianism in relational terms: 'The definition of myself as a lesbian cost me in my life and has also clarified certain things. It is a very complicated thing. I think I am now a lesbian. That has changed a certain focus in my life. Being lesbian is almost an epistemological position that goes beyond commitment. I don't know any vision of sexuality, sexual community and relationships that satisfies me.'

19 See Janice Raymond, *A Passion for Friends*, (Boston and London, The Women's Press, 1986), p. 7.

20 ibid., p. 23.

21 Ursula King, *Voices of Protest, Voices of Promise*, The Hibbert Lecture, London, Hibbert Trust, 1984.

22 See Leila Berg, *Death of a Comprehensive*, London, Penguin, 1968.

23 Simone Weil, *Waiting on God* (London, Fontana, 1951), p. 114.

24 Iris Murdoch, *The Sovereignty of the Good* (London, Routledge and Kegan Paul, 1970), p. 37.

25 Nelle Morton, *Educating for Wholeness*, Address to World Federation of Methodist Women, Dublin, 1976.

26 See Mary Field Belenky *et al.*, *Women's Ways of Knowing* (New York, Basic Books, 1986), p. 218.

27 Sara Ruddick, 'Maternal Thinking', in *Feminist Studies* 6, Summer 1980.

28 *Women's Ways of Knowing*, loc. cit.

29 Adrienne Rich, 'Natural Resources', in *The Dream of a Common Language*, New York and London, W. & W. Norton, 1978.

30 Ivan Illich, *De-Schooling Society*, London, Penguin, 1973; Paulo Freire, *Pedagogy of the Oppressed*, London, Penguin, 1972, tr. Myra Bergman-Ramos; Leonardo Boff, *Ecclesio-Genesis – Basic Communities Re-invent the Church*, Brazil, 1977; New York, Dublin and Sydney, Orbis, 1986, tr. R. B. Barr.

31 For example, Gustavo Gutierrez, *A Theology of Liberation, History, Politics and Salvation,* Lima, 1971; Maryknoll, NY, Orbis, 1973.

32 George Worgul, *From Magic to Metaphor – A Validation of Christian Sacrament,* New York, University Press of America, 1980. The theme is also developed by such contemporary writers on the sacraments as Bernard Cooke, *Sacraments and Sacramentality,* Mystic, Connecticut, 23rd Publications, 1983, and Tad Guzie, *A Book of Sacramental Basics,* New Jersey, Paulist Press, 1982.

33 E. Dussel, 'The Bread of the Eucharistic Celebration as a Sign of Justice in the Community', in *Concilium* vol. 152, no. 2 (1983), pp. 56–65 tells the now celebrated story of Bartolomé de Las Casas, the Spanish priest in Mexico, who could not celebrate the Eucharist because, on meditating on the text of Ecclesiasticus 34.21, he realized that the bread he was blessing was the life of the poor. He freed his slaves and devoted himself to the work of justice. He could then once more celebrate the Eucharist.

34 Tissa Balasuriya, *The Eucharist and Human Liberation,* London, SCM, 1979.

35 Monica Hellwig, *The Eucharist and the Hunger of the World,* New Jersey, Paulist Press, 1979; Thomas Cullinan, *The Passion of Political Love,* London, CIIR, 1982.

36 Rosemary Ruether, *Sexism and God-Talk* (London, SCM, 1983), p. 138.

37 John Robinson has rightly declared, (in *The Body,* London, 1952, quoted by Rosemary Haughton, *The Passionate God* (London, Darton, Longman, and Todd, 1979), p. 174): 'It is almost impossible to exaggerate the materialism and crudity of Paul's doctrine of the church as literally now the Resurrection-Body of Christ'.

38 Elizabeth Schüssler-Fiorenza, *In Memory of Her* (London, SCM, 1983), p. 350.

39 Marjorie Suchocki, *God, Christ and Church,* op. cit., (New York, Crossroads, 1985), p. 206.

40 Rita Brock, 'The Feminist Redemption of Christ', in *Visions of Christian Feminism* (San Francisco, Harper and Row, 1984), p. 67.

41 Sam Keen, *The Passionate Life: Stages of Loving,* San Francisco, Harper and Row, 1983.

Index

Abelard, Peter 114–15, 185

Anselm 110; atonement theory of 112–16, 124–5, 194

atonement: and Feminist theology 13–14, 109–10, 118–25, ch. 7 *passim*; Greek model 110–12; Latin model 112–16, 124–5, 145, 194; modern models 116–18; in process thought 127–131; and social processes 194; in penal theory 195; Bushnell's types 195

Atwood, Margaret 15, 51, 71, 82, 119, 148, 180

Balasuriya, T 171, 204

Beauvoir, Simone de 20, 181

Belenky, Mary Field 202

Berdiaev, Nicolas 22

Bettelheim, Bruno 28, 183

birth: as symbol 138–143; loss of symbol 143–6, 199

Blanchefleur 120

Blandina 135

Brock, Rita Nakashima 108, 158, 174–5, 193, 202, 204

Brown, Joann Carlson 180

Browning, Don S 131–2, 190

Bushnell, Horace 133–4, 195

Capra, Fritjof 33, 183

Cassandra, 55, 187

Castillejo, Irene Claremont de 160, 187

Chodorow, Nancy 25–7, 182

Christ: example of power-in-relation 95–103; and women in the Gospels 98–103; and Mary 101–3; passion for justice 105; victim symbolism 122–3; seen in suffering woman 135–7; in Shaker belief 138; and childbirth image 145–6; and cross symbolism 150–2; Body of 170–3

Christ, Carol 64, 188

Christa 13, 134, 137, 179

Christus Victor 111

Collins, Sheila 121, 179, 196

Condren, Mary 145, 201

Connectedness with nature 42–52

Cox, Harvey 185; *see* Nature

creation-centred spirituality 5–6, 178

cross and suffering of women 12–14; 173; and Via Purgativa 72; and Holocaust 91–3, 100–1; and Dark Night 75–80; and atonement 118–25; as central symbol 150–2

Daly, Mary re-membering 10, 188–9; witch-hunt 16–17, 180; critique of Whitehead 29–30, 184; cross theology and suffering 121, 144–5, 146, 179, 196; and eternal woman 21; new naming 56; male saviour 123, woman identified universe 163

Dark Night of the Soul 74–80

death 146–50

Demeter and Persephone 29–30, 48, 53, 183; *see* myth

Dillard, Annie 51, 186

Dinnerstein, Dorothy 19, 181

Douglas, Ann 134, 199

Eckhart, Meister 70–1, 115, 140, 148, 156, 189

King, Ursula 164, 203
Koestler, Arthur 32, 183
Kohlberg, Lawrence 204
Kung, Hans 124, 139, 197

lesbianism: definition of 203; and
    mutuality 161-5
Lessing, Doris: Martha Quest 34,
    132, 148, 183; journey to identity
    of Martha Quest 63-83
liberation: feminist theology as
    critical study of 7-11; limits of
    liberation theology 3-4, 10-11,
    153-7; feminist spirituality of
    153-7
Lord, Audre 103-4, 193
Luther, Martin 12, 179

madness 198
matriarchy 44-6
Meland, Bernard 127-9, 191, 198
memory, dangerous memory 9-10,
    94-5; as redemptive tool 65-7,
    93-5
Merchant, Caroline 186
Metz, Jean-Baptist: and dangerous
    memory 9-10, 94-5, 179; criticism
    of Schillebeeckx 94, 192
Miller, Jean Baker 26-7, 183
Moltmann, Jürgen ix, 36, 91-2, 121,
    139, 191, 195-6, 196-7
Morton, Nelle 157-8, 167, 168, 177,
    202
motherhood: and God 56-8, 140-3,
    200; and marriage 39; societal
    experience 182; of Rachel 29-30,
    141-3; of woman in Rev. 143; and
    Virgin Mary 143-5
mutuality: basic energy of creation
    85-8; in life of Jesus 85-108; and
    Resurrection 103; and feminist
    ethics 157-65, 203; and education
    165-9; and Sacraments 169-74;
    and prayer 174-6

mysticism: 72-4; and Dark Night
    74-80
myth: Demeter and Persephone
    29-30, 48, 53; Isis 29, 53; Inanna
    29, 53; Psyche and Eros 48, 77;
    see femininity, myths of; Eternal
    Woman

Nature: as context for redemption
    38-60; and Schleiermacher 43;
    and Otto 43-4; source of whole-
    ness for women 48-52; in
    Christian symbolism 51-2;
    naturistic epiphanies 65; critique
    of attitudes towards 47, 184; as
    dying mother 40; in context of
    At-one-ment Process 138-43;
    opposed to artefact 185
neo-Jungianism 23, 46, 182; see
    Ulanov, Ann
Neumann, Erich 18, 180, 186
Niebuhr, Reinhold: sin as pride 17,
    130, 180
Norwich, Julian of 142, 150

obedience, critique of 124
Ochs, Carol: patriarchy, matriarchy
    45-6, 185; 62; and via purgativa
    71, 190; re-imaging of death
    148-50, 201
ordination of women: and poems of
    Charles Williams 66; and Vatican
    197
Osiek, Carol 72, 180
Otto, Rudolph 43-4, 185

Pan, Kwok Lui 92, 197
patriarchy: and 'nekrophilic' im-
    agery 121; dating of 179
Perpetua 135-7, 164
personal, limits of 39; in marriage
    164-5
Plaskow, Judith 180

power: re-imaged as mutuality-in-relation, as erotic 103–5, 139; *see* God as power-in-relation

Process thought 28–37; and the Dark Night 78–80; and atonement 127–31; and Christology 172

Psyche and Eros 48, 77; *see* myth

psychology and gender difference: Freudian perspective 20, 181; neo-Jungian perspective 23, 182; Maccoby and Jacklin 182; *see* Gilligan, Carol; Miller, Jean Baker

psychotherapy and atonement 131–3

Quest genre: in feminist literature 186; *see* the Holy Grail

Radegunde 166

Ragnell, Dame 41–2

Raymond, Janice 162, 203; *see* female friendship and lesbianism

redemption: language of 1–3; and liberation 7–10; and creation 4–7; as reclaiming 2, 10; as re-membering 10; as self-affirmation ch. 4 *passim*; as building right relation ch. 5 *passim*; and language of grace 174–6

Rich, Adrienne ix, 1, 46–7, 55, 77, 144, 150, 177, 180, 190

Rogers, Carl client centred therapy 198

Rossetti, Christina 118–19, 196

Rowbotham, Sheila 22, 181

Ruddick, Sara 168, 203; *see* education and maternal thinking

Ruether, Rosemary Radford 7, 8, 178; the Fall and women 12, 179; anthropology 20–1; redemptive woman 134; soteriology 123, 197; relation between Christianity and establishment 199

Russell, Letty 7, 178

Sacraments and redemptive mutuality 169–74

Santmire, Paul 47, 184

Scanzoni, Letha Dawson 203

Schillebeeckx, Edward: and redemption 11–14, 177; critique of Metz 94

Schleiermacher, Friedrich: and nature 43, 184; and atonement theory 117, 195

Seattle, Chief 40, 184

Shange, Ntoshake 186

Shields, David 150, 202

sin: and 'guilt' of women 11; and victim status of women 15–19; as passivity 17–19, 63; as blocking relationality 36; as refusal of exchange 107

Sobrino, Jon 36, 180

Soelle, Dorothee primacy of liberation over creation 32, 85, 140, 147, 200

Spretnak, Charlene 29–30; and Capra, Fritjof 40, 184

Stanton, Elizabeth Cady 12

Starhawk 54, 187; *see* Wicca movement

Stone, Merlin 185; *see* matriarchy

Suchocki, Marjorie Hewitt 34, 78, 98, 109–10, 132, 174, 183, 184, 192, 193, 204; *see* Process thought, Dark Night

Systems theory 32–3, 183

Teresa of Avila, 63, 70–1, 72, 164, 189

Thistlewaite, Susan Brooks 12–13, 122

Tillich, Paul 39, 180; God-above-God 56; ground of our being 88; Latin view of atonement 113, 121, 195; method of correlation 177;

Hannah Tillich's biography 180
Trible, Phyllis 141-2, 197; journey of a metaphor 200

Ulanov, Ann 23, 182; see psychology and gender difference
Underhill, Evelyn 62, 188

victim: womens' refusal of status 15, 51, 122-3; see Atwood, Margaret, Cross and suffering of women
vulnerability: and God 58; and women 13-14

Walker, Alice 77, 82-3, 191
Ward, Mary 166
Weil, Simone: spirituality of waiting 68, 167; and Dark Night 78; and mysticism 72-3; suffering and creation 146-7, 189; attitude to eating 201
Welch, Sharon 3, 87, 94, 177, 179; recovery of subjugated knowledges; dangerous memory 9-10
Wendel, Elizabeth Moltmann: and goddess religion 44, 98; and crucified woman 137; and Martha legend 142, 192; and women in Mark's Gospel 98, 178
Whitehead, Alfred North 34-5, 47, 59, 183; see Process thought
Whitehead, J.D. power and sensitivity as virtue 202
Whitmont, Edward 24, 184; see Ragnell, Dame
Wicca movement 54, 178
Wiesel, Eli 90-2, 191; see Holocaust
Williams, Charles 66, 107, 189; concept of coinherence 193; and mutuality of forgiveness 196
Williams, Daniel Day 86, 118, 119-21, 127; and atonement 130-1; Macquarrie's appreciation of 197
Wilson-Kastner, P., and Kastner, G.R. 199
Womanist theology 7-8, 178
'Woman Church' 172-3
Woolf, Virginia: moments of being 65, 188-8; and Christina Rossetti 196
Worgul, George 170-4, 204

Young, Frances 142, 147, 151, 201

DATE DUE

12/12/02	